Postcard History Series

Allen County

in Vintage Postcards

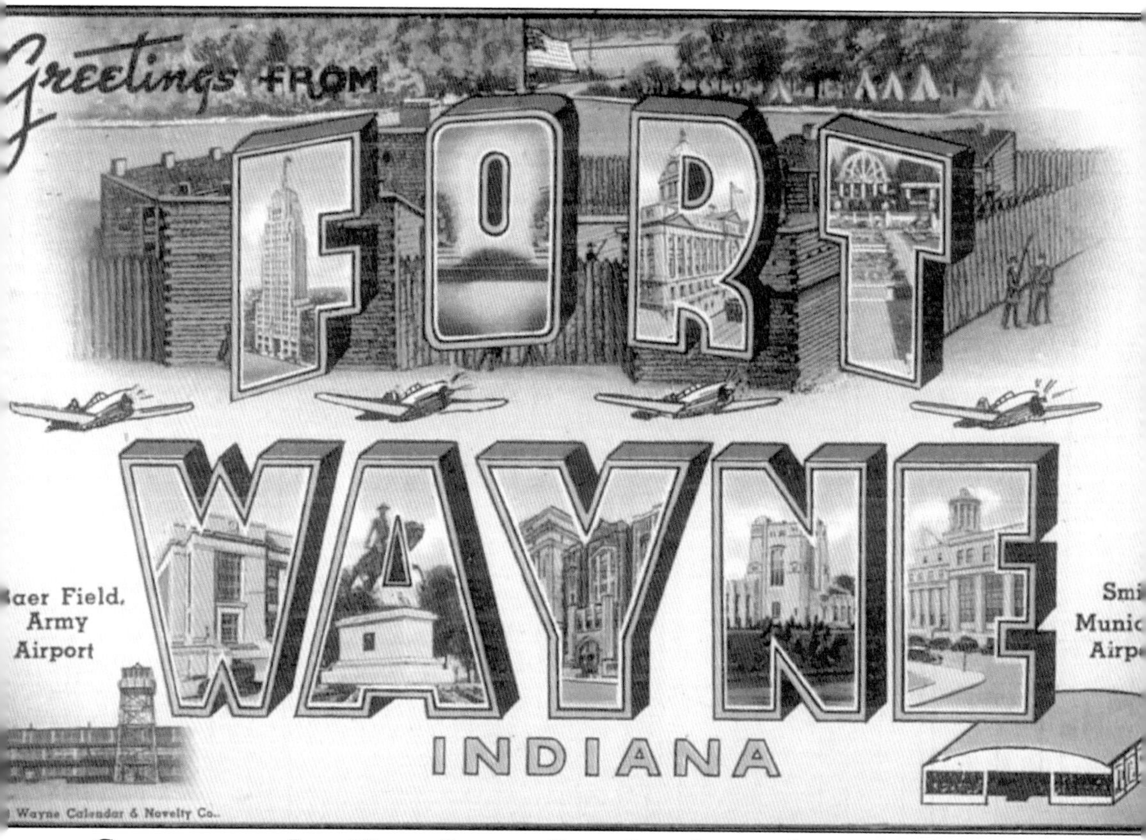

GREETINGS FROM FORT WAYNE, INDIANA. "Large Letter" postcards were popular. This linen card features Fort Wayne landmarks within the letters.

POSTCARD HISTORY SERIES

Allen County

IN VINTAGE POSTCARDS

John Martin Smith

ARCADIA PUBLISHING

ISBN 978-0-7385-1915-9

Published by Arcadia Publishing
Charleston, South Carolina

Printed in the United States of America

Library of Congress Catalog Card Number: 2001093311

For all general information contact Arcadia Publishing at:
Telephone 843-853-2070
Fax 843-853-0044
E-Mail sales@arcadiapublishing.com
For customer service and orders:
Toll-Free 1-888-313-2665

Visit us on the Internet at www.arcadiapublishing.com

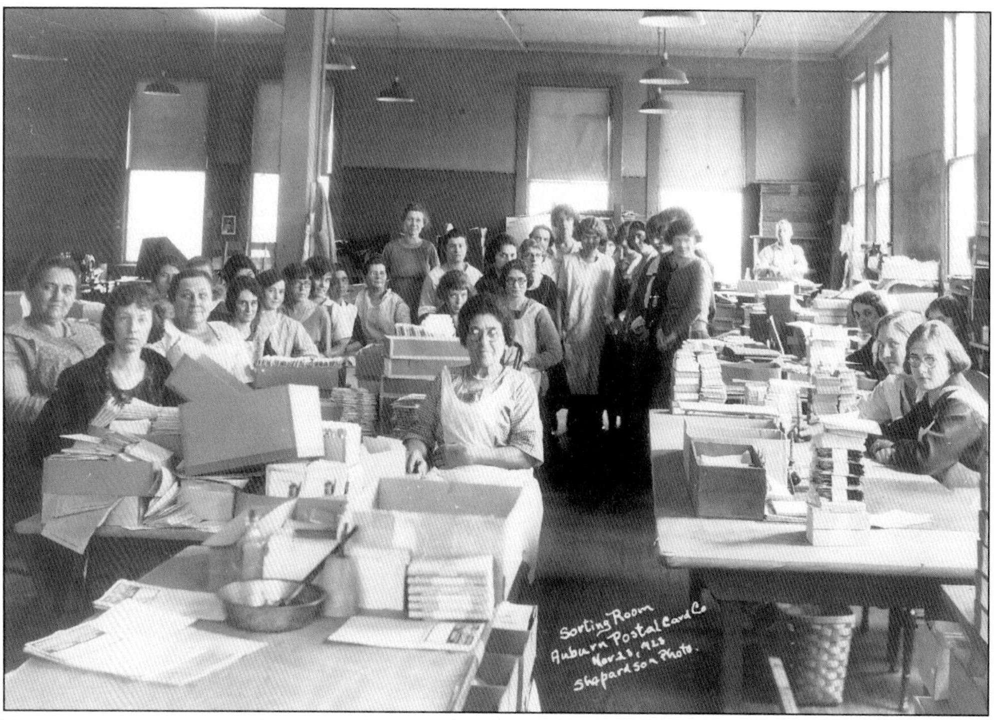

MAKING POSTCARDS. This is an image of Auburn Postcard Company employees (same as Noble and Steuben).

CONTENTS

ACKNOWLEDGMENTS

The author is indebted to several people who have contributed to

this production of this book:

My wife, Barbara Clark Smith, has participated in the collection of these postcards for nearly 40 years. I thank her for her patient search through thousands of postcards at antique shows and antique malls to find those relevant to Northeastern Indiana.

My son and lawyer partner, Thompson Smith, has made law office facilities available to assist in the production of this book. His paralegal, Tricia Hertsel, has done the computer input and organization. My secretary of 32 years, Sharon George, has also assisted.

Arcadia editor Ann Fugman has been of great assistance in getting the book into print in accordance with the high standards of Arcadia. The quiet behind-the-scenes efforts of a good editor always makes an author look good!

Lastly, I am indebted to those photographers and merchants who had the foresight and vision to create and distribute the original postcards. While postcards have a fleeting, ephemeral quality to them, those "packrats" who have collected and saved them have provided us with a legacy of our towns that would have otherwise been lost after the click of the camera and the thunk of the postmark!

John Martin Smith

INTRODUCTION

After my grandfather died in 1961, we found a box of old postcards which were exchanged between my grandmother, Viola Smith, and her sister, Iona. They both lived in Butler, Indiana. I arranged the cards in chronological order and scanned the messages. Some were postmarked the same day.

With a little research and questions to my father, Walter M. Smith, who served as postmaster in Butler from 1950 to 1976, I found that beginning in 1907, there was mail delivery twice each day in the town. Therefore, the sisters could exchange messages the same day—i.e. "Can you and Carl come for supper at 6PM? Iona"—"Yes, I will bring an apple pie, Viola"

Some of the cards had floral and holiday scenes on the front and others had real photographs of buildings located in Butler. Postage was 1¢. I later sorted out the scenes of buildings and started looking for others. At antique shops, flea markets, antique malls, and auctions I found more postcards from Butler. This search then expanded to all of Northeastern Indiana. Over a period of about 30 years I have accumulated hundreds of postcards. One of the best sources now is Ebay on the Internet. Since most of the postcards were sent away from their place of origin, many are listed for sale from places far from Northeastern Indiana. This source has enabled me to augment the collection presented here.

The history of the use of postcards centers around United States Postal Laws and Regulations. The printed format of postcards also enables one to generally date postcards. The sequence is as follows:

1893–1898 Pioneer Cards

These cards are quite rare and are sometimes labeled as "Souvenir Postcards."

1898–1901 Private Mailing Cards

These cards are labeled "Private Mailing Card" on the address side and usually also state "Authorized by Act of Congress of May 19, 1898."

1901–1907 Undivided Backs

Postal regulations did not permit a message on the back – just the address. This was also true of the Pioneer and Private Mailing Cards.

1907–1915 Divided Backs

On March 1, 1907, the United States Postal Service approved the divided back card which permitted the address on the right side and a message on the left side of the back. This change made the use of postcards much more prevalent as a means of communication.

1915–1930s White Borders

A change in printing techniques resulted in a printed image with a narrow white border.

1935–1955 Linens

These cards were printed on cardboard stock with a "linen" like surface. The publisher started with a photograph but modified it to make an idyllic image that was also colorized.

1945–Present Chromes
These cards are printed in color on a slick stock.

The foregoing date categories overlap considerably. Sometimes the same basic photographs were used for several postcard versions. Pre-linen cards were frequently colorized in various ways. For example, a black and white image would be overprinted with a brick color on a brick building. The Auburn Postcard Company was known for its "Blue Sky" cards which were a black and white image with the sky overprinted in light blue.

From about 1900–1915, many cards were "Real Photo" cards. That term is used to describe a photograph printed by the photographer directly onto postcard stock. Sometimes only a single postcard was made. Usually, the number of cards printed was limited. Real photo cards are sought by collectors due to their relative rarity and sharp, clear image. Real photo cards were also issued in the 1940s and 1950s. A real photo card and a printed card can be distinguished quite easily by magnifying the image—a printed card will have a pattern of small dots to create the contrast, whereas a real photo card will have a solid image.

The bulk of the images in this book date from 1910–1915, which was the golden era of postcard production. It is likely that the local use of postcards waned after the telephone came into general use. As automobile travel increased, postcards were used by tourists to send a photograph and message back home. Many persons also collected postcards which led to friends and relatives sending them postcards for their collection.

There were several local postcard companies in Bryan, Ohio; Fort Wayne, Indiana; and Auburn, Indiana. The Auburn Postcard Company was a major international publisher of postcards. The Whitten-Dennison Post Card Company moved to Auburn from Maine in 1910. They built a small factory on East Seventh Street adjacent to Cedar Creek which employed five women. The name of the company was changed to Auburn Post Card Manufacturing Company in 1913, and to Auburn Greeting Card Company in 1929. In 1933, D.E. Messenger acquired the company and changed the name to Messenger Corporation, which is still in operation at 318 E. Seventh Street and is a major printer of religious calendars and printed materials for the funeral home industry.

How were the subjects of postcards chosen? Generally, they were chosen by local merchants on the basis of what would sell in their drugstore, restaurant, or bookstore. In some cases the scenes selected were designed to show off the town. The most common are scenes of the courthouses and principle streets. They were ordered in quantities of 500–1,000, so the merchant wanted to make sure that they would sell.

The images selected for this book are designed to present a representative selection of images for Steuben County. The space and format of the book did not permit the use of all cards in our collection for this county. In some cases, the messages on the back are as interesting as the image on the front. I have incorporated some of these in my interpretations. The bold type in my captions repeats the caption of the card. If the date is not contained in the caption and the card is postmarked, the postmarked date is stated "*c.* 19—." If the card is not postmarked, or if the postmark is not readable, no date is stated. I then supplement the caption with other information when appropriate. Some images simply speak for themselves, so I refrain from any further comment.

While not originally intended to document a town or place historically, I find that they are a great source of local history and images that is otherwise unavailable. As buildings are restored to their original design, a postcard may be the only source of a period image of that particular building.

I sincerely hope that my readers enjoy and use the image and captions contained herein to appreciate their heritage and sense of place.

John Martin Smith

One

Churubusco

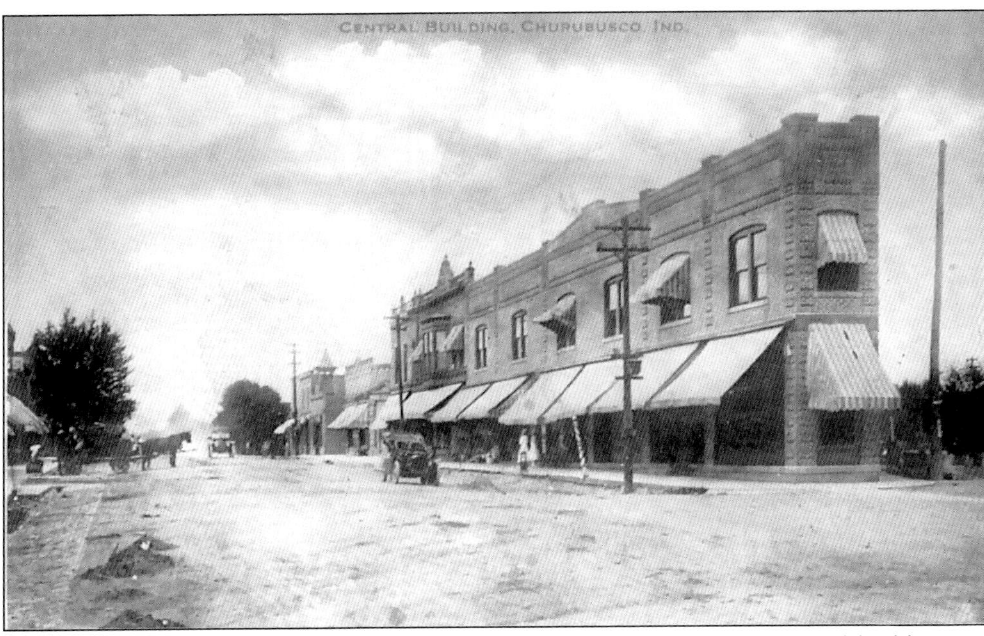

Central Building, Churubusco, Indiana. This unusual triangular shaped building is a Churubusco landmark, *c.* 1918.

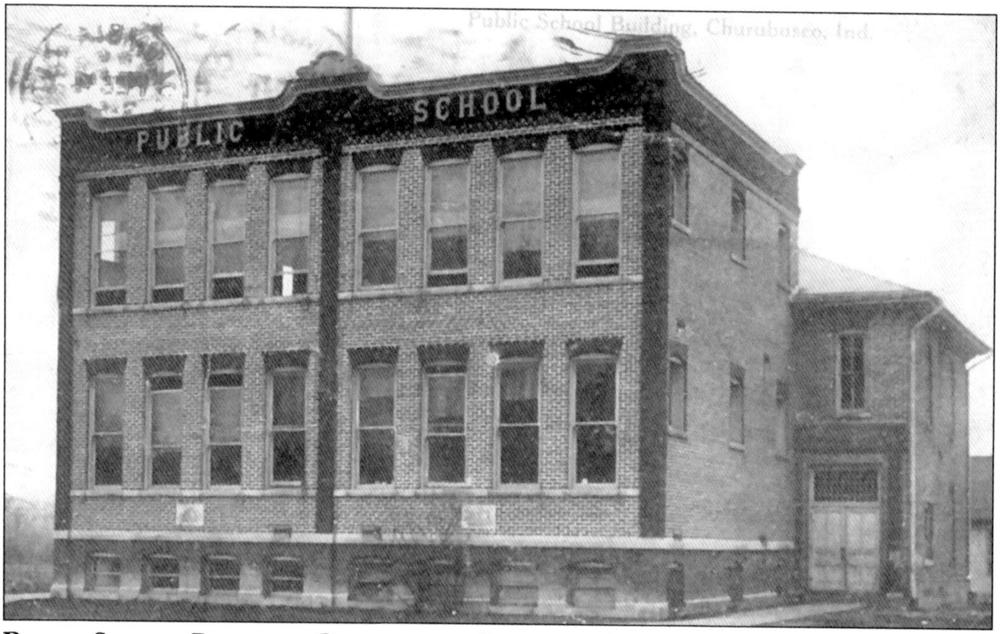

Public School Building, Churubusco, Indiana. The windows of this building faced south to provide maximum daylight, *c.* 1916.

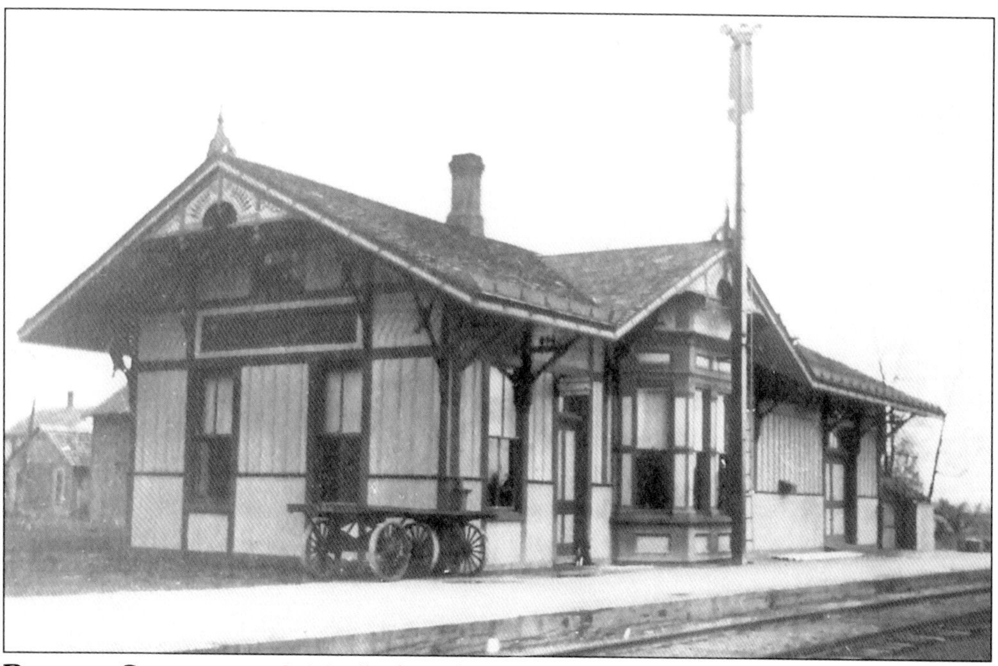

Depot at Churubusco. Originally the Eel River Railroad, this depot was built when the line was owned by the Wabash Railroad. It was later owned by the Pennsylvania Railroad. (Note: This image is not a postcard.)

Two

Fort Wayne

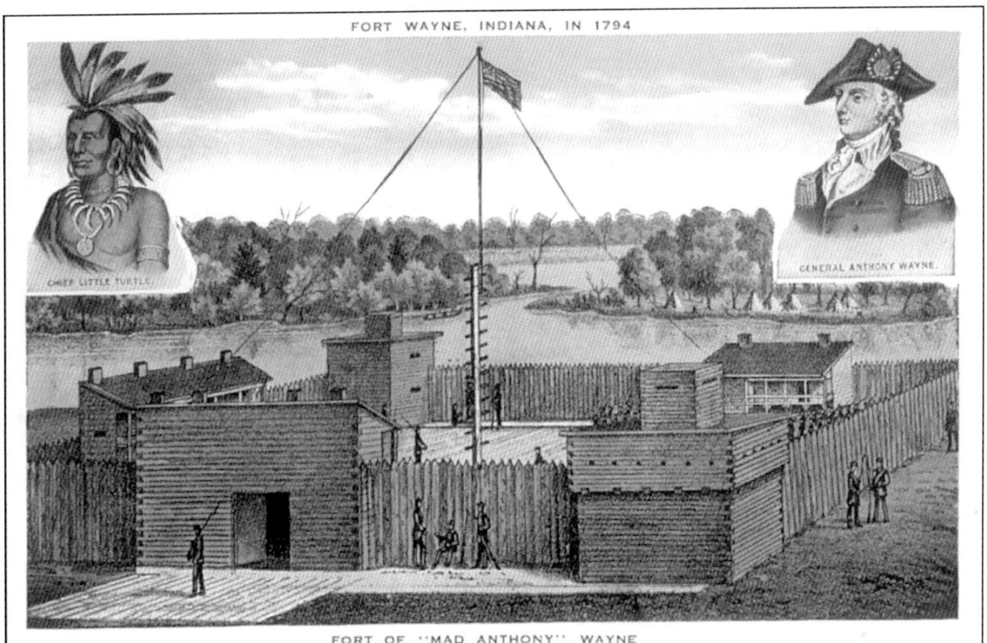

Fort of "Mad Anthony" Wayne, Fort Wayne, Indiana (in 1794). A small triangular park known as Old Fort Park marks the site of this wooden stockade. On the 22nd of October, 1794, following the defeat of the natives by Major General Anthony Wayne, this fort was dedicated. The tribal leader in these Indian wars was Little Turtle, chief of the Miamis. After a succession of commandants, the fort was evacuated in 1819. The last blockhouse was torn down in 1856. Old Fort Park is on East Main Street (Old Fort Place), four squares east of the Allen County Courthouse.

OLD FORT WAYNE

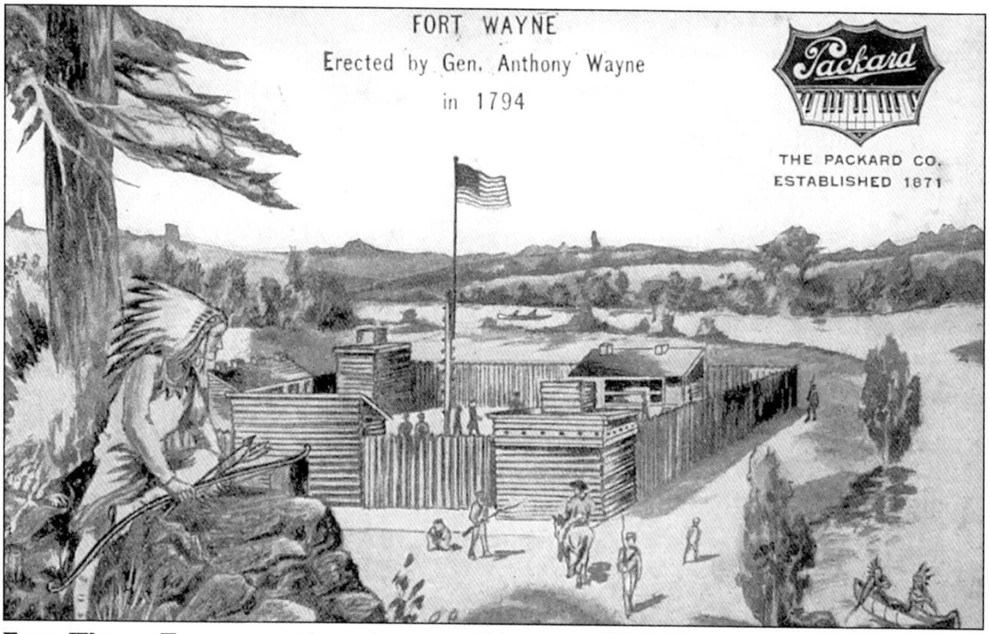

FORT WAYNE, ERECTED BY GEN. ANTHONY WAYNE IN 1794. This artist's conception of the "Old Fort" was published by the Packard Co., which manufactured pianos and organs in Fort Wayne.

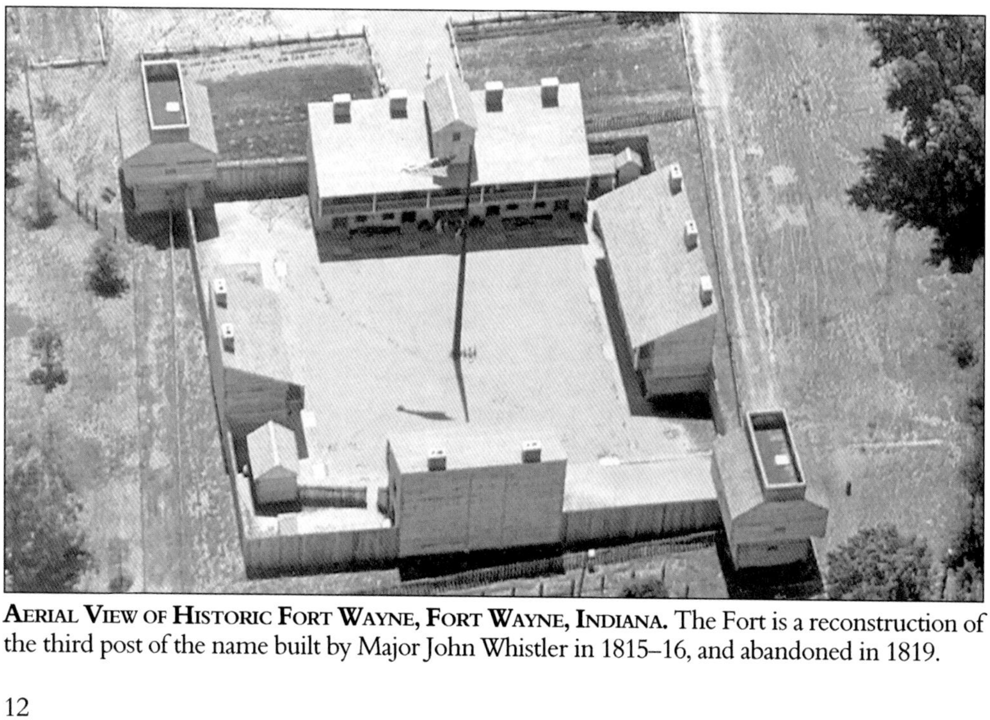

AERIAL VIEW OF HISTORIC FORT WAYNE, FORT WAYNE, INDIANA. The Fort is a reconstruction of the third post of the name built by Major John Whistler in 1815–16, and abandoned in 1819.

Allen County Courthouse

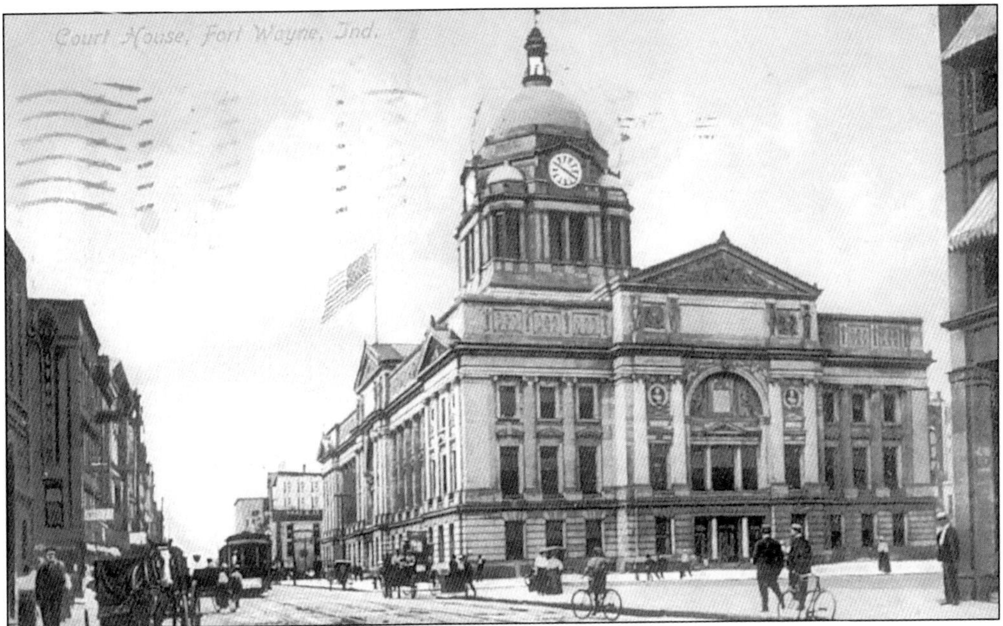

Courthouse, Fort Wayne, Indiana, c. 1909. The cornerstone of Allen County's fourth courthouse was laid on November 17, 1897. The building was designed by Mahurin and Mahurin, prominent Fort Wayne architects.

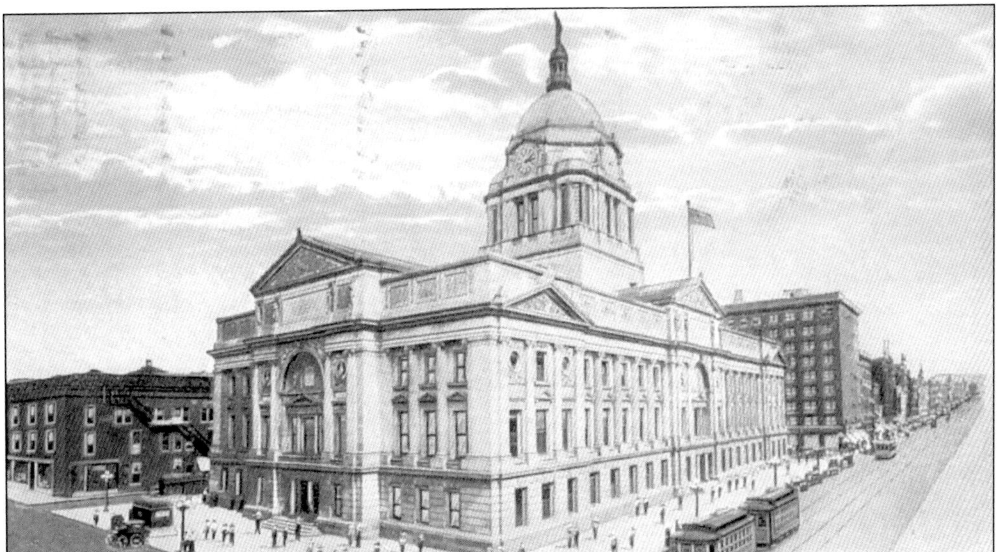

Allen County Court House, Fort Wayne, Indiana, c. 1924. The building is constructed of Vermont granite and Indiana limestone. A weather vane made of copper, representing liberty, caps the dome.

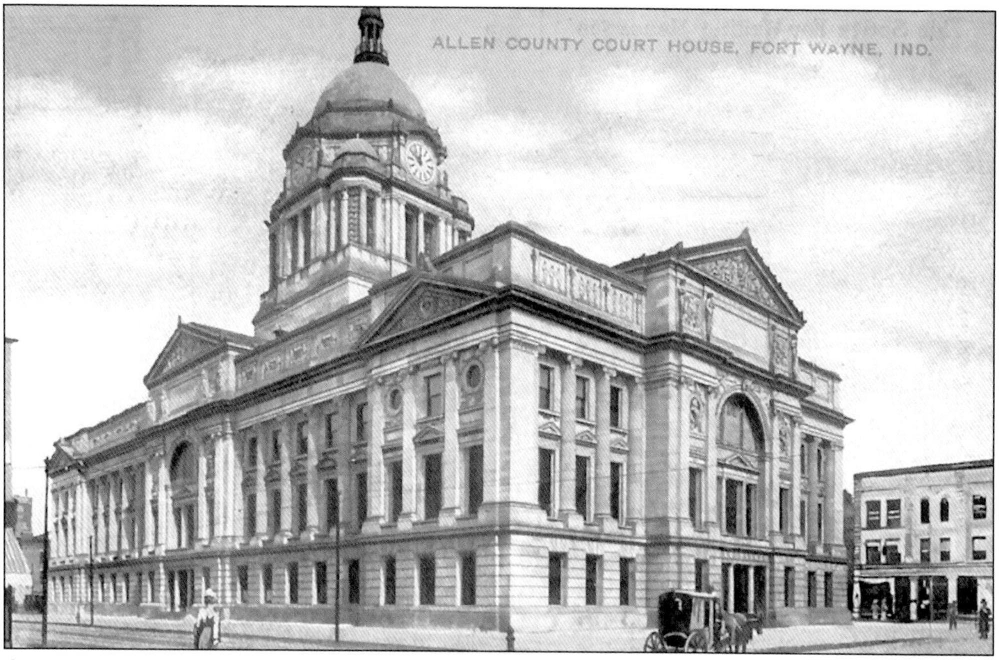

ALLEN COUNTY COURTHOUSE, FORT WAYNE, INDIANA, *c.* 1907. This grand building was the subject of many postcards.

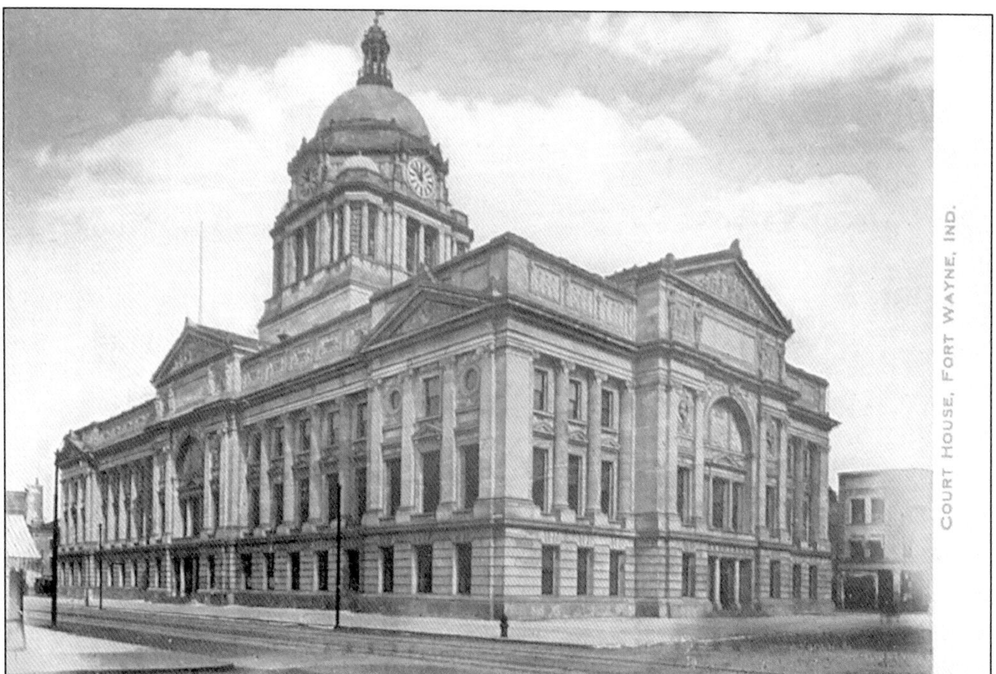

COURTHOUSE, FORT WAYNE, INDIANA, *c.* 1908. The interior of the dome features four large murals painted by Charles Holloway.

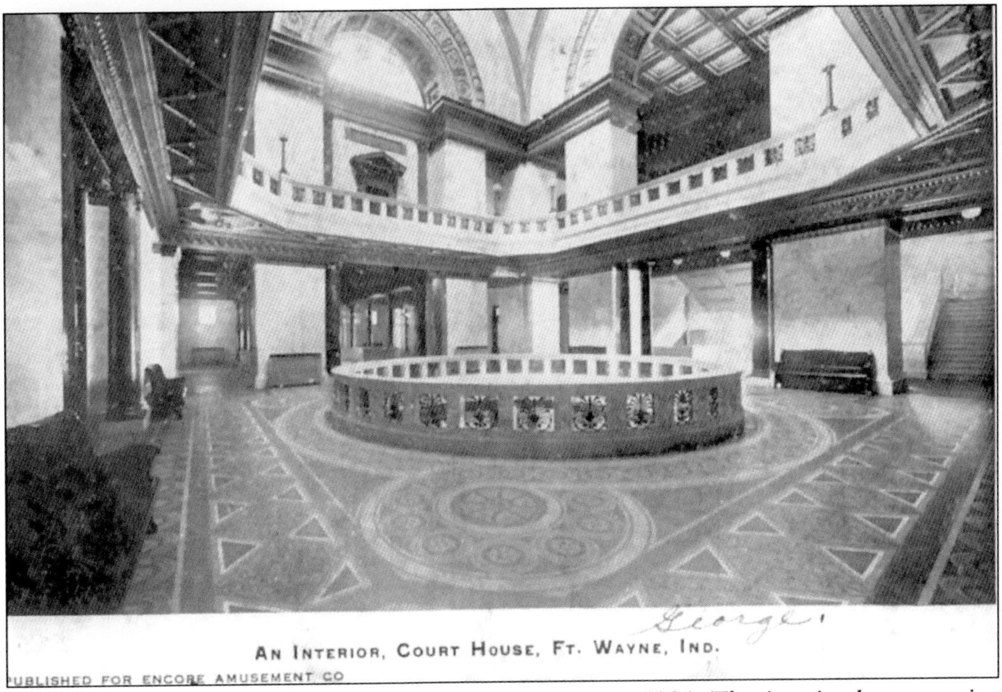

An Interior, Courthouse, Fort Wayne, Indiana, *c.* 1906. The interior has extensive granite, marble, and scagliola.

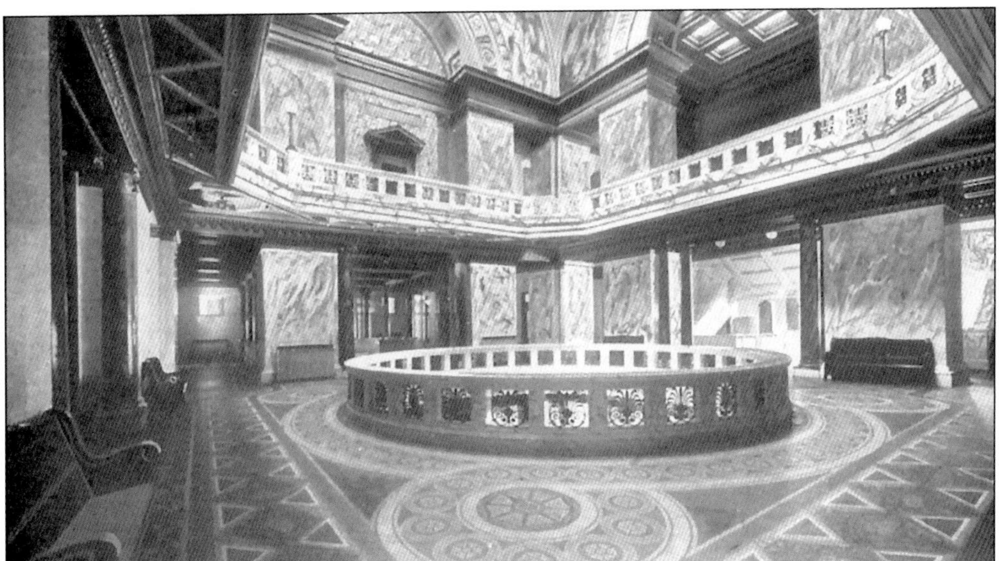

Office Floor Of Rotunda, Main Staircase, Courthouse, Fort Wayne, Indiana. The message states: "Sat. A.M. Am at Viola's now. Am planning on coming Wed. but they are coaxing me to stay for all the doings. There is a dance every night until Thurs. is the last as I wouldn't get there till Fri. Frank is afraid he will get homesick if he comes. He don't know yet for sure. I don't know what to do about staying. You can stay at home and help if I am not there. Why don't you folks write? Were you expecting me home today? It is snowing and blowing today. Write any place and I will get it some way. C.W."

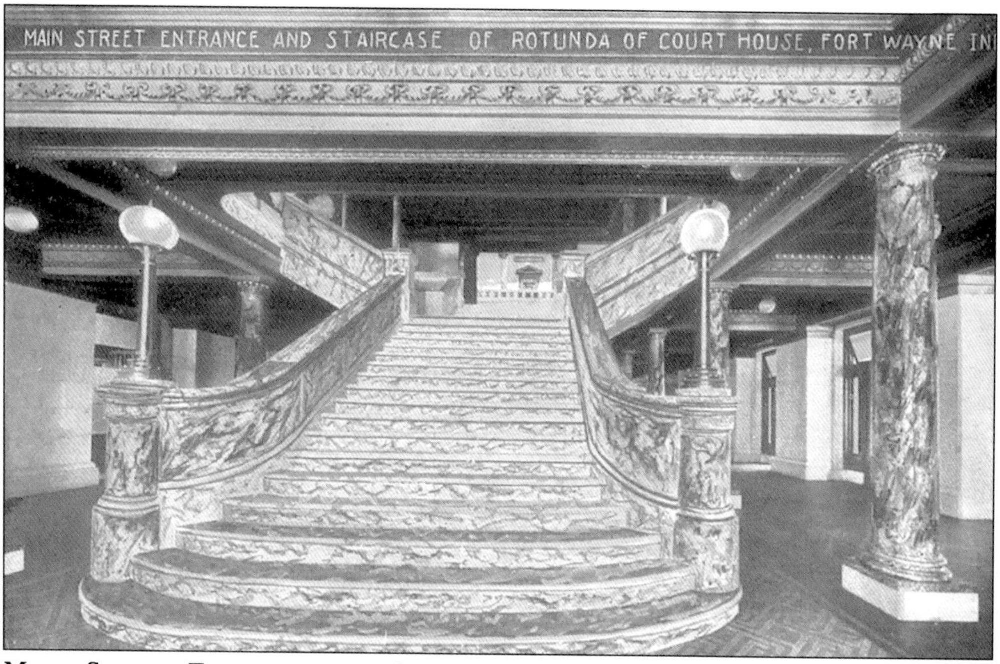

Main Street Entrance and Staircase of Rotunda of Courthouse, Fort Waynea, Indiana.

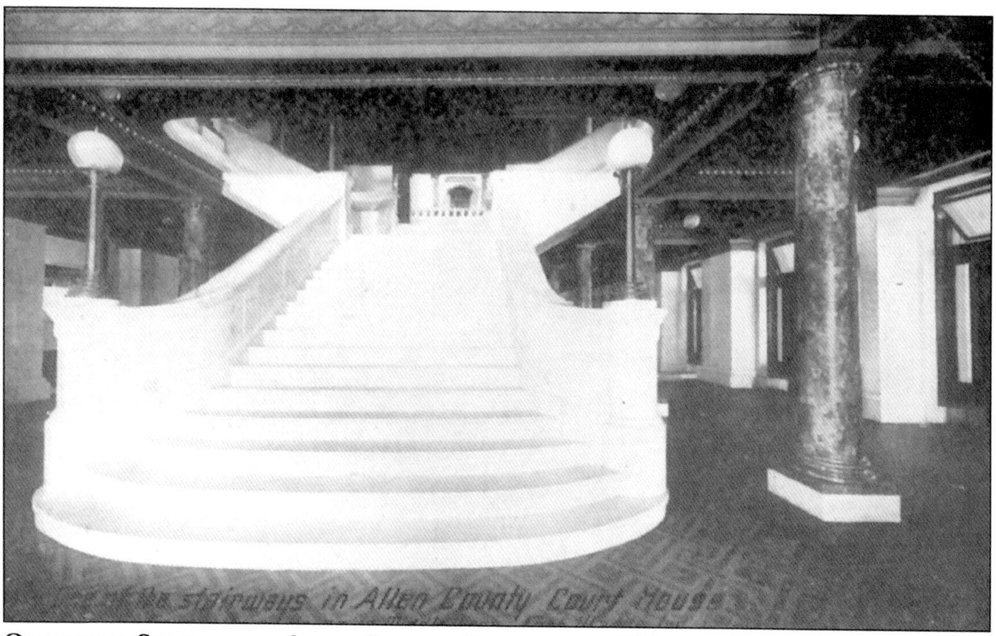

One of the Stairways in Allen County Courthouse. This courthouse is in Middle West, Fort Wayne, Indiana.

ALLEN COUNTY INSTITUTIONS

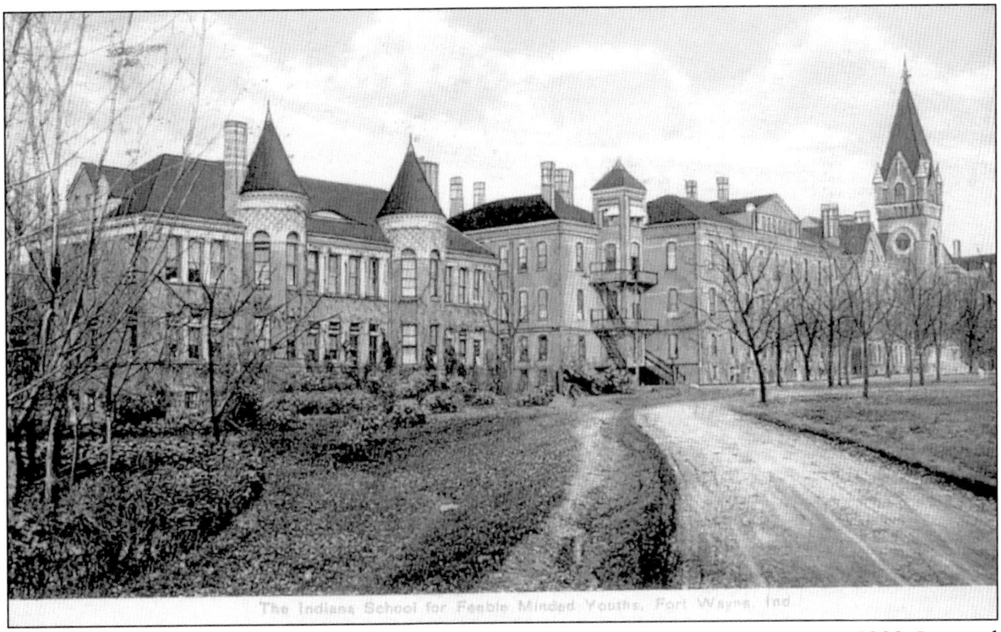

THE INDIANA SCHOOL FOR FEEBLE MINDED YOUTHS, FORT WAYNE, INDIANA, *c.* 1909. Located on East State Street, these buildings housed mentally ill youth.

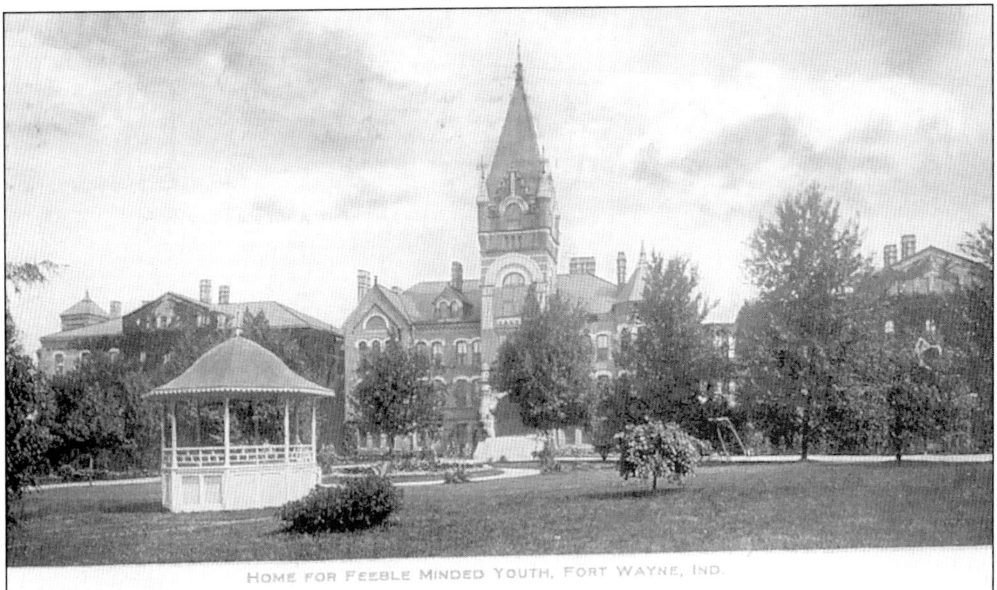

HOME FOR FEEBLE MINDED YOUTH, FORT WAYNE, INDIANA, *c.* 1912. This is another view with the gazebo.

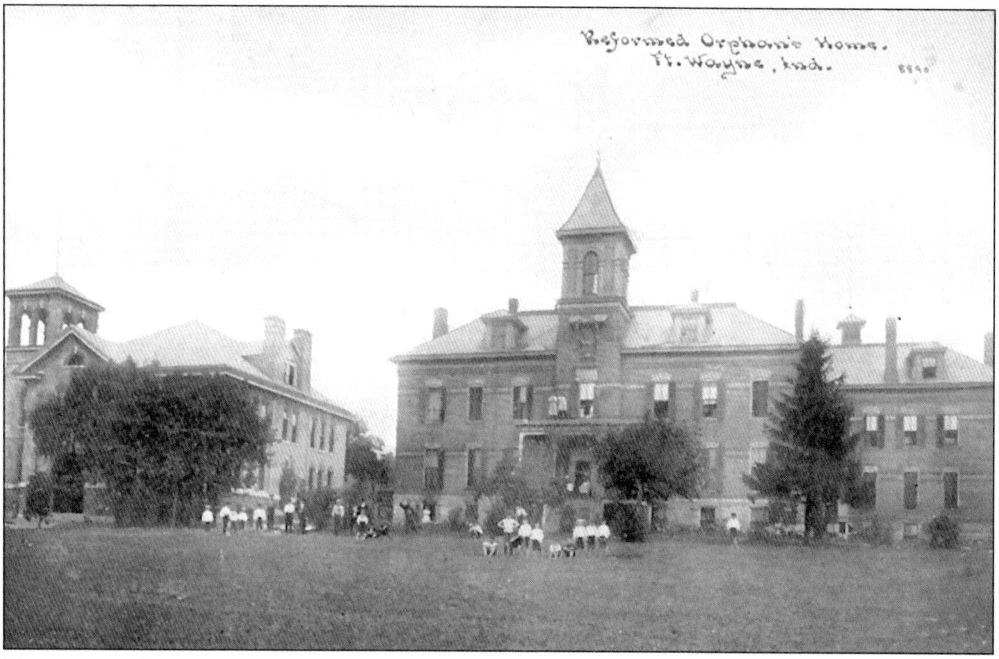

REFORMED ORPHAN'S HOME, FORT WAYNE, INDIANA. Many religious organizations had homes for orphans.

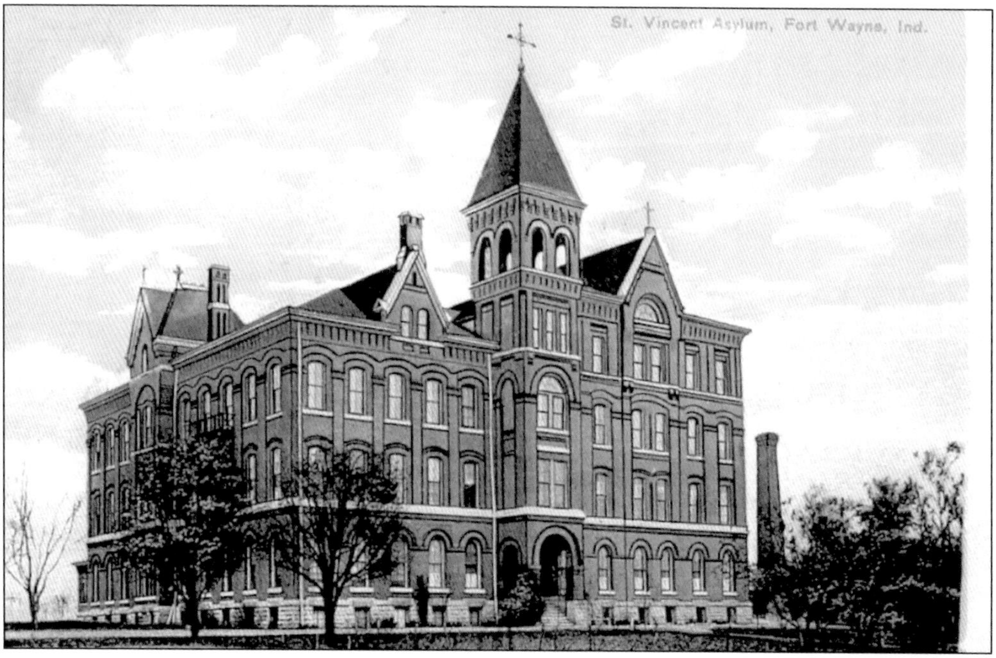

ST. VINCENT ASYLUM, FORT WAYNE, INDIANA, *c.* 1909. This Catholic institution provided care for less fortunate persons.

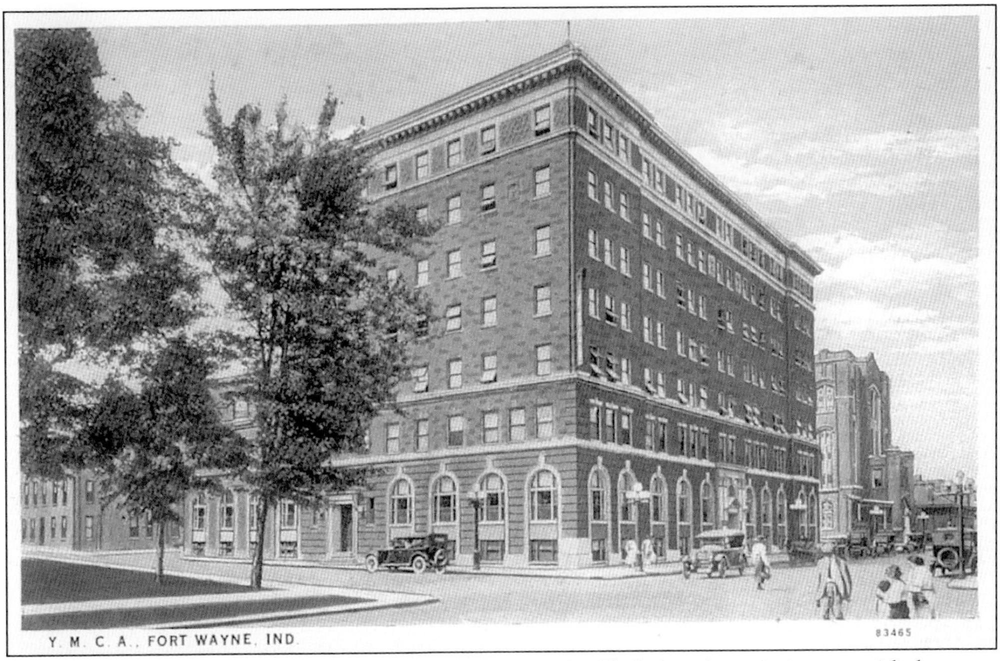

Y.M.C.A. Fort Wayne, Indiana. The Young Men's Christian Association provided rooms and athletic facilities for young men who came to Fort Wayne to work or attend school.

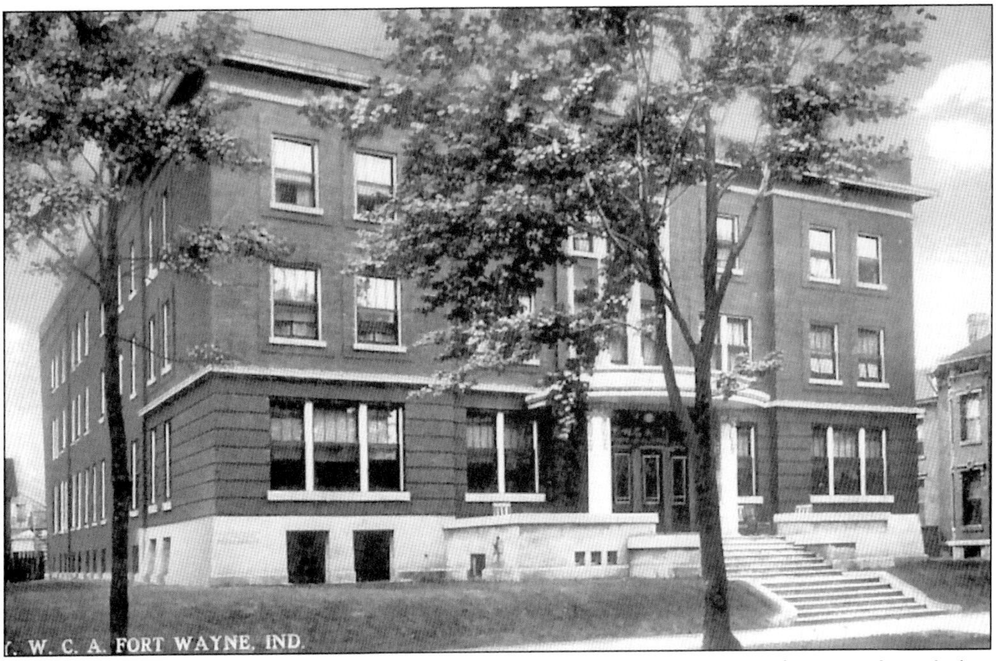

Y.W.C.A. Fort Wayne, Indiana, c. 1916. The Young Women's Christian Association provided similar facilities for young women.

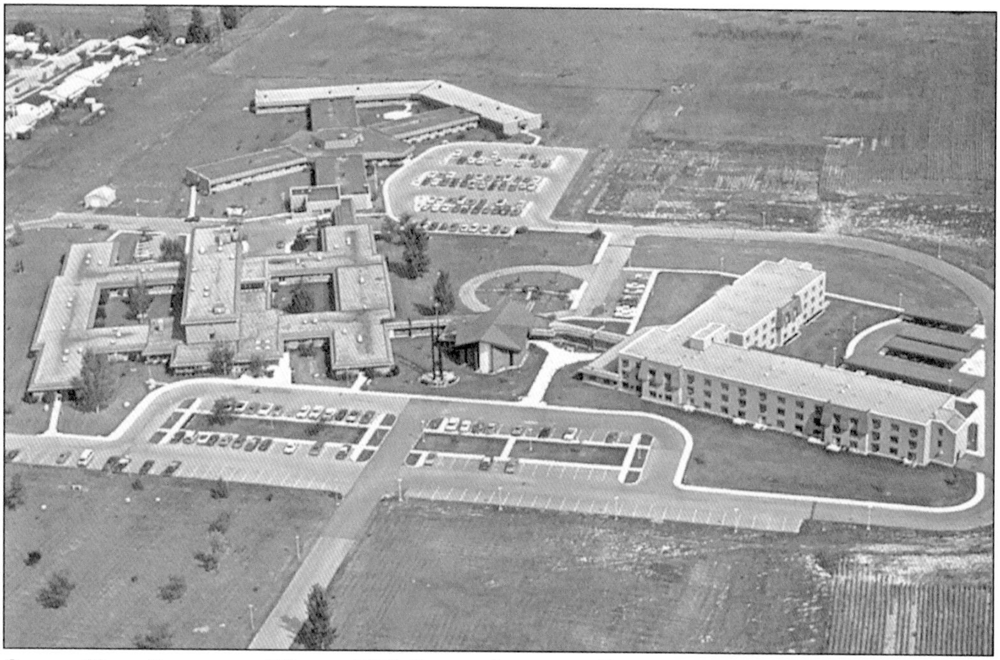

AERIAL VIEW, LUTHERAN HOME, 6701 SOUTH ANTHONY BOULEVARD, FORT WAYNE, INDIANA. This extensive facility provides housing and services for elderly persons.

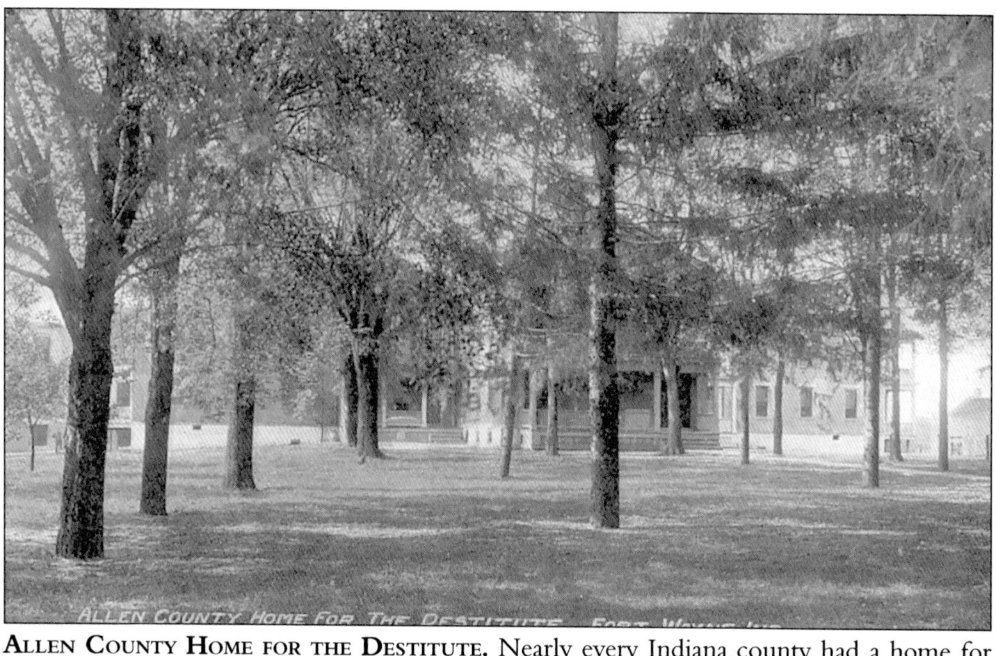

ALLEN COUNTY HOME FOR THE DESTITUTE. Nearly every Indiana county had a home for those who were unable to support themselves.

CATHEDRAL SQUARE

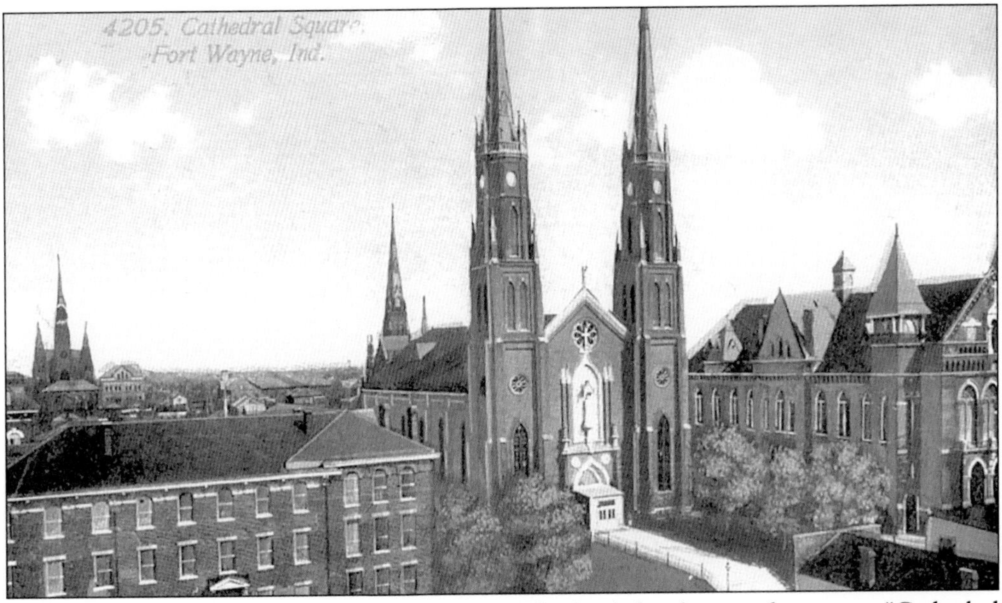

CATHEDRAL SQUARE, FORT WAYNE, INDIANA. The land that became known as "Cathedral Square" was acquired in the 1850s. The first Catholic church was known as St. Augustine's. The Cathedral of the Immaculate Conception was constructed in 1859.

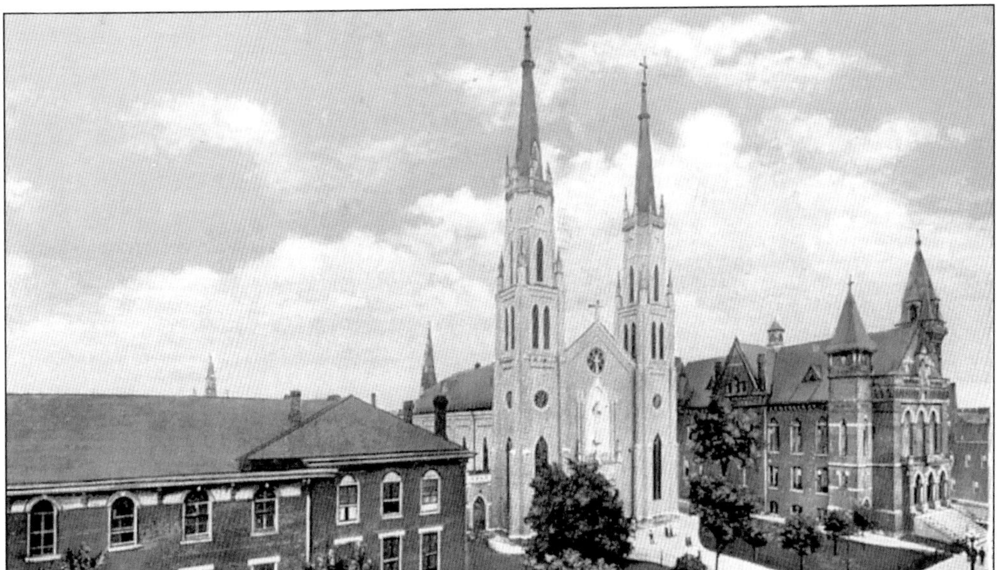

ST. AUGUSTINE'S ACADEMY, CATHEDRAL, CENTRAL CATHOLIC HIGH SCHOOL, FORT WAYNE, INDIANA. Cathedral Square was the location of the major Catholic institutions of the Catholic church.

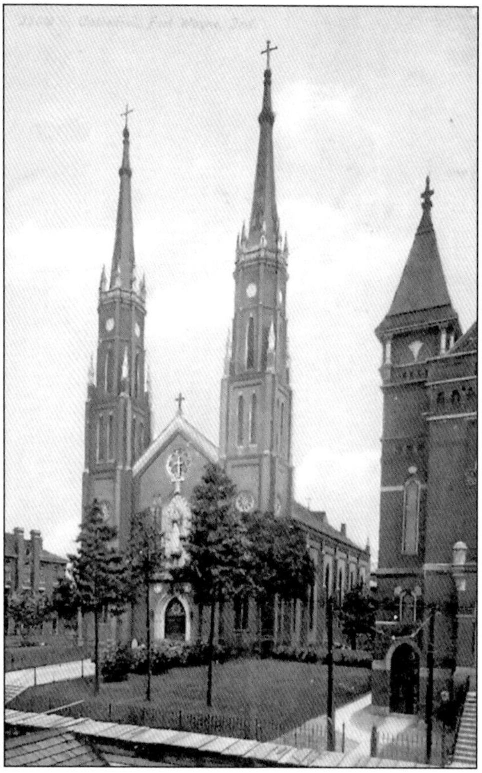

Cathedral, Fort Wayne, Indiana, *c.* 1907. The original construction was of brick.

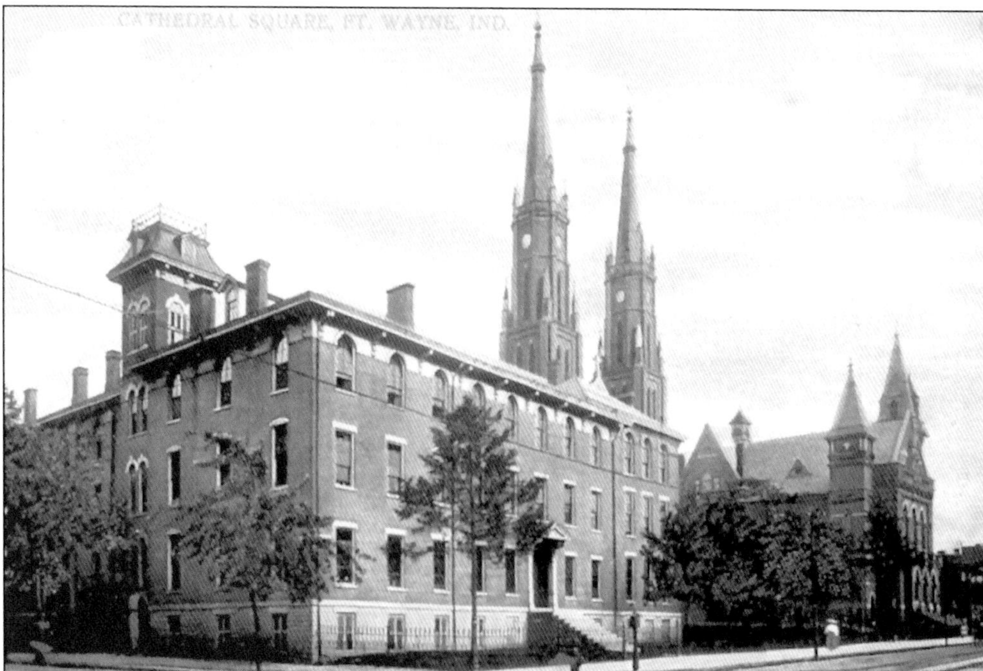

Cathedral Square, Fort Wayne, Indiana. This is a view from the rear showing St. Augustine's Academy.

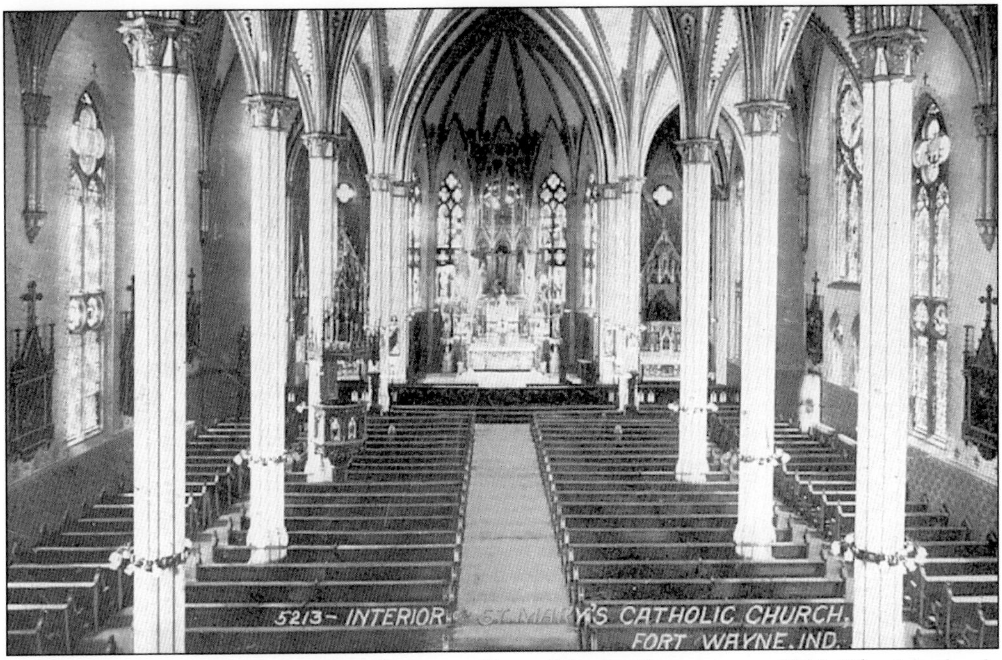

INTERIOR ST. MARY'S CATHOLIC CHURCH, FORT WAYNE, INDIANA, C. 1914. The interior is similar to European cathedrals.

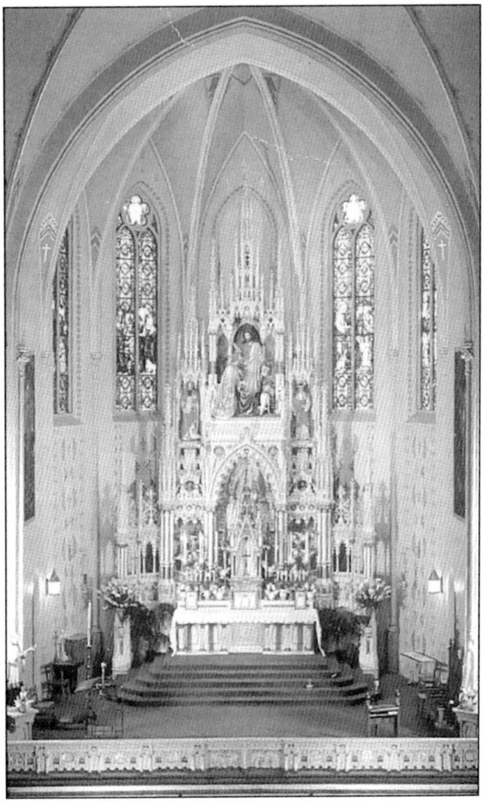

CENTER ALTAR, SAINT PETER'S CATHOLIC CHURCH, SAINT PETER'S SQUARE, FORT WAYNE, INDIANA. The interior detail is outstanding.

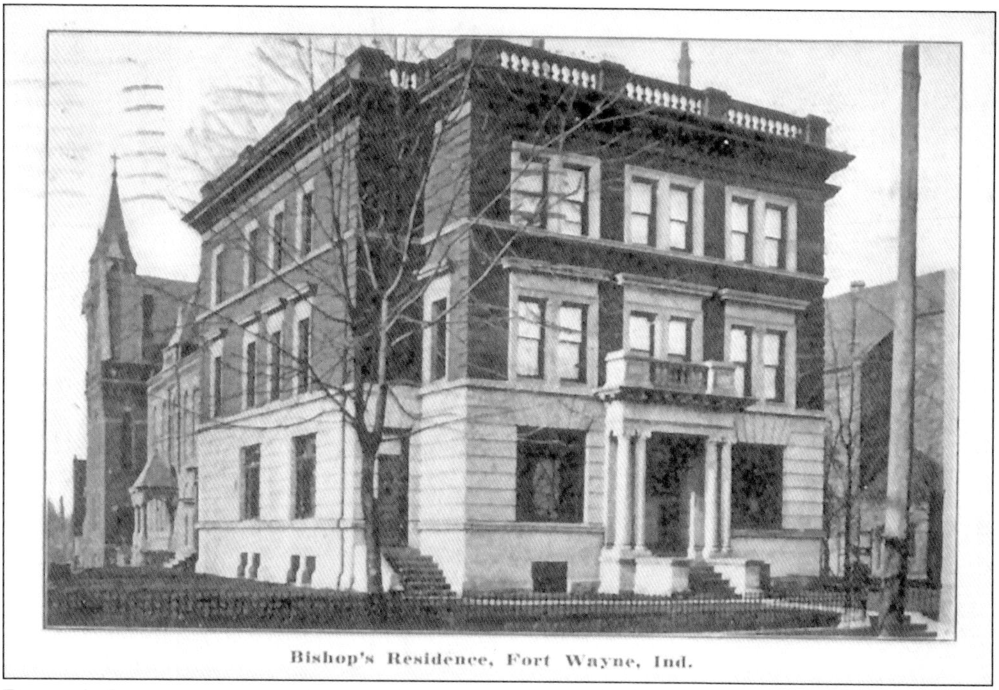

Bishop's Residence, Fort Wayne, Indiana, *c.* 1911. The building provided a residence plus office space for the Bishop and support staff.

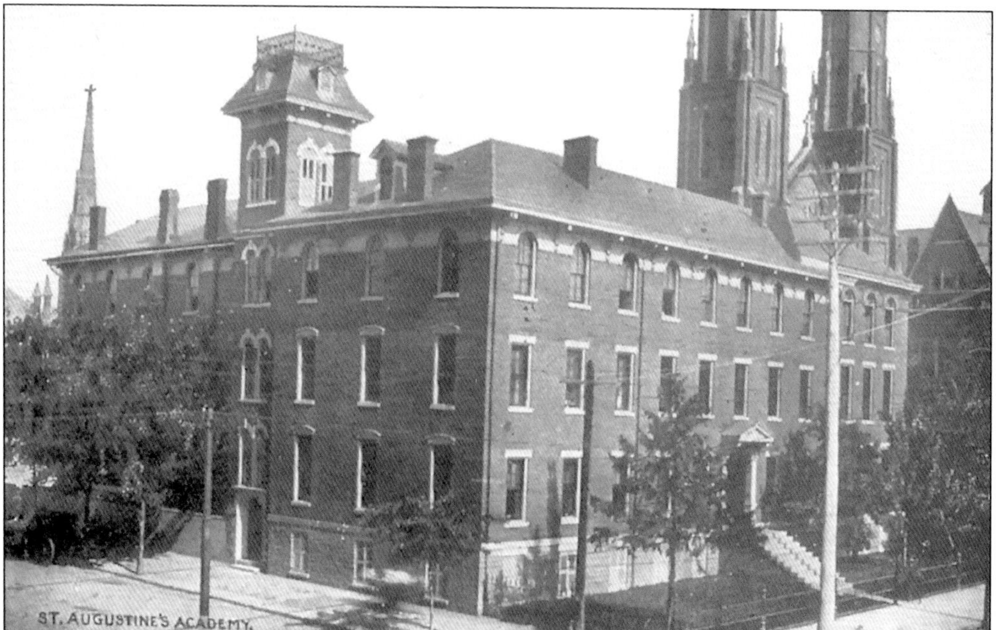

St. Augustine's Academy, Fort Wayne, Indiana. St. Augustine's Academy for Girls was operated by the Sisters of Providence.

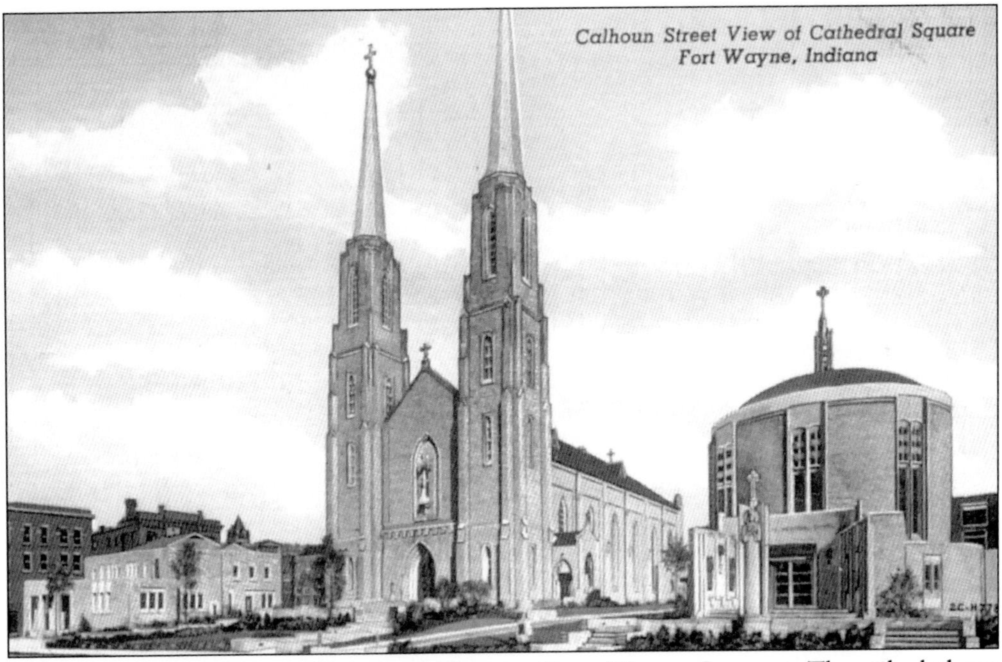

Calhoun Street View of Cathedral Square, Fort Wayne, Indiana. The cathedral was extensively renovated in the 1950s.

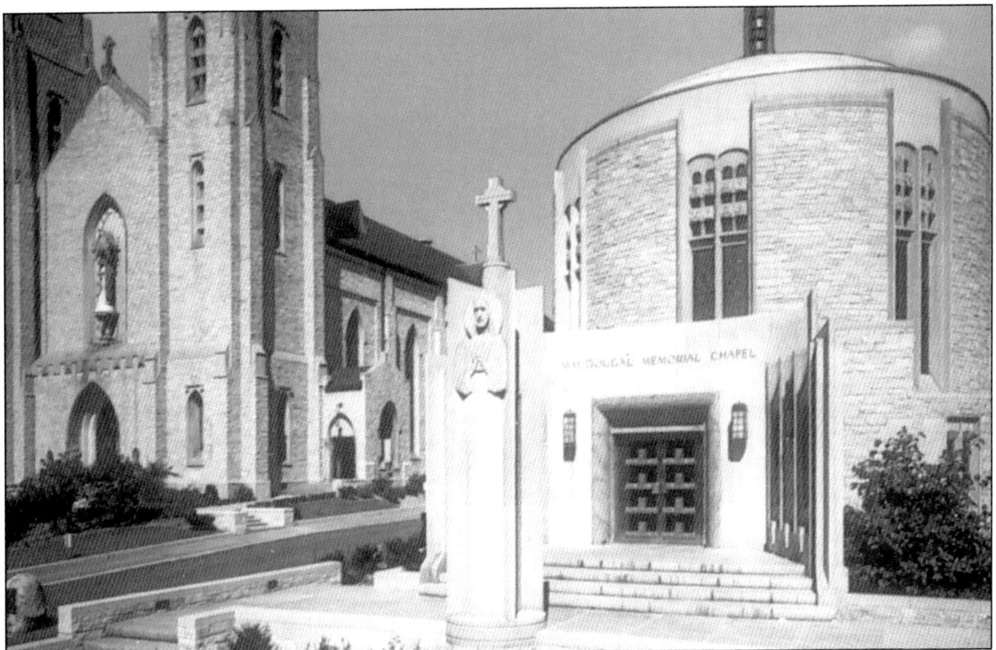

MacDougal Chapel, Cathedral Square, Fort Wayne, Indiana. The MacDougal Memorial Chapel was added to the complex in the 1950s.

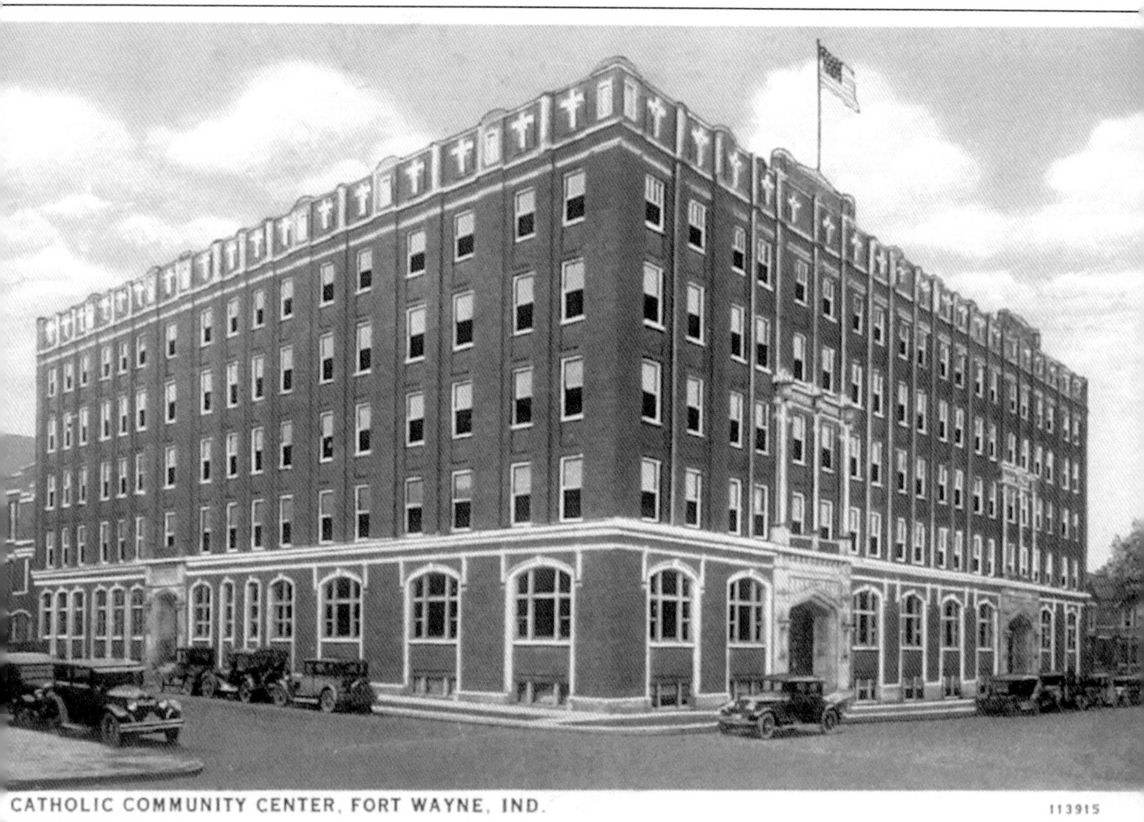

CATHOLIC COMMUNITY CENTER, FORT WAYNE, INDIANA. This building provided many of the same facilities for Catholics as did the Y.M.C.A. for Protestants.

ALLEN COUNTY PUBLIC BUILDINGS

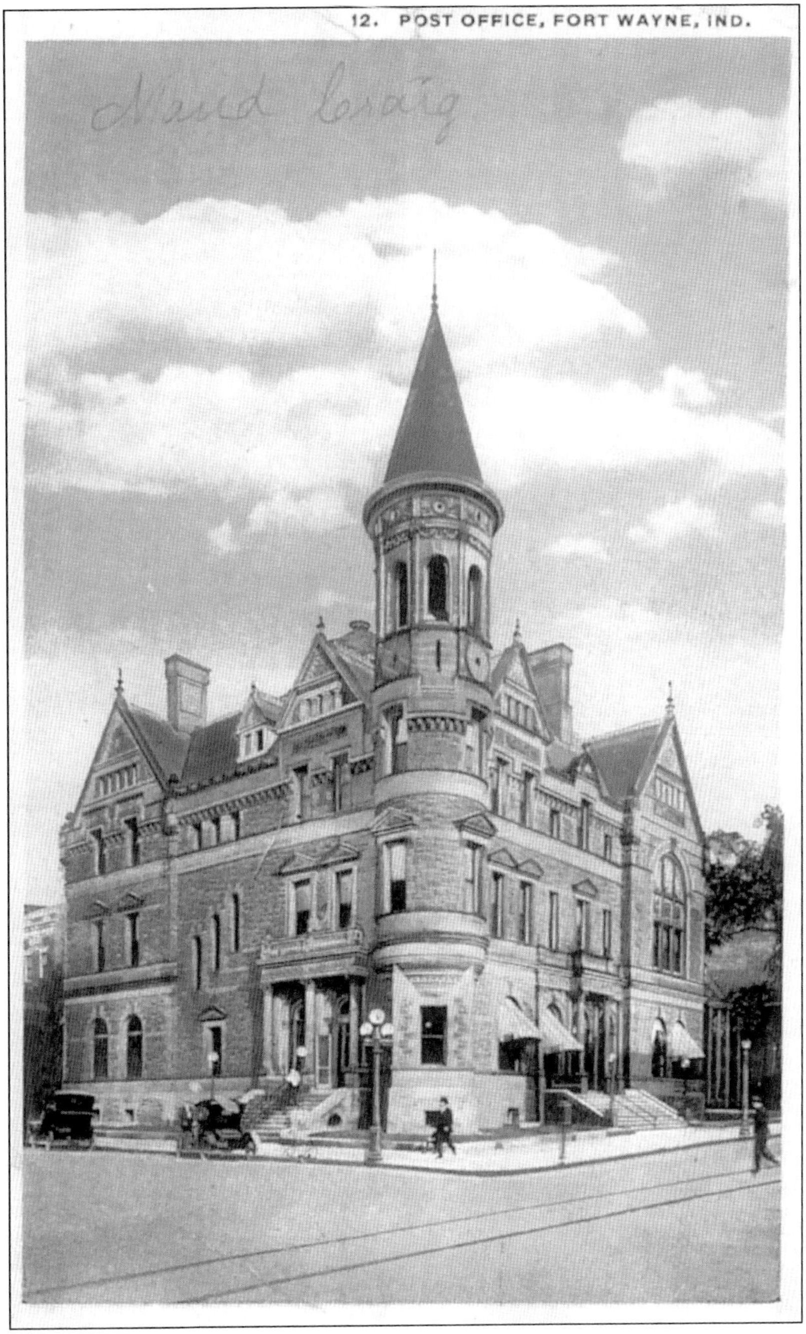

POST OFFICE, FORT WAYNE, INDIANA. The post office was an outstanding building. Note the trolley tracks in the foreground.

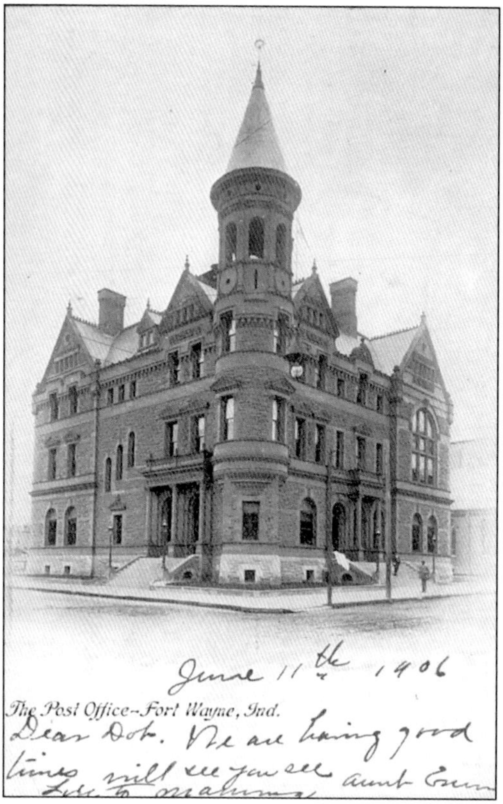

The Post Office, Fort Wayne, Indiana, c. 1906. The message states: "June 11th, 1906. Dear Dot. We are having good times—will see you all—Love to mamma—Aunt Erma."

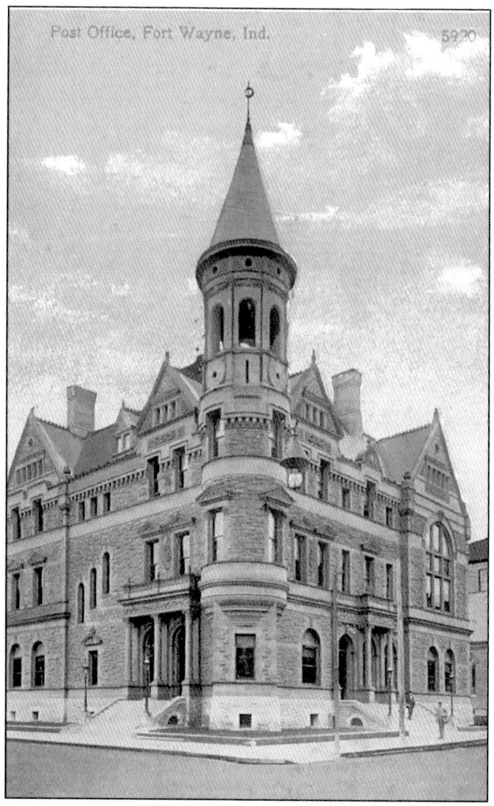

Post Office, Fort Wayne, Indiana. This shows another view, which has been sanitized.

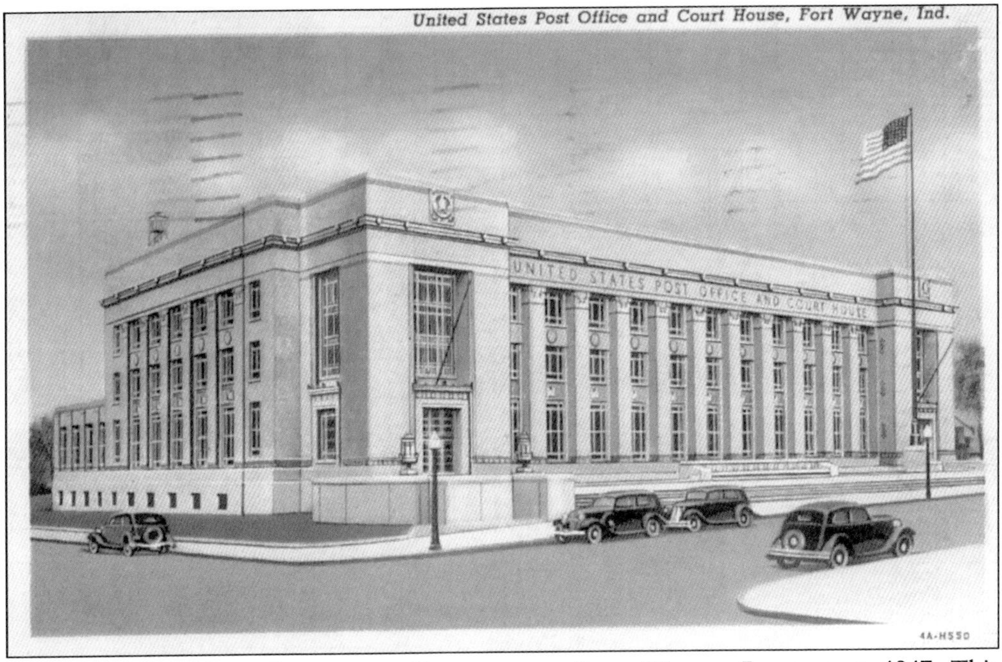

UNITED STATES POST OFFICE AND COURTHOUSE, FORT WAYNE, INDIANA, *c.* 1947. This building housed the post office, federal courts, and federal offices.

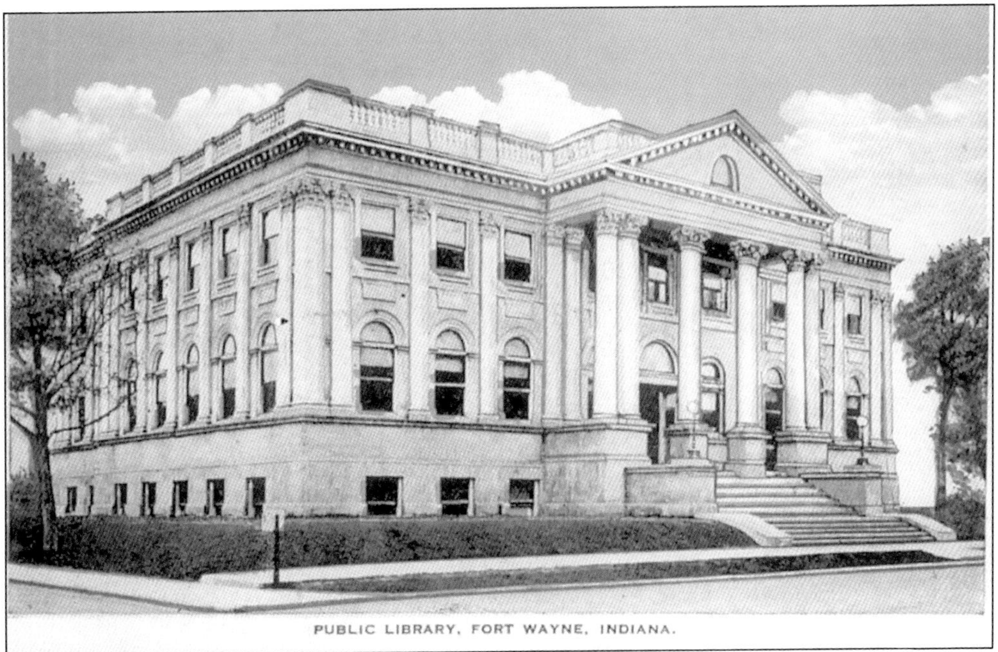

PUBLIC LIBRARY, FORT WAYNE, INDIANA. The library was a classical structure of large proportions.

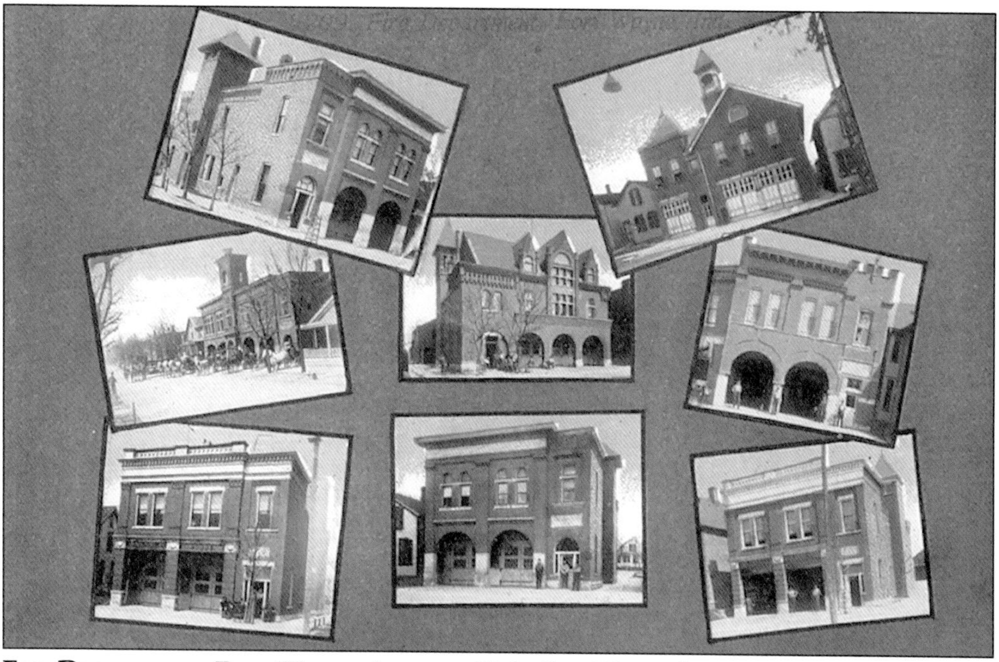

Fire Department, Fort Wayne, Indiana. Eight Fort Wayne fire stations are shown. These were strategically located within the city to provide quick responses to fire calls.

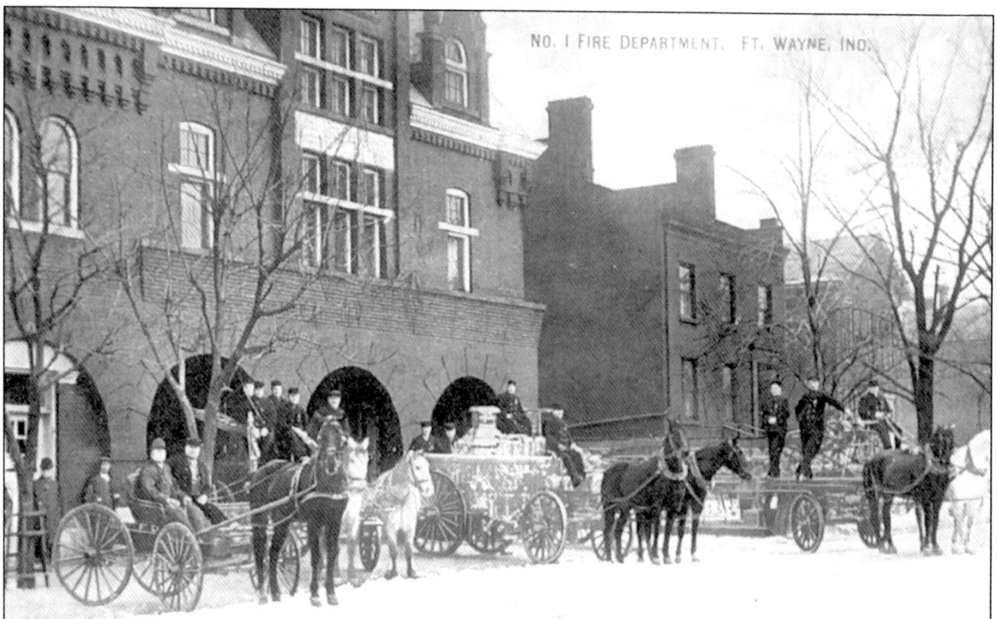

No. 1 Fire Department, Fort Wayne, Indiana. Horse-drawn steam powered pumps were used to fight fires.

Schools

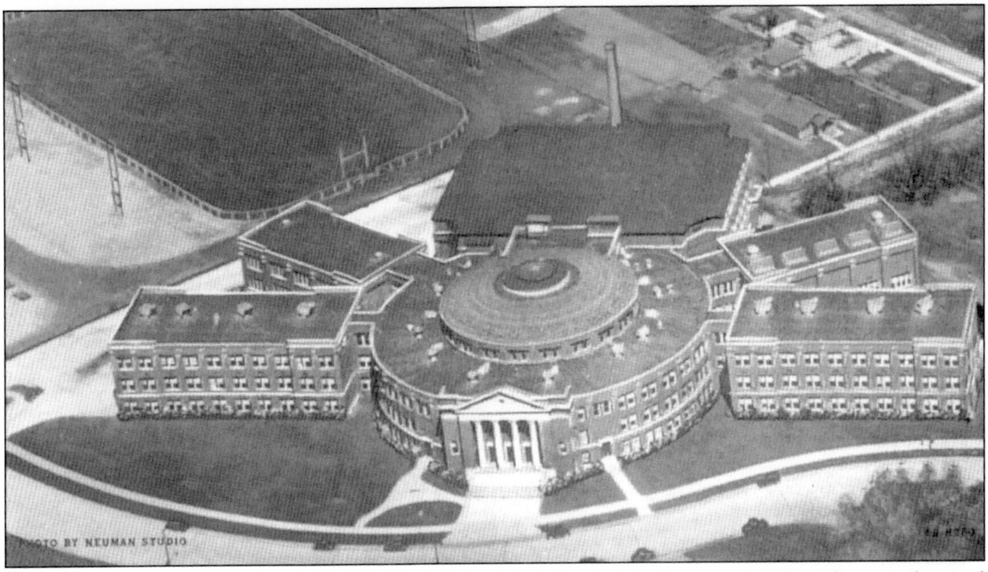

Aerial View of North Side High School, Fort Wayne, Indiana, *c.* 1948. The neoclassical complex of buildings was constructed in the 1920s on the banks of the St. Joseph River to serve students living on the north side of Fort Wayne. Its gymnasium was the home floor of the National Basketball Association's Fort Wayne Zollner Pistons until 1957.

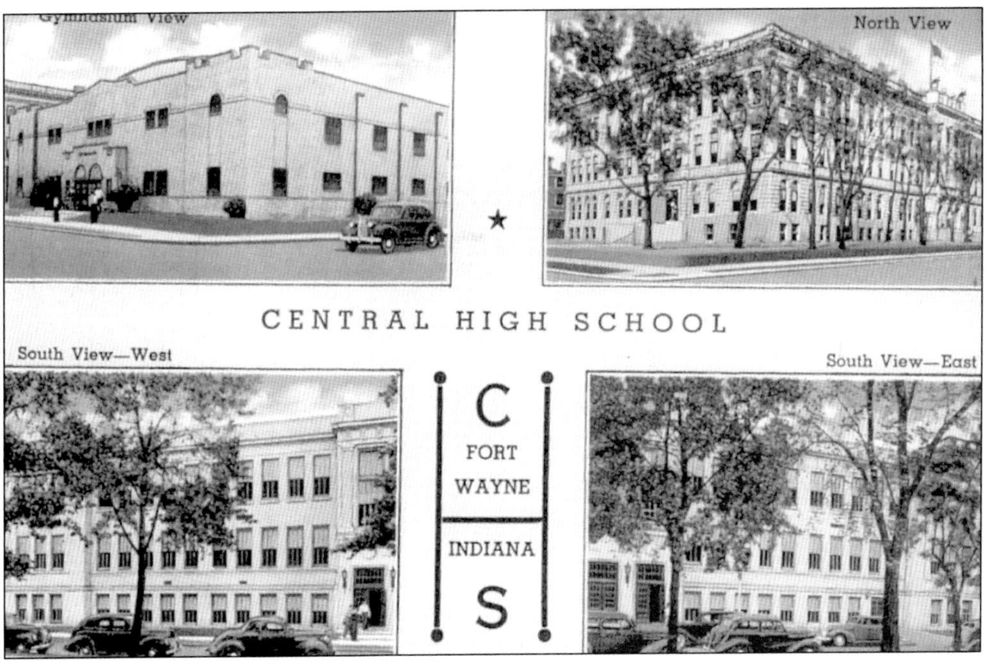

Central High School, Fort Wayne, Indiana.

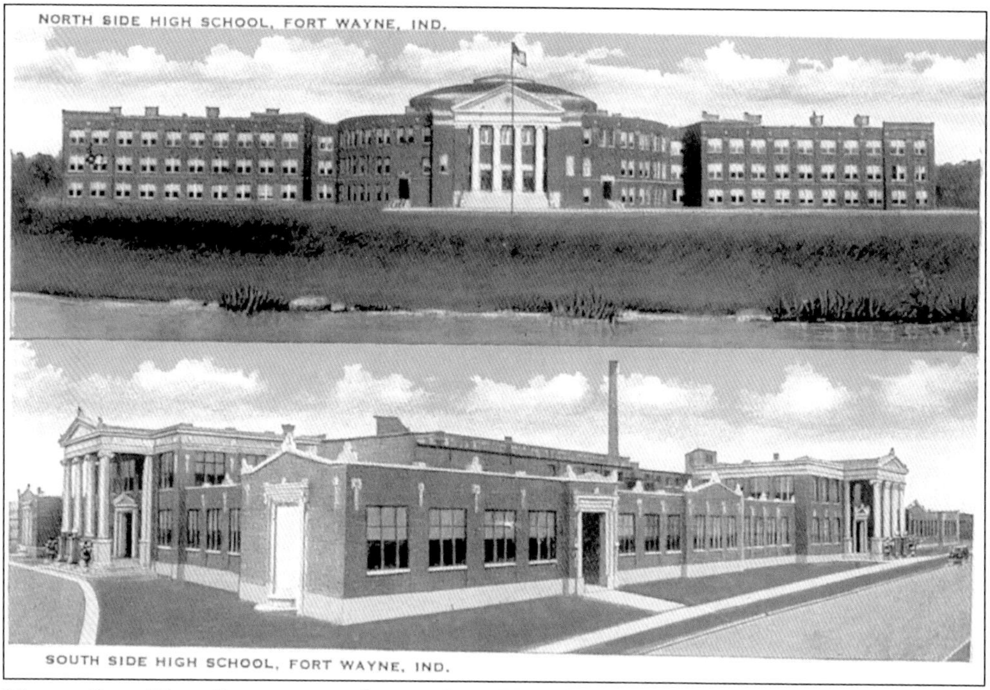

North Side High School and South Side High School, Fort Wayne, Indiana. South Side High School was also built in the 1920s. It has several nationally known alumni, including Shelley Long, Bill Blass, and Dr. Nancy Snyderman.

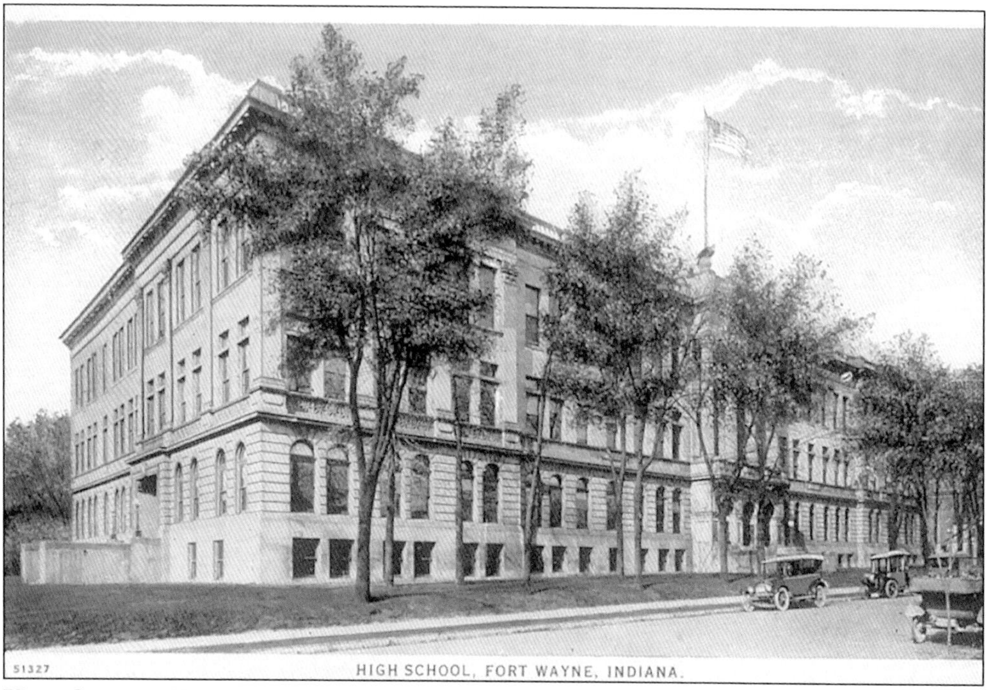

High School, Fort Wayne, Indiana. This is another view of Central High School.

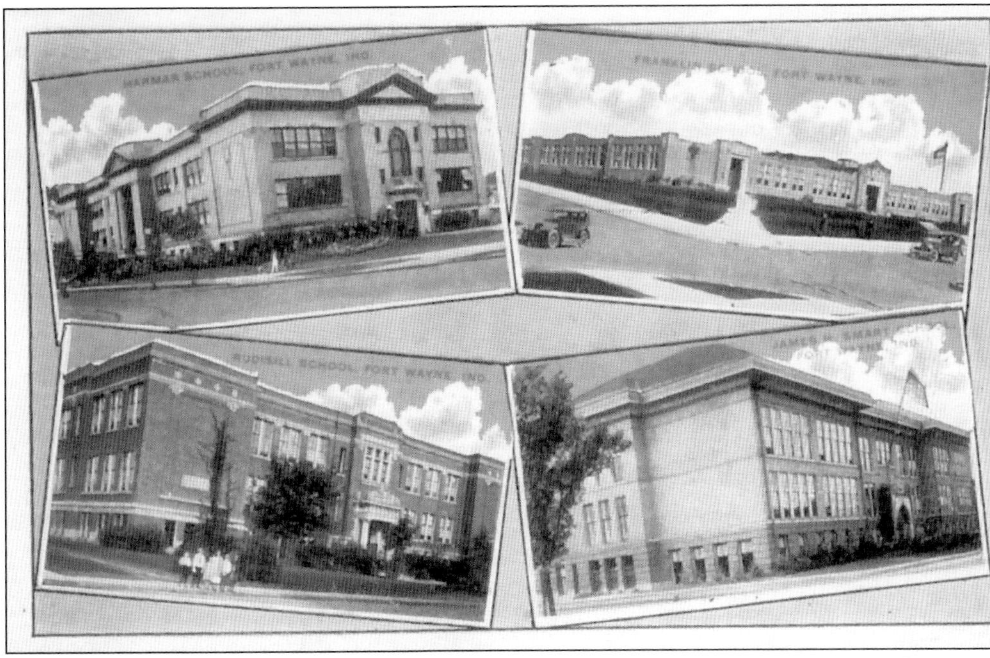

HARMAR SCHOOL, FORT WAYNE INDIANA; FRANKLIN SCHOOL, FORT WAYNE, INDIANA; RUDISILL SCHOOL, FORT WAYNE, INDIANA; AND JAMES H. SMART SCHOOL, FORT WAYNE, INDIANA. Elementary schools were located in Fort Wayne neighborhoods so that most elementary students could walk to school.

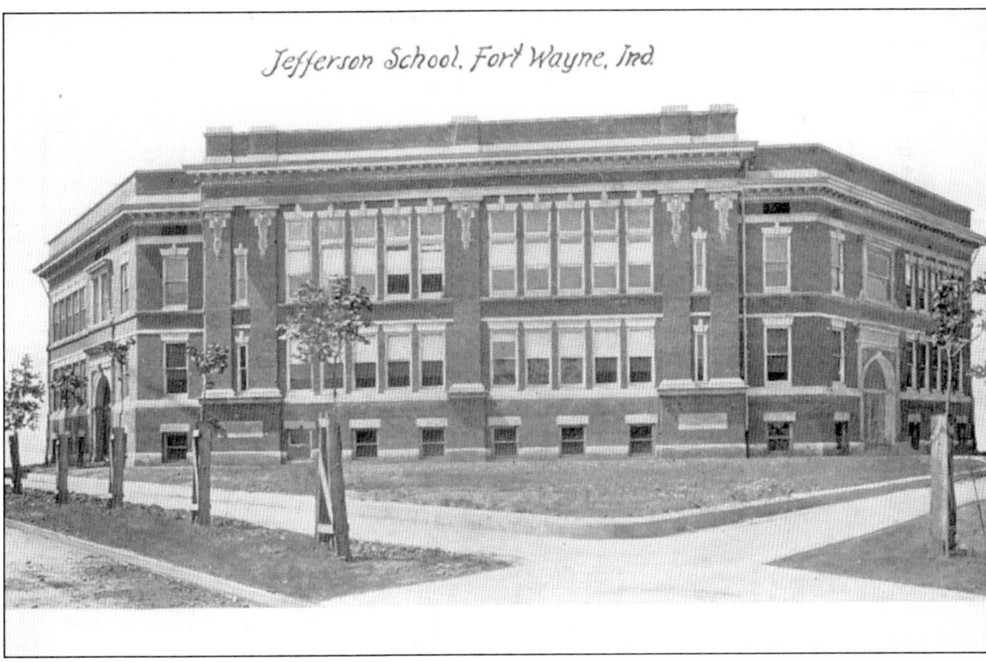

JEFFERSON SCHOOL, FORT WAYNE, INDIANA.

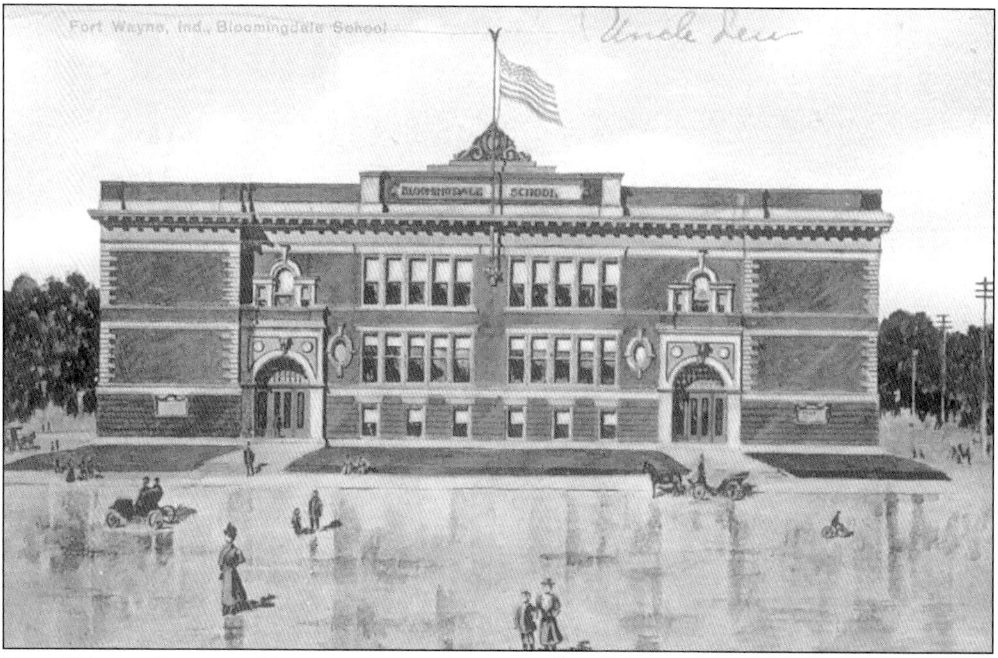

FORT WAYNE, INDIANA, BLOMMINGDALE SCHOOL. Shown here is an artist's conception of the neighborhood school.

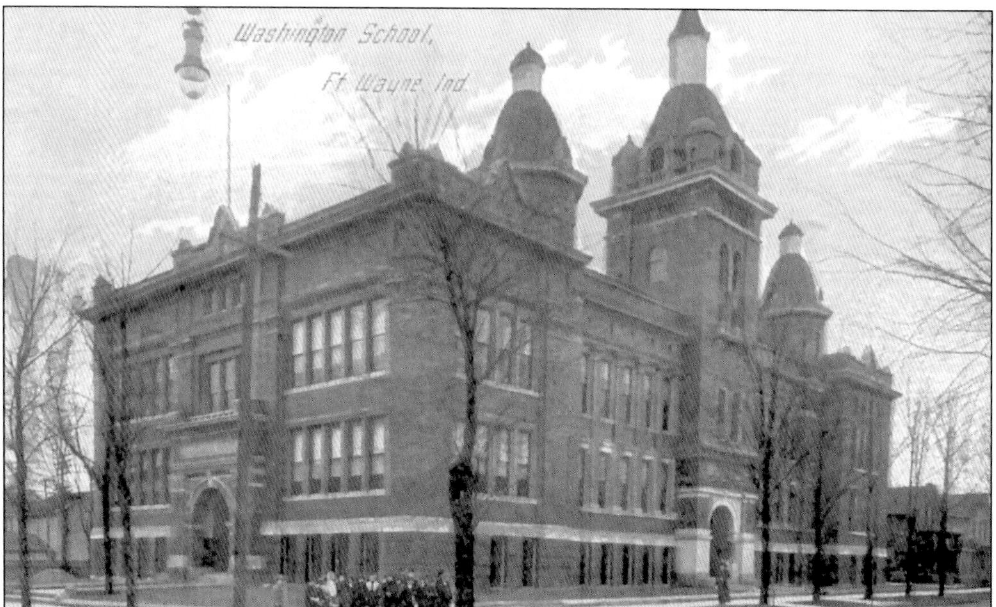

WASHINGTON SCHOOL, FORT WAYNE, INDIANA, C 1912. The message on the card states: "Do not remember your names exactly so you may have your choice of cards. Having a very fine time. Idilia B."

COLLEGES

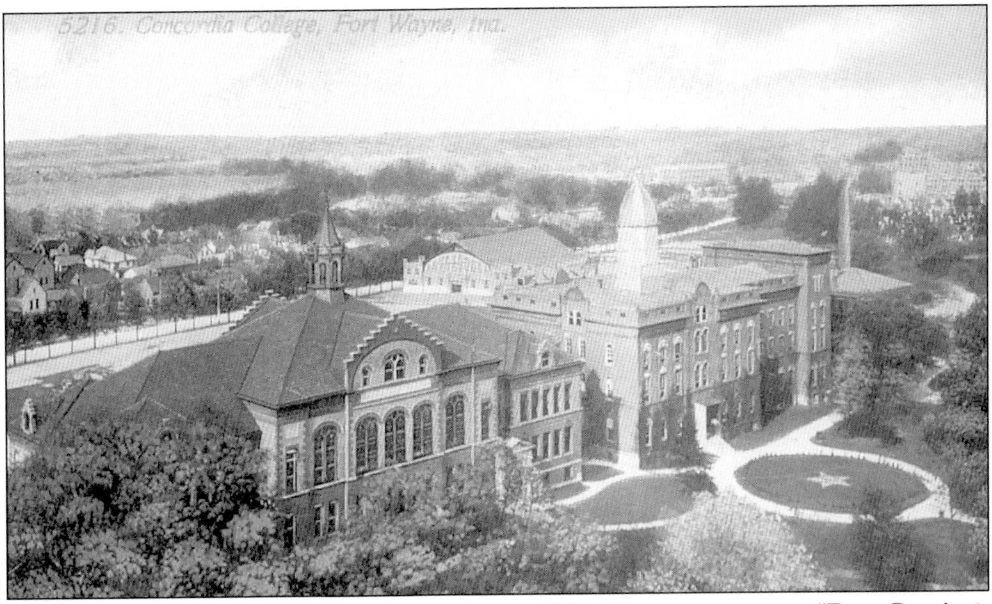

CONCORDIA COLLEGE, FORT WAYNE, INDIANA, *C.* 1913. The message states: "Dear Cousin & all. I received your welcome card, it found me all real well, the babies are getting along fine, I am up & around, I feel, purty good, but be a long time, to get back in strength. I named them, Lewis Herman, Lucile Fredica. They are doing fine, come & see them, we have bad weather rain, good bye. Write soon."

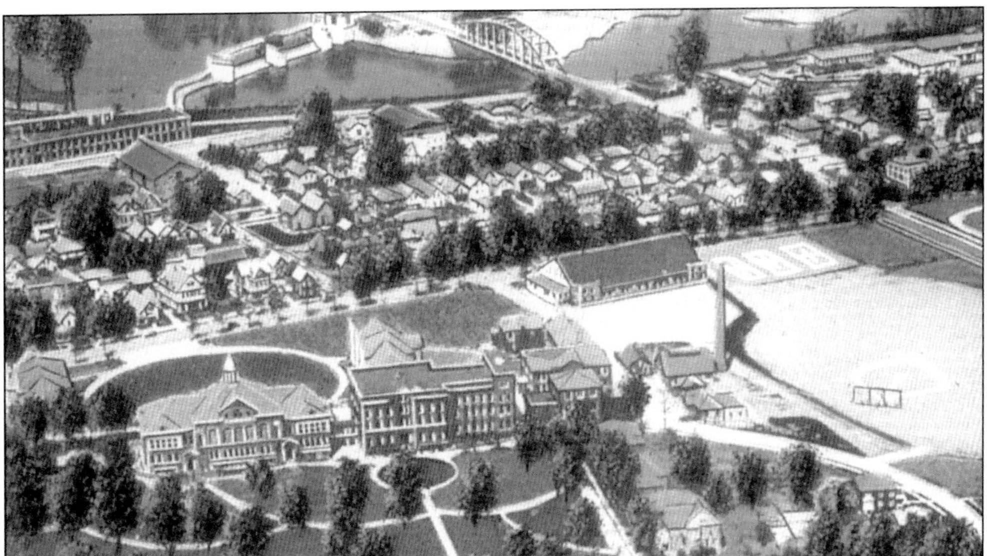

A VIEW OF CONCORDIA COLLEGE, FORT WAYNE, INDIANA. The college was originally located east of the downtown area.

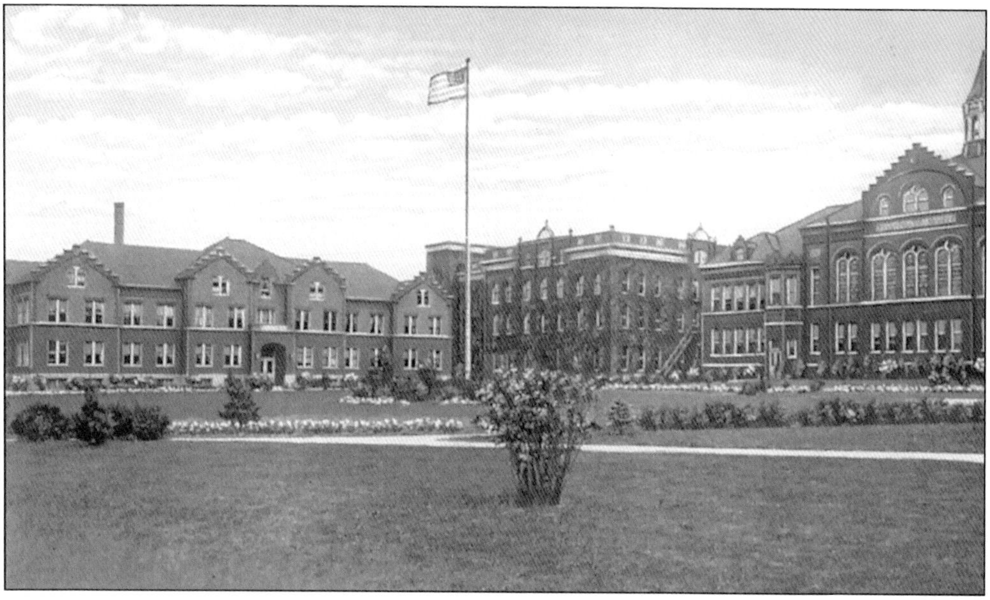

Sectional View of Concordia College, Fort Wayne, Indiana. The college buildings faced a large green area.

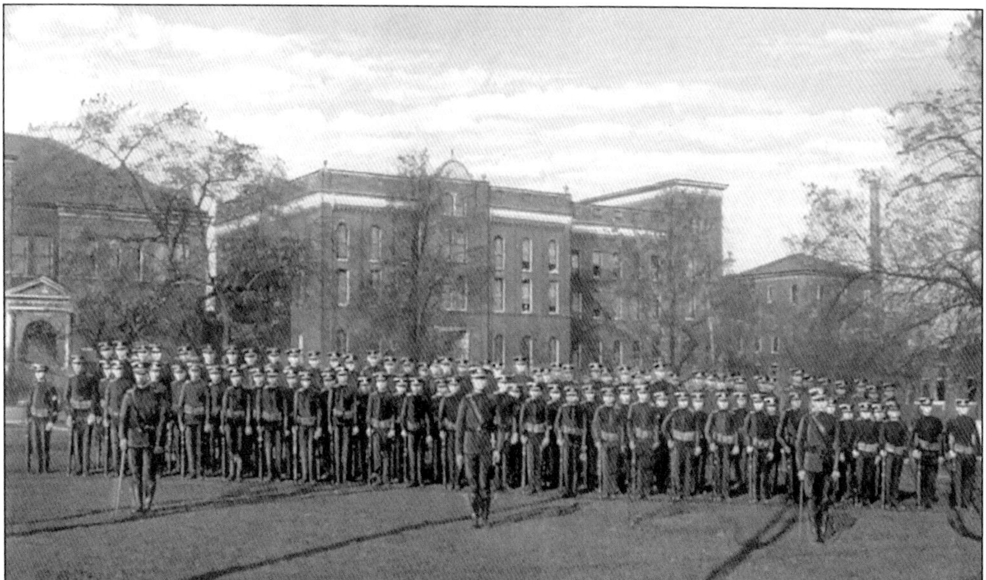

Concordia Cadets, Concordia College, Fort Wayne, Indiana. The Concordia Cadets provided military training for students.

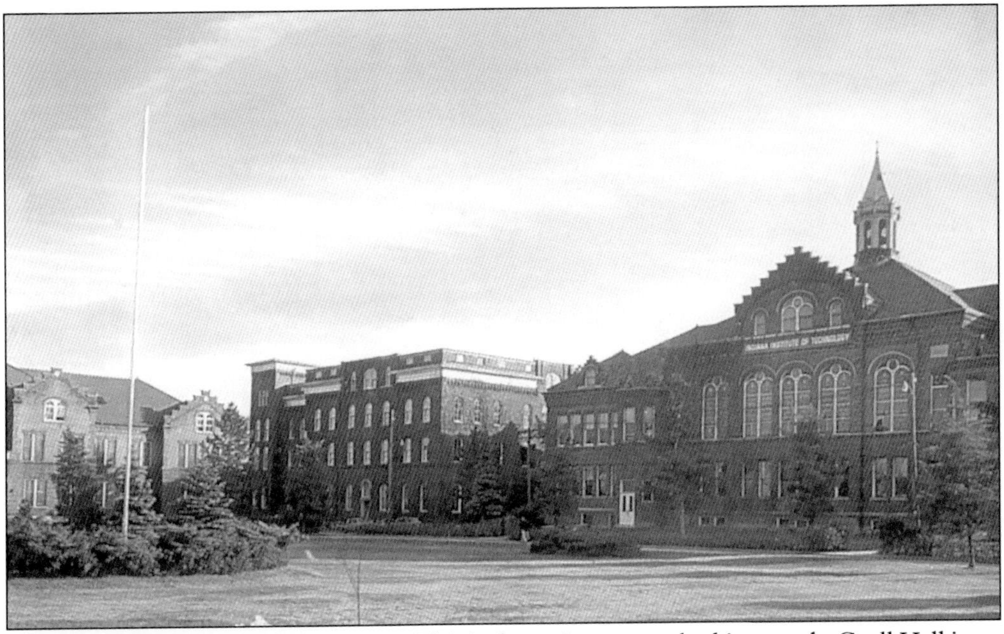

INDIANA INSTITUTE OF TECHNOLOGY. This is the main campus looking south; Crull Hall is on the left, Hanser Hall is in the center, and Shick Hall is on the right, at 1600 East Washington Boulevard, Fort Wayne, Indiana. After Concorida College moved to a new site on the north edge of Fort Wayne, the Indiana Institute of Technology acquired the campus.

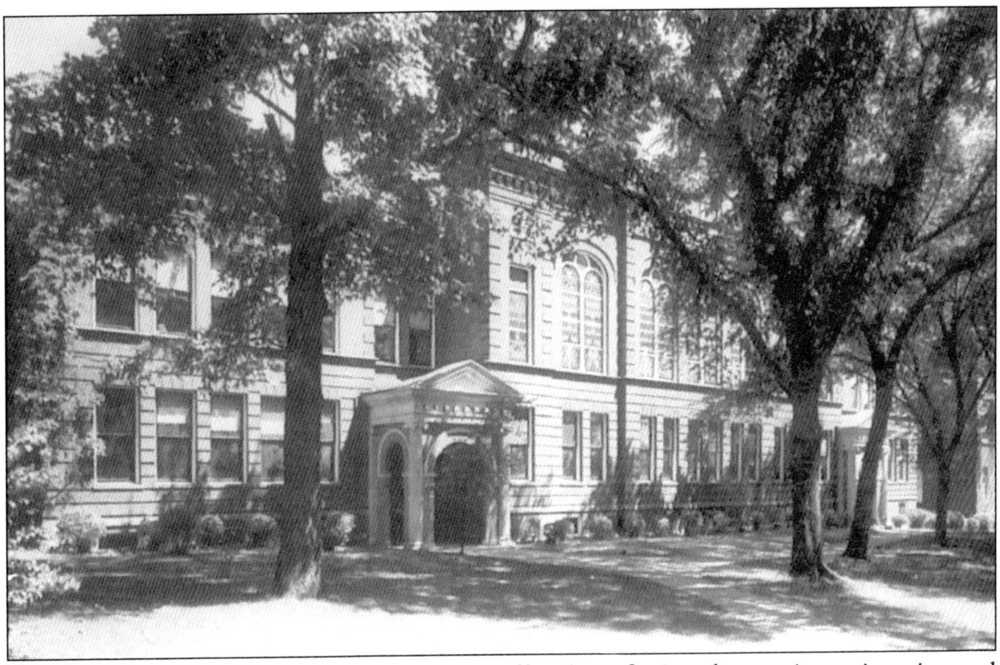

INDIANA TECHNICAL COLLEGE. This school offered conferring degrees in engineering and science, with 23 buildings located on a beautiful 20-acre campus at 1600 East Washington Boulevard in Fort Wayne, Indiana.

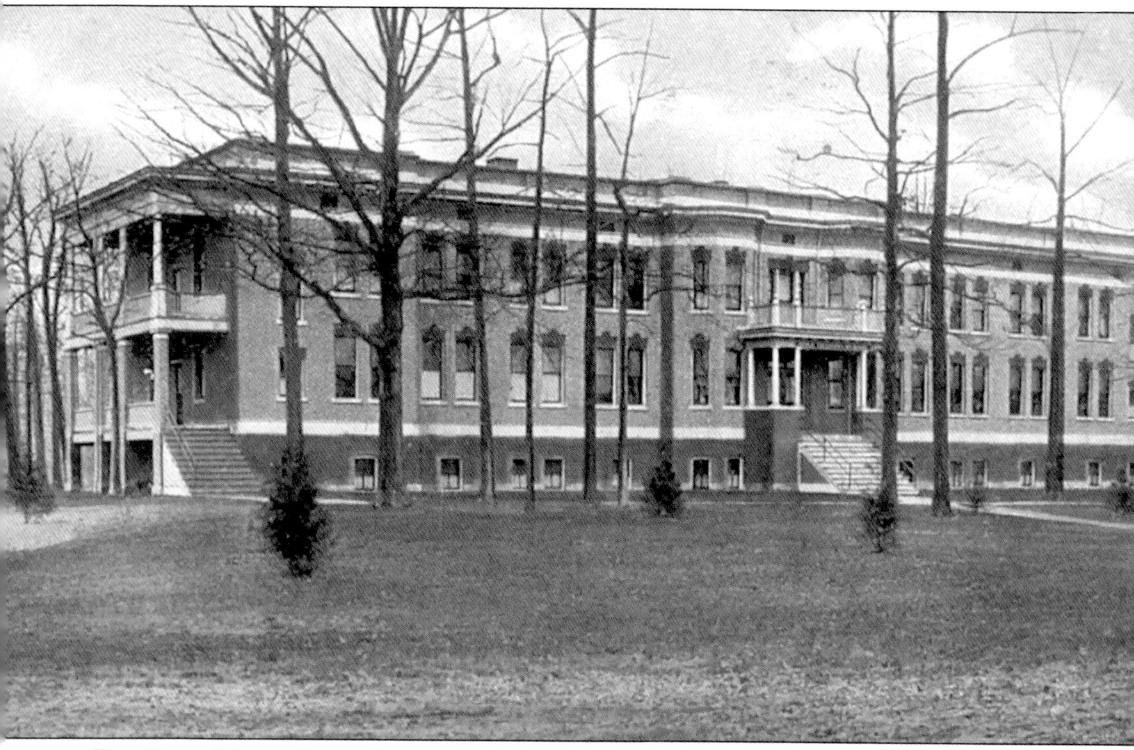

THE FORT WAYNE BIBLE TRAINING SCHOOL, FORT WAYNE, INDIANA, *C.* 1908. The message on this card states: "Mon Aug 3—4 p.m. All 8 of us have seen the sights took dinner out at Robison Park Had a jolly circus. We are going now to Columbia City and then in wagon to Lune Lake."

HOSPITALS

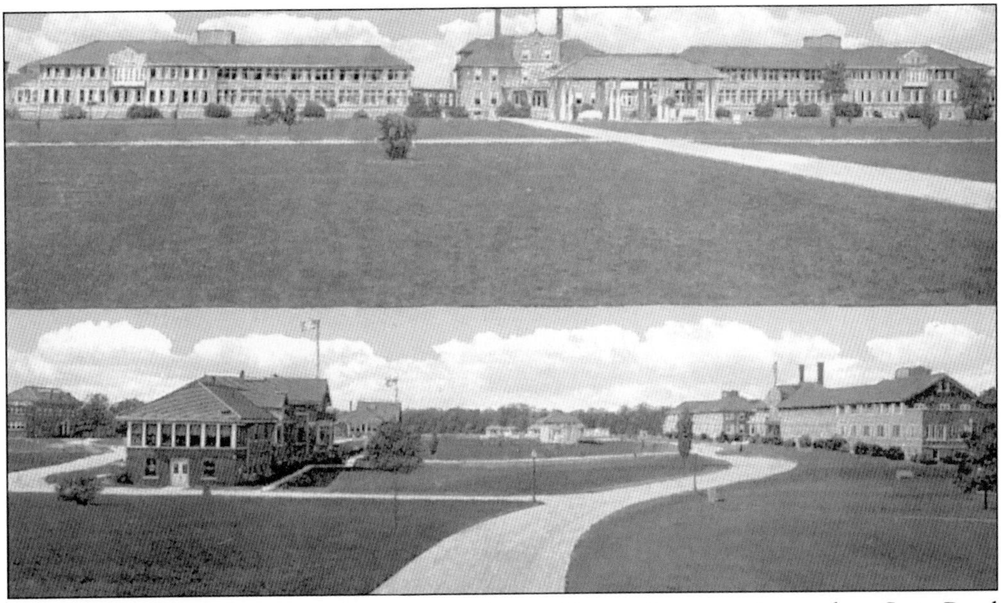

IRENE BYRON TUBERCULOSIS SANATORIUM, FORT WAYNE, INDIANA. Located on State Road 3, north of Fort Wayne, this complex of buildings provided a facility for the isolation and treatment of patients with the highly contagious disease of tuberculosis.

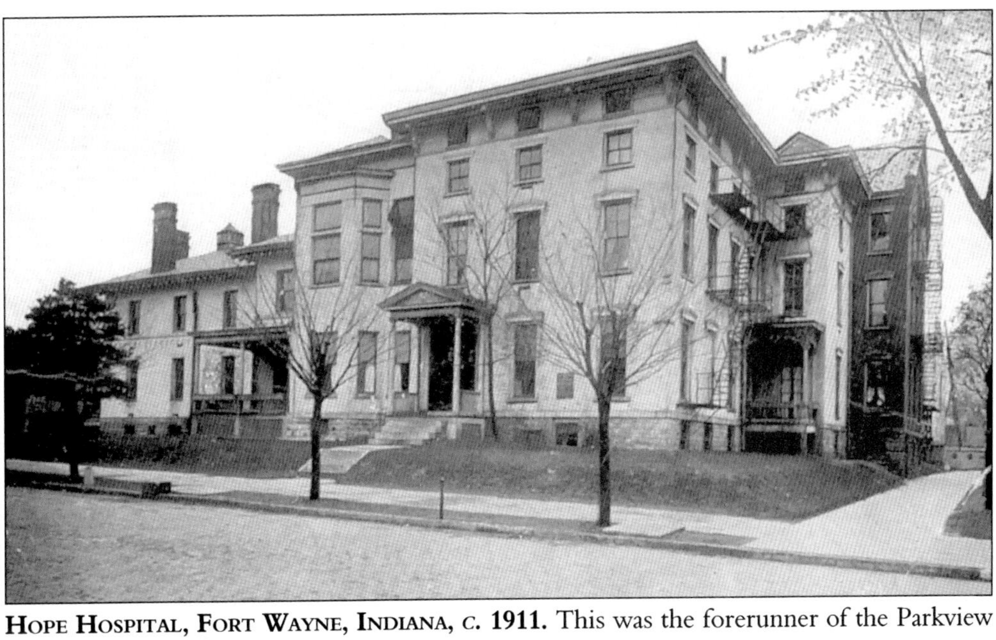

HOPE HOSPITAL, FORT WAYNE, INDIANA, *c.* 1911. This was the forerunner of the Parkview Memorial Hospital.

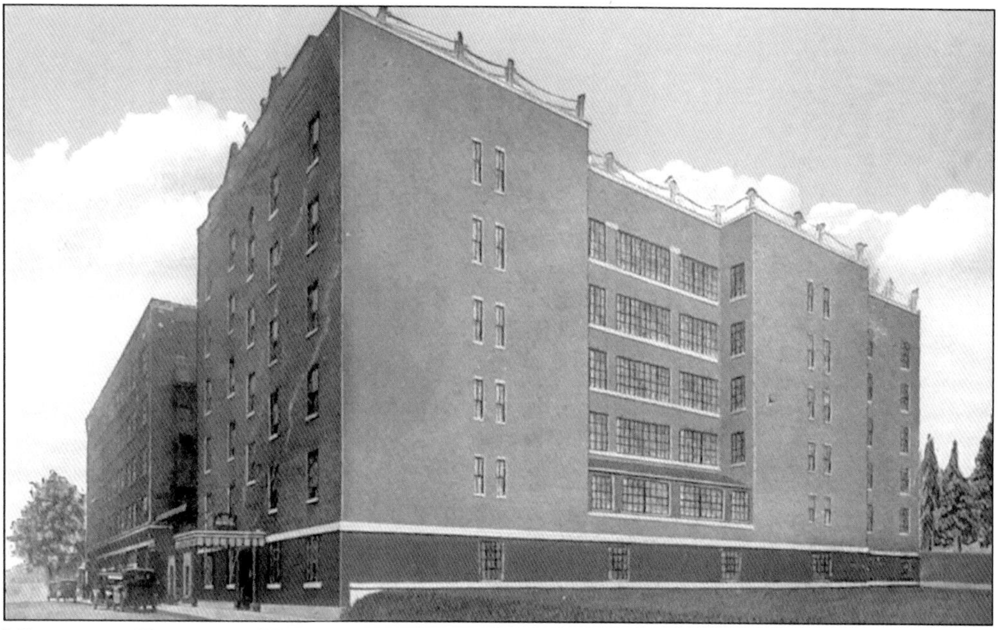

METHODIST EPISCOPAL HOSPITAL, FORT WAYNE, INDIANA. The Methodist Hospital was also a forerunner to Parkview Memorial Hospital.

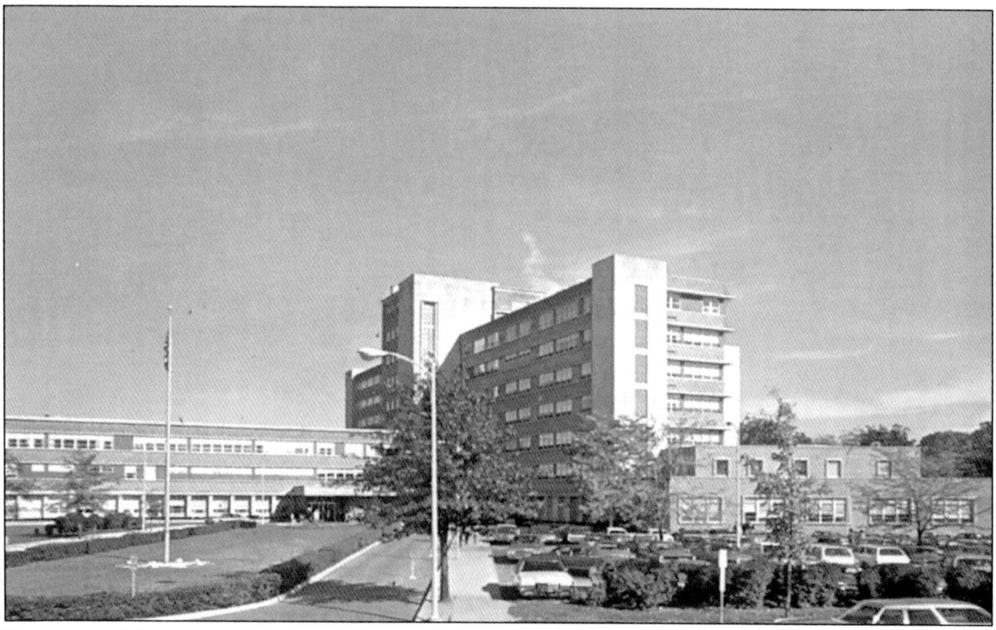

PARKVIEW MEMORIAL HOSPITAL, FORT WAYNE, INDIANA. This hospital was located on an 18-acre wooded tract on East State Boulevard at Randallia Avenue.

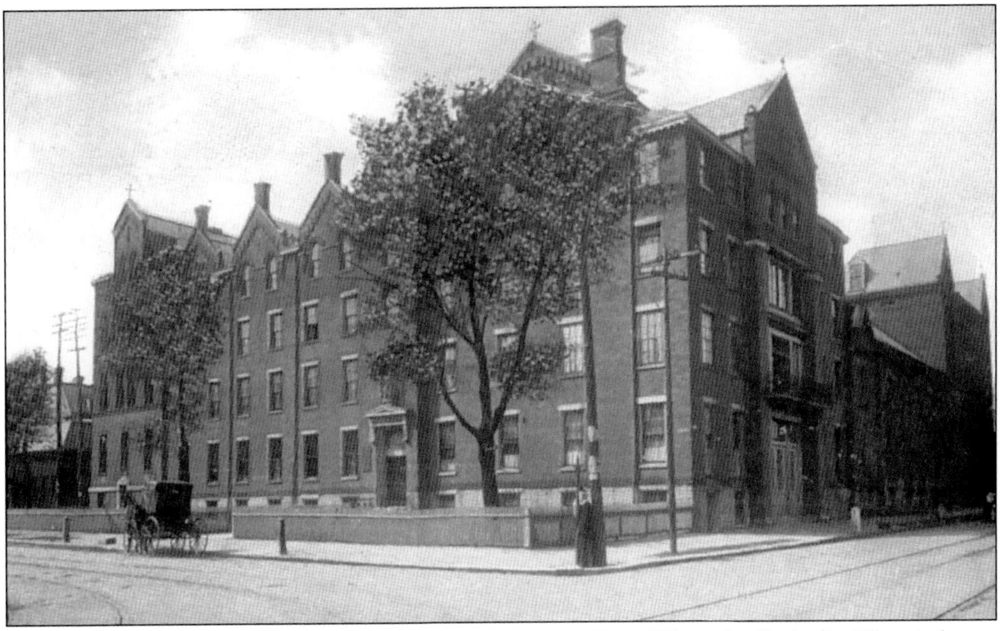

SAINT JOSEPH'S HOSPITAL, FORT WAYNE, INDIANA. Fort Wayne's Catholic Hospital was located at Broadway and Berry Streets.

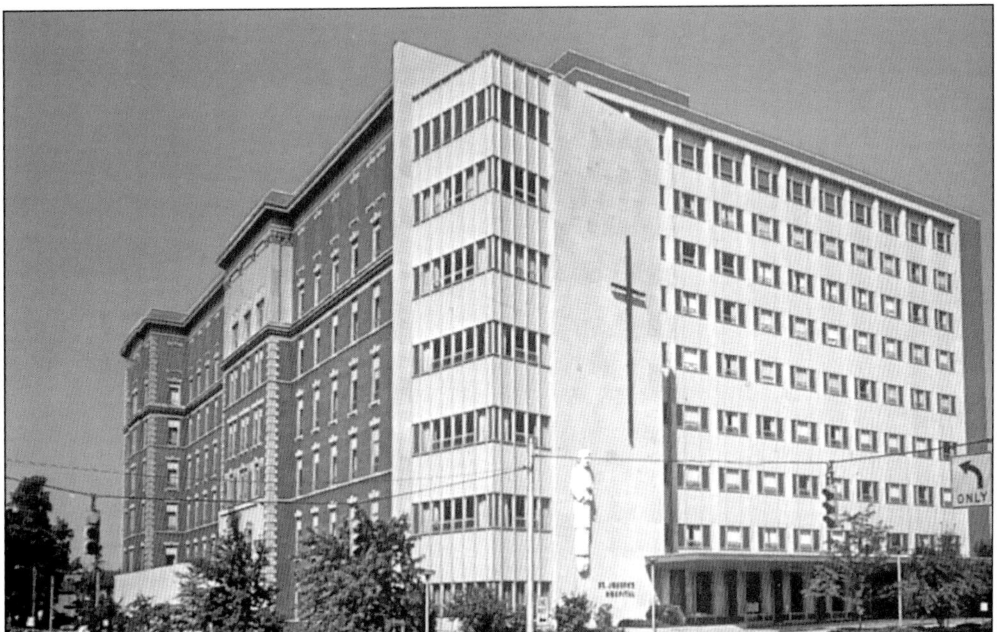

ST. JOSEPH HOSPITAL, FORT WAYNE, INDIANA. This hospital was located at 700 Broadway at West Berry Street, Fort Wayne, Indiana.

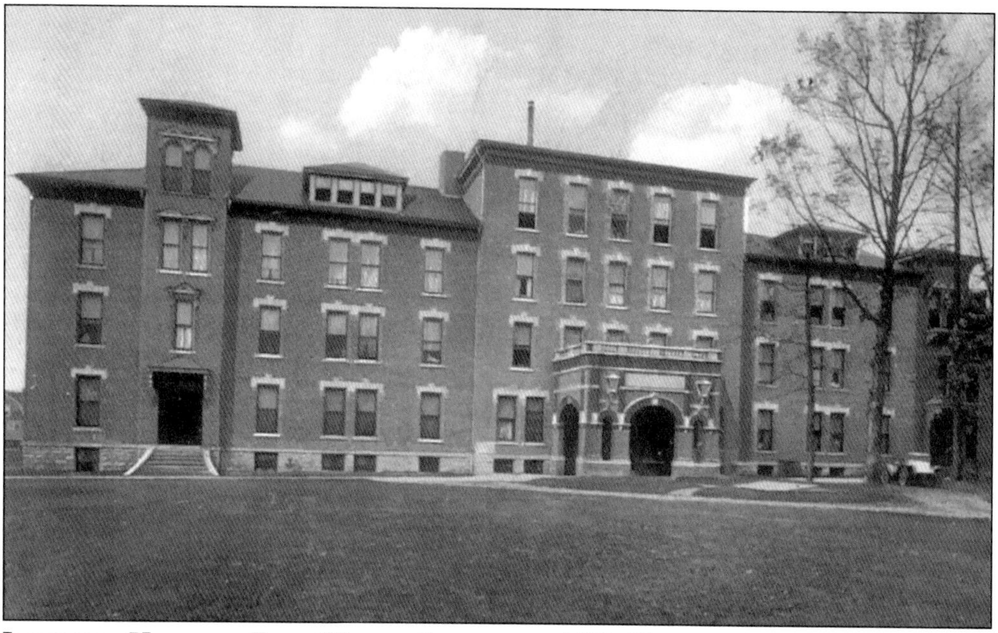

Lutheran Hospital, Fort Wayne, Indiana, c. 1909. The message on this card states: "Dear Sister and Brother. I will drop you another card. We are having a good time think Sabrina is getting weaker all the time. This is the hospital where she was operated in just before Xmas. Mama has to stay with her all the time, but she seems to enjoy it. Well Good Bye this time, Emma."

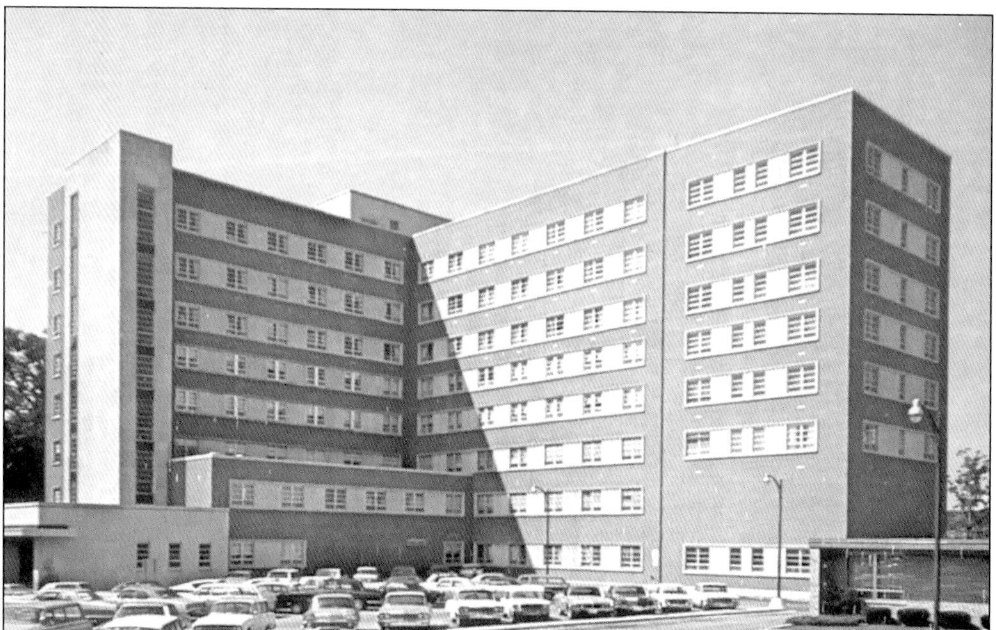

Lutheran Hospital. Northeastern Indiana's largest general hospital, this was located at 3024 Fairfield Avenue in Fort Wayne, Indiana.

CHURCHES

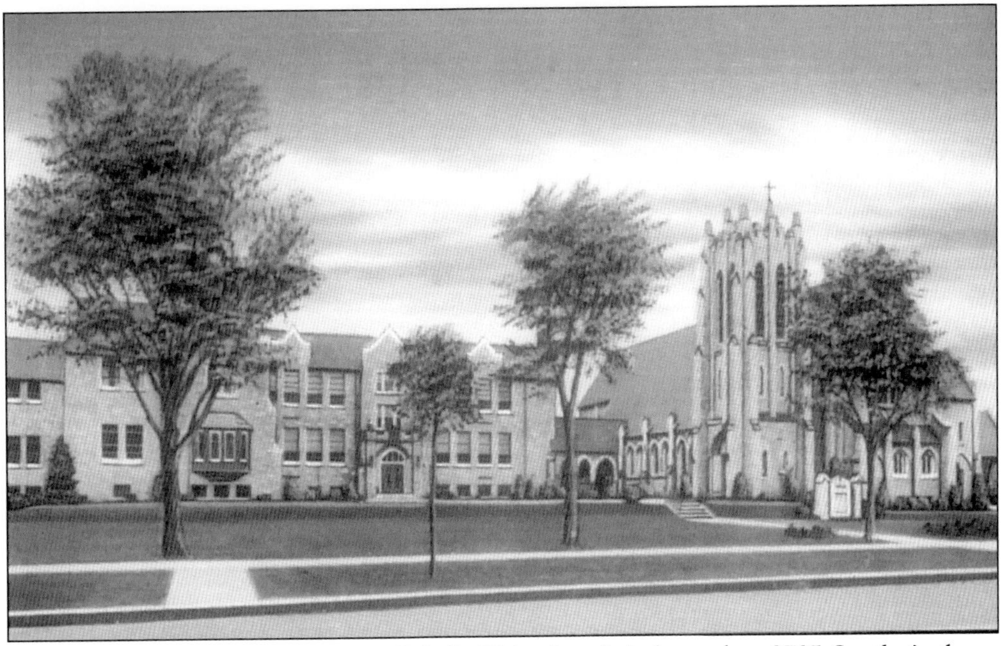

BETHLEHEM LUTHERAN CHURCH, U.A.C. This church is located at 3705 South Anthony Boulevard, Fort Wayne, Indiana.

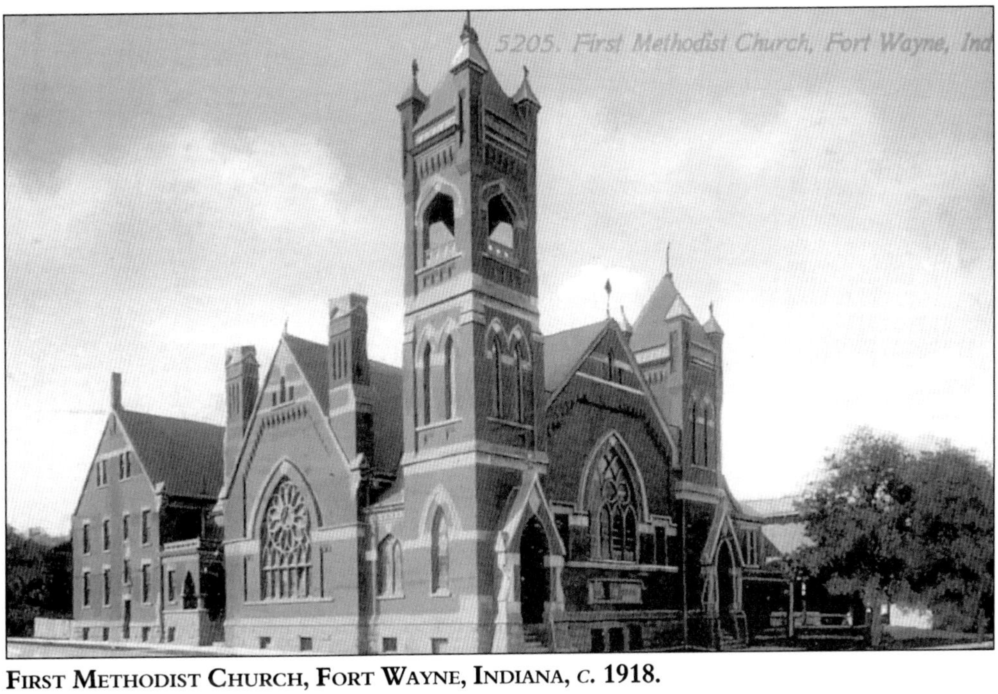

FIRST METHODIST CHURCH, FORT WAYNE, INDIANA, *C.* 1918.

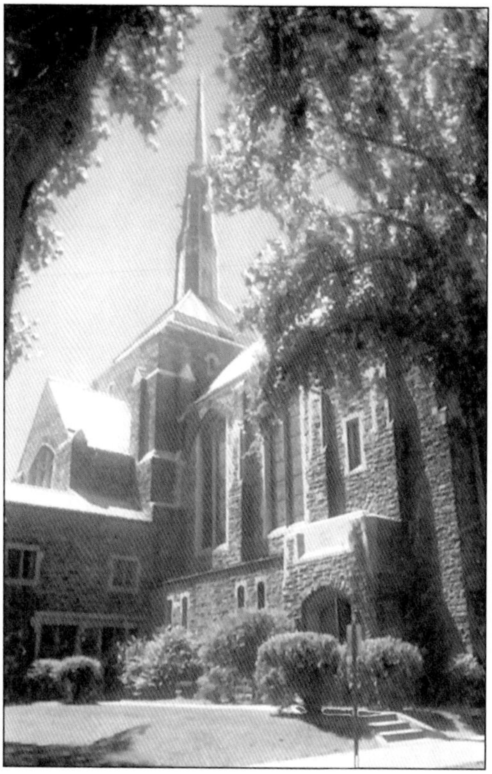

TRINITY ENGLISH EV. LUTHERAN CHURCH, FORT WAYNE, INDIANA. This church was founded in 1846, by Paul Hartzell Krauss, D.D., Pastor. It was the first exclusively English-speaking Lutheran congregation in northern Indiana. The church and parish buildings—1925 A.D.—are the work of the late great Gothic architect Bertram G. Goodhue.

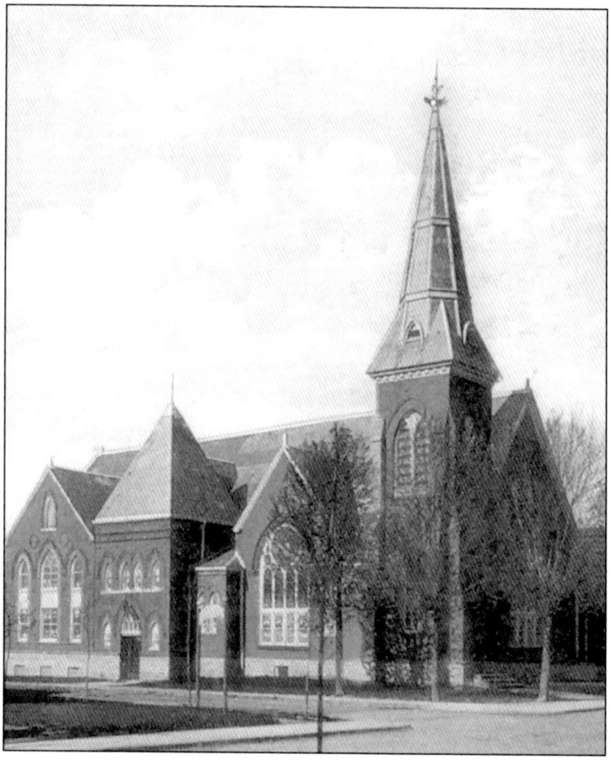

PRESBYTERIAN CHURCH.

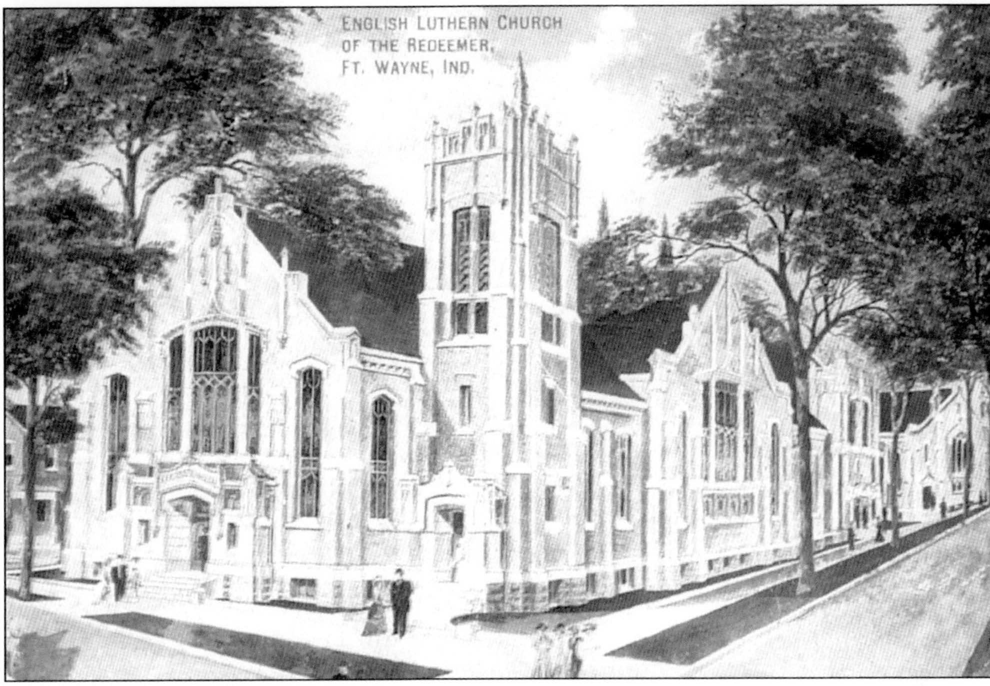

English Lutheran Church of the Redeemer, Fort Wayne, Indiana, *c.* 1911. Shown here is an artist's conception, which was probably commissioned by the architect before construction began.

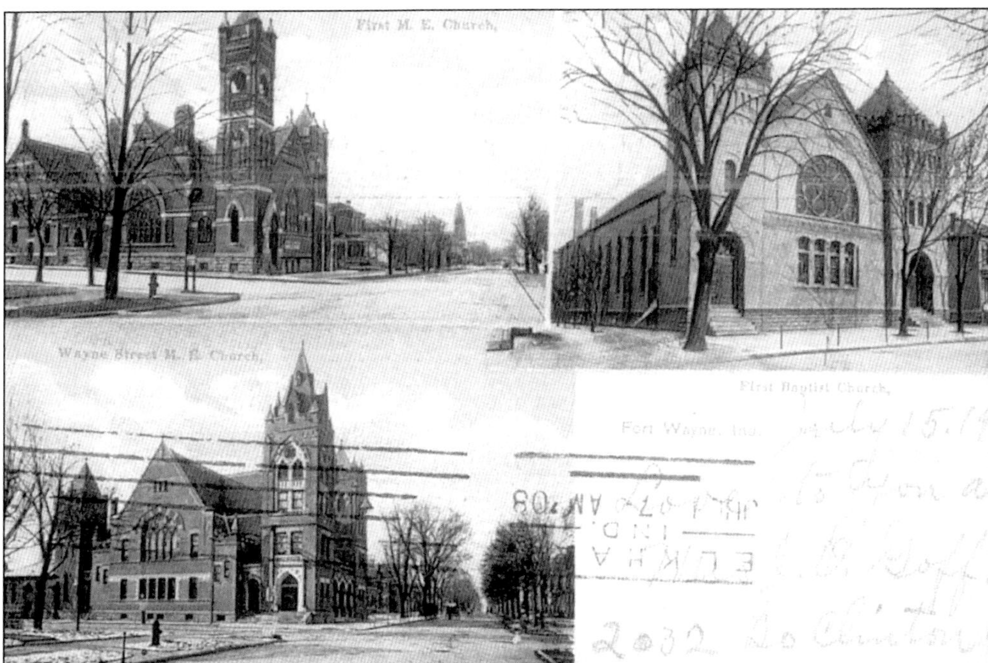

First M.E. Church, Wayne Street M.E. Church, First Baptist Church, Fort Wayne, Indiana.

LODGES AND CLUBS

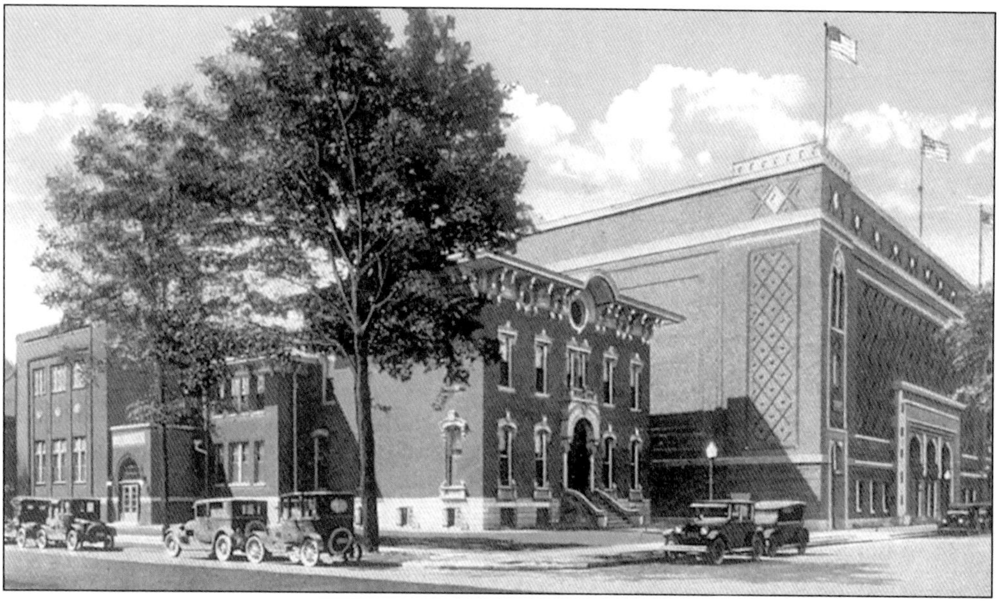

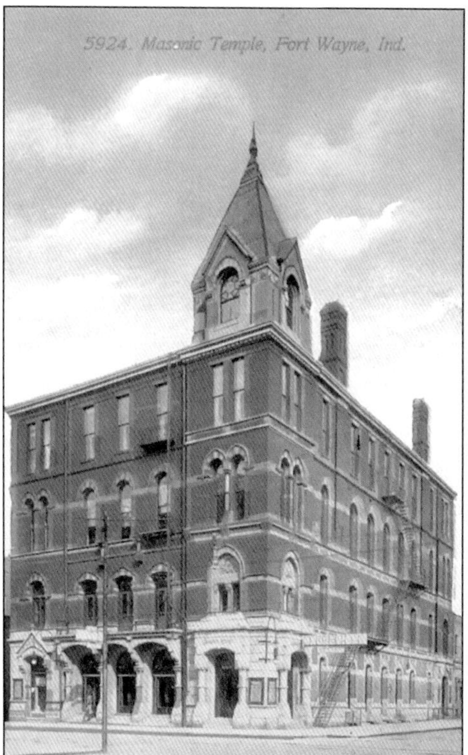

NEW SHRINE TEMPLE, FORT WAYNE, INDIANA.

MASONIC TEMPLE, FORT WAYNE, INDIANA.

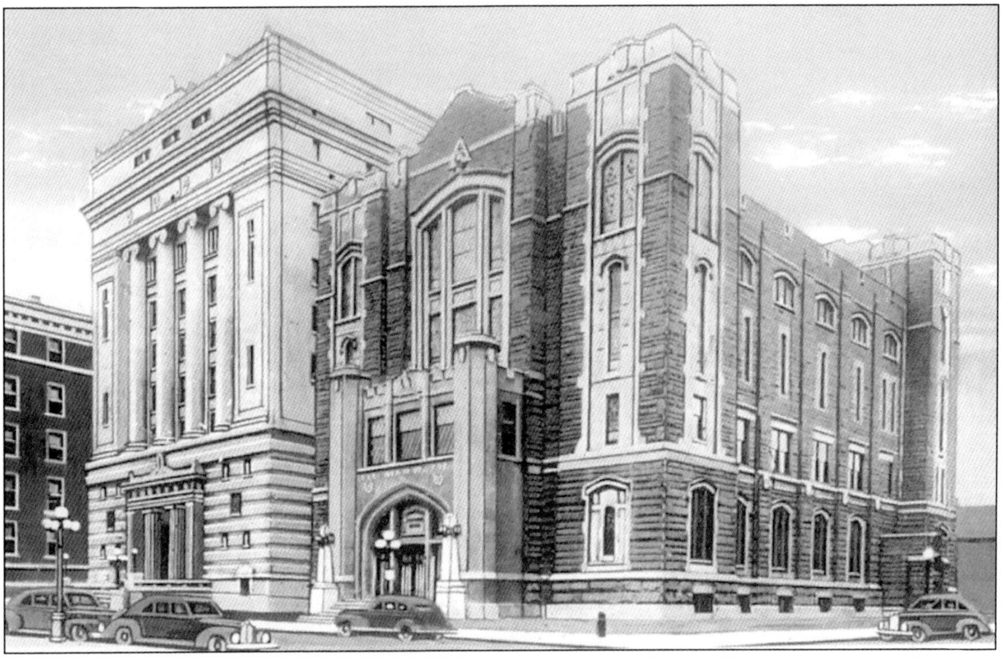

MASONIC TEMPLE AND SCOTTISH RITE CATHEDRAL, FORT WAYNE INDIANA.

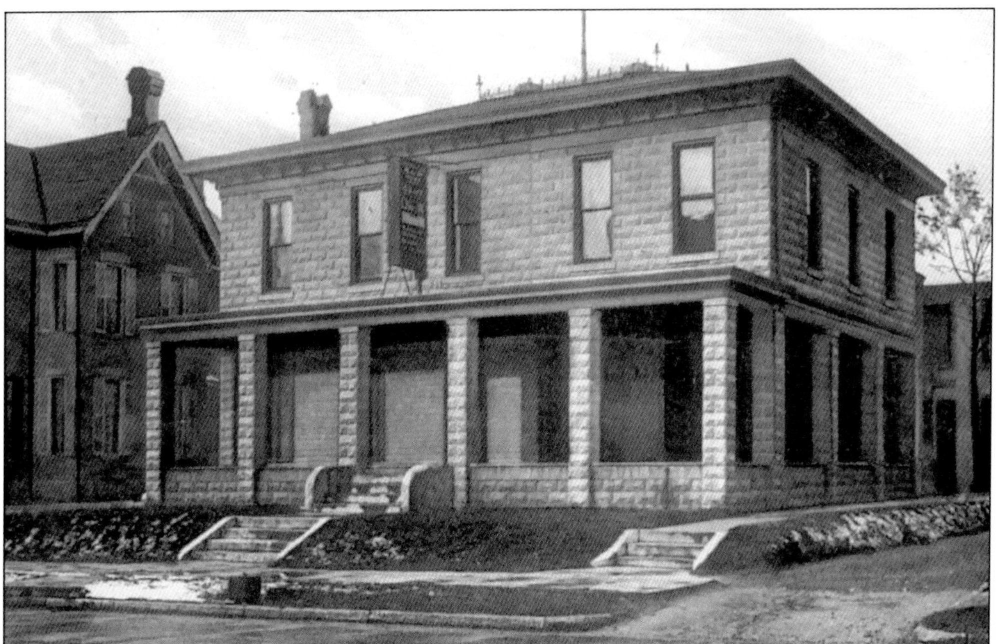

K.O.F.P. HOME, FORT WAYNE, INDIANA, *c.* 1909.

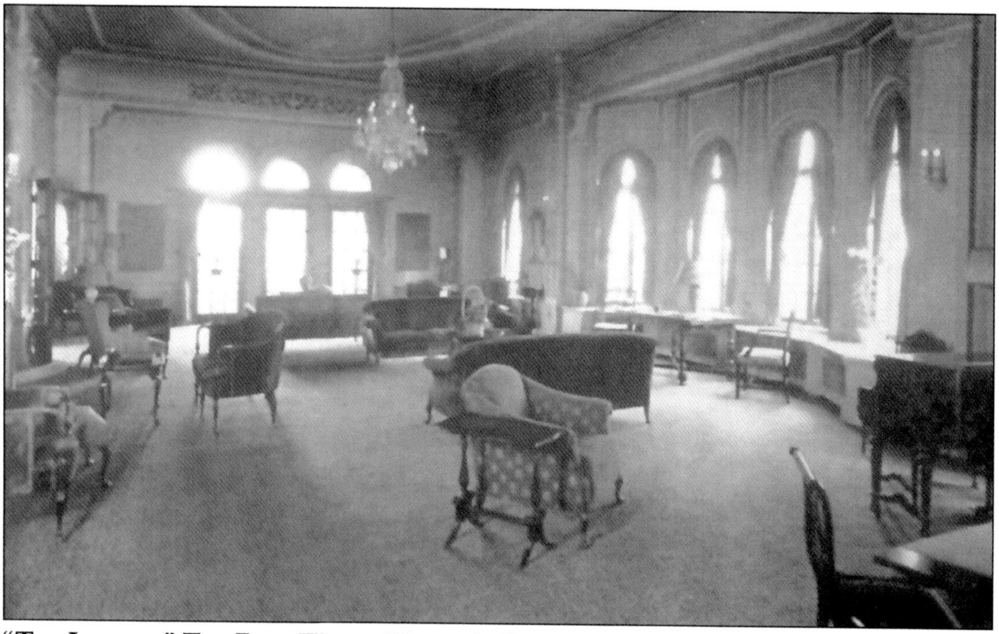

"The Lounge," The Fort Wayne Woman's Club.

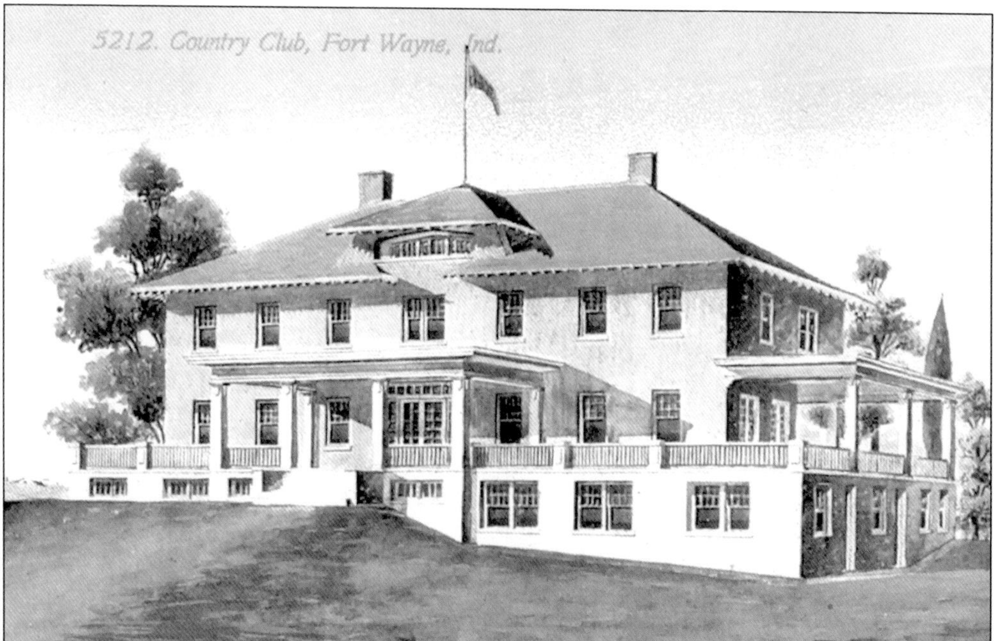

Country Club, Fort Wayne, Indiana, *c.* 1912.

Rivers and Bridges

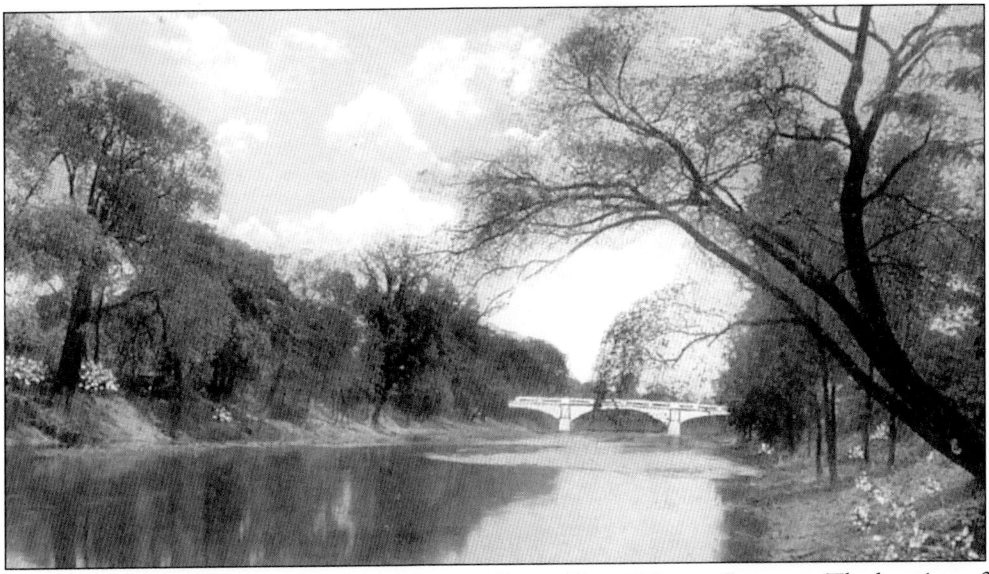

Harmer's Ford, Historic Spot on Maumee River, Fort Wayne, Indiana. The location of Harmer's Ford includes a small section of the Maumee River and the adjacent banks, three-fourths of a mile east of the courthouse. It marks the site of the slaughter of the troops of Gen. Josiah Harmer on October 20, 1790, by the Miamis and Chief Little Turtle. Directions are as follows: East Main car to corner of Harmer and Washington Bd-E; walk north three squares to river bank; Ford is a few rods east of Harmer Street. The term "East Main Street Car" refers to the trolley.

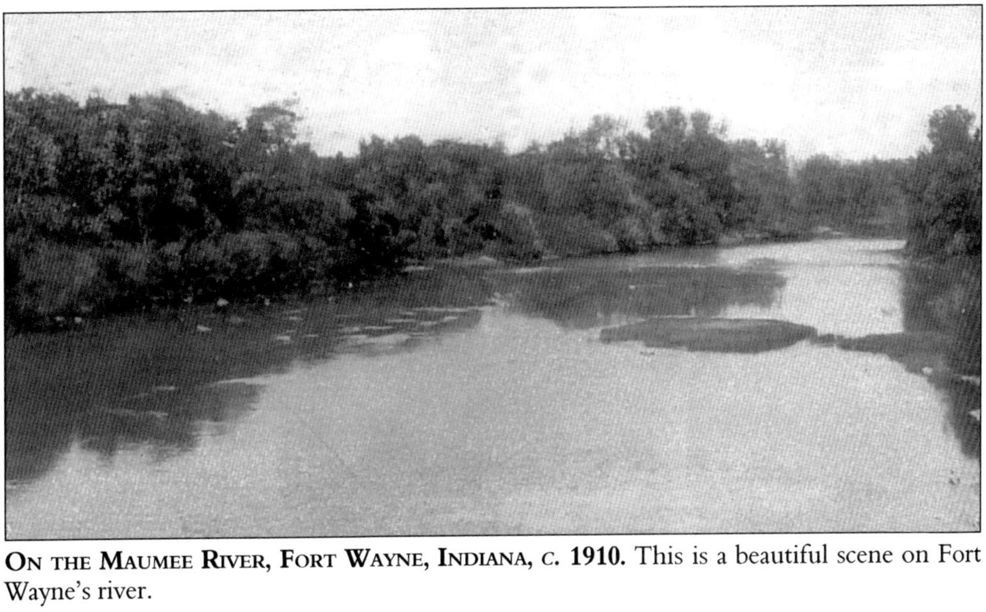

On the Maumee River, Fort Wayne, Indiana, *c.* 1910. This is a beautiful scene on Fort Wayne's river.

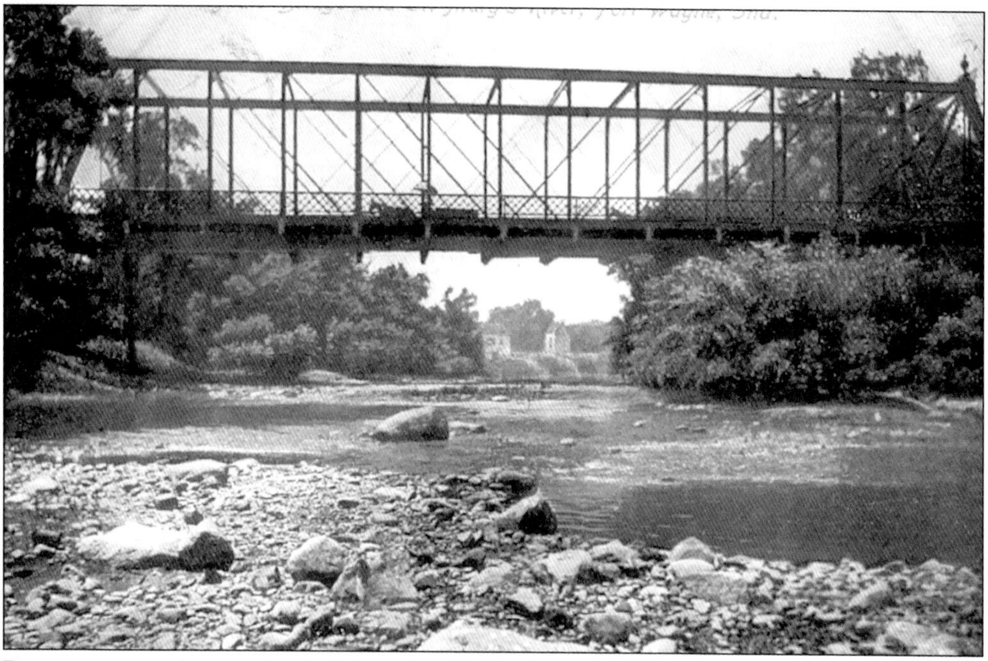

Bloomingdale Bridge and St. Mary's River, Fort Wayne, Indiana. Steel bridges were an improvement over wooden structures. They were located high above the river in order to avoid floodwaters.

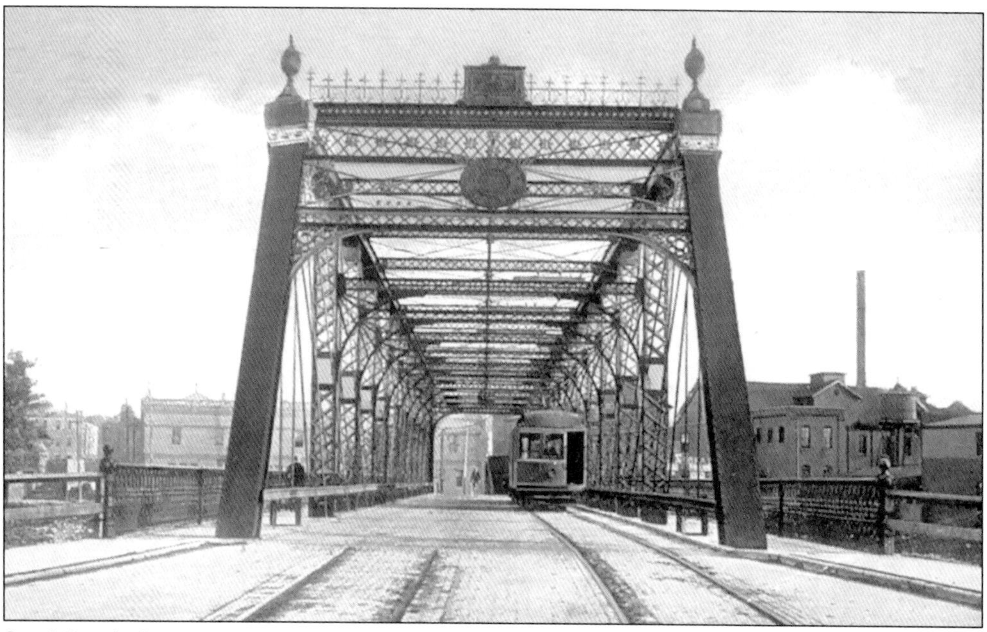

St. Mary's Bridge, Fort Wayne, Indiana, c. 1913. This message states: "Hello Esther! How's the weather up there? Looked for you girls last Mon. P.M. on the 5.23. I went to Lake James. Talk about tan I'm the real thing—I'm growing a new skin. Did you get to go? I'll write (if I can stand the strain) someday this week. With love Ida."

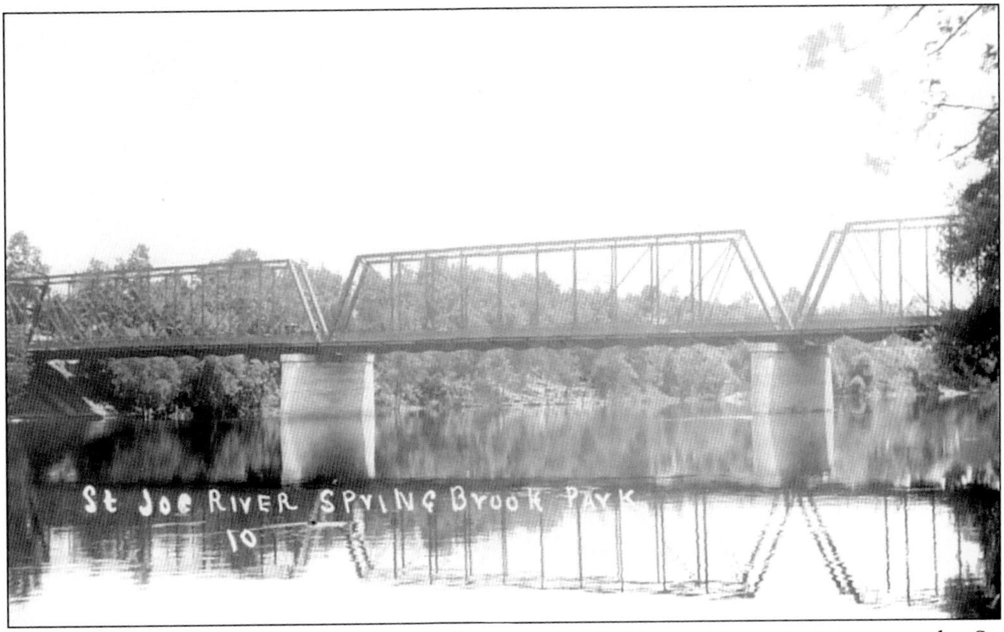

ST. JOE RIVER SPRING BROOK PARK. A three-section bridge was necessary to cross the St. Joseph River.

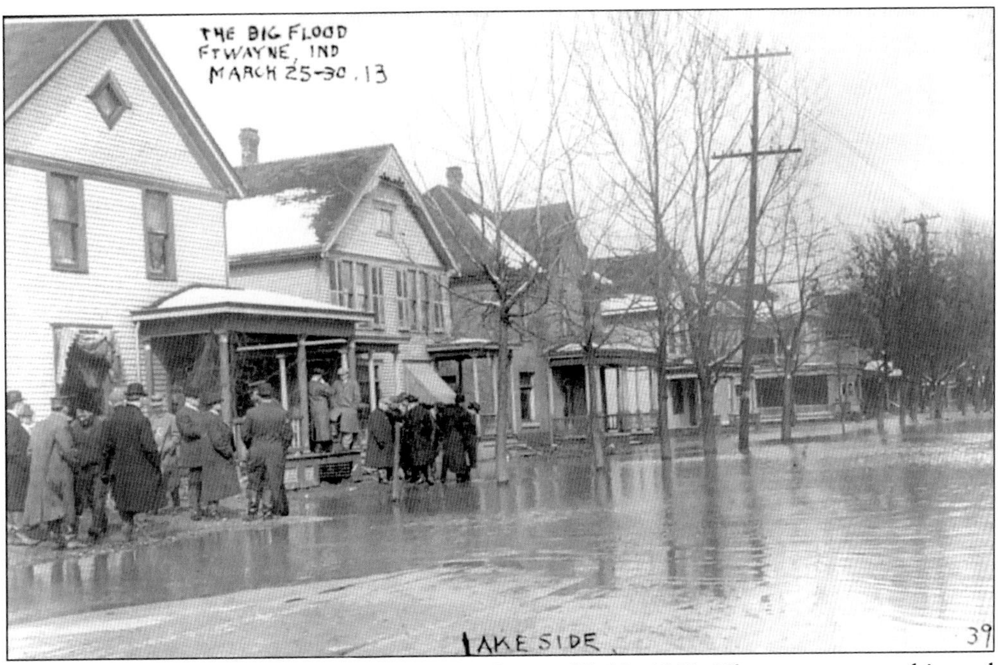

THE BIG FLOOD, FORT WAYNE, INDIANA, MARCH 25–30, 1913. The message on this card states: "This is Mothers House taken as the water was going down her floor was about 5 inches above the water."

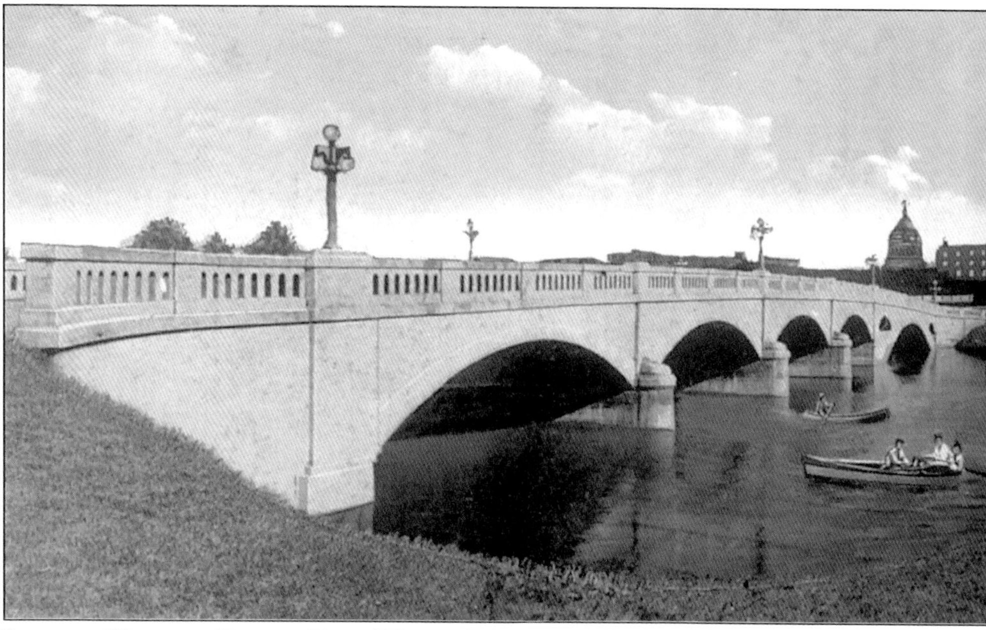

LINCOLN HIGHWAY BRIDGE, FORT WAYNE, INDIANA, *c.* 1922. The Lincoln Highway was one of the first transcontinental highways across the nation. It became a major route for tourists traveling by automobile.

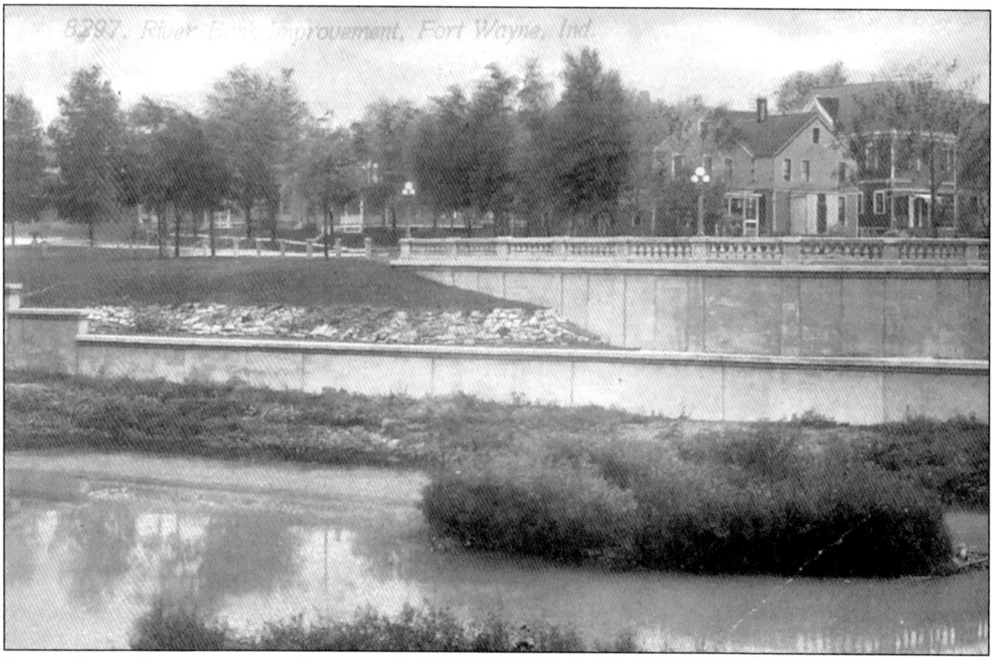

RIVER BANK IMPROVEMENT, FORT WAYNE, INDIANA, *c.* 1912. Fort Wayne has been plagued by flooding from its rivers.

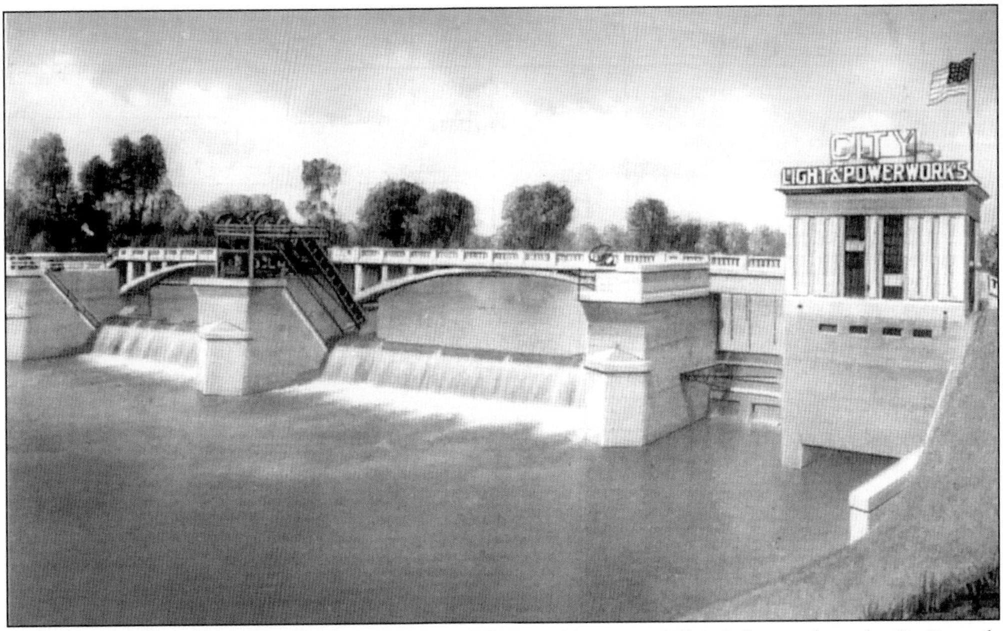

MUNICIPAL DAM AND POWER PLANT, FORT WAYNE, INDIANA. This is located on the St. Joseph River on North Anthony Street.

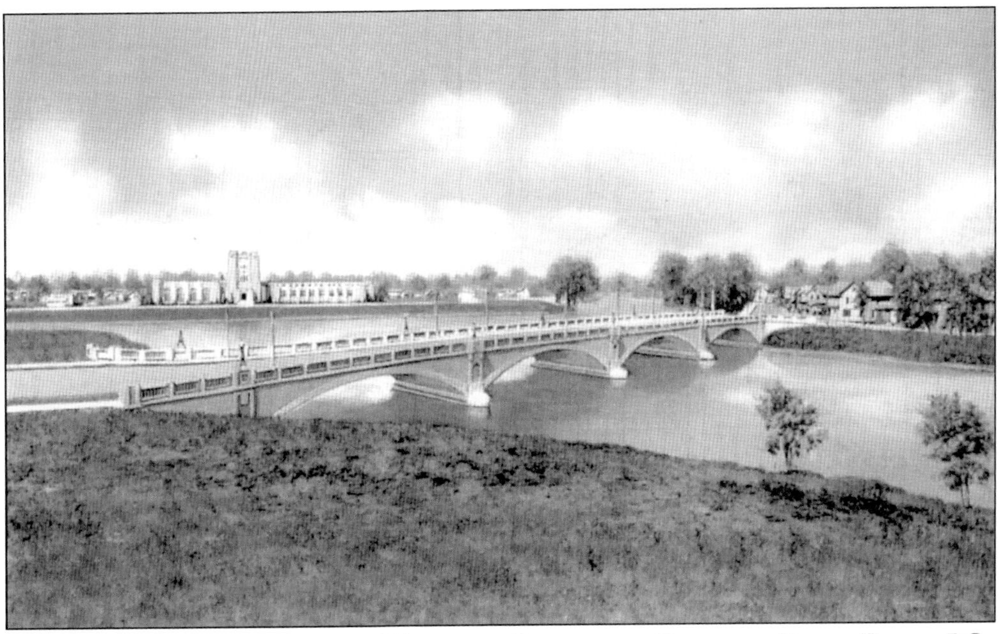

COLUMBIA AVENUE BRIDGE AND MUNICIPAL FILTRATION PLANT AT THREE RIVERS J.C., FORT WAYNE, INDIANA. Built in 1926, the Columbia Street Bridge connects the Lakeside neighborhood to the downtown area. The Three Rivers Filtration Plant was dedicated in 1933, and provided Fort Wayne with state of the art facilities.

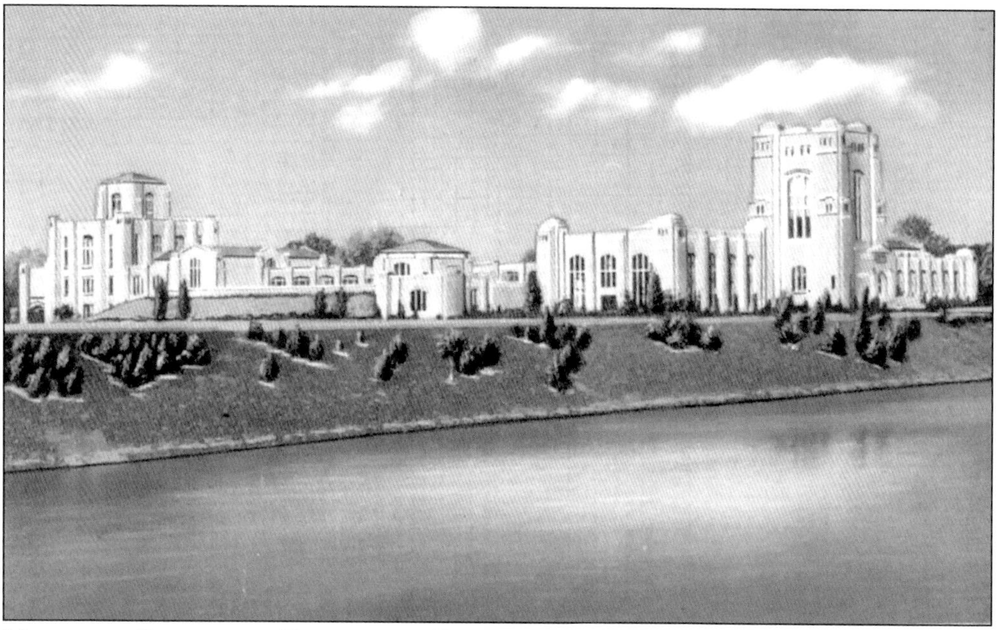

Municipal Filtration Plant and Reservoir, Fort Wayne Indiana. The Gothic architecture has provided a handsome setting for a necessary government function.

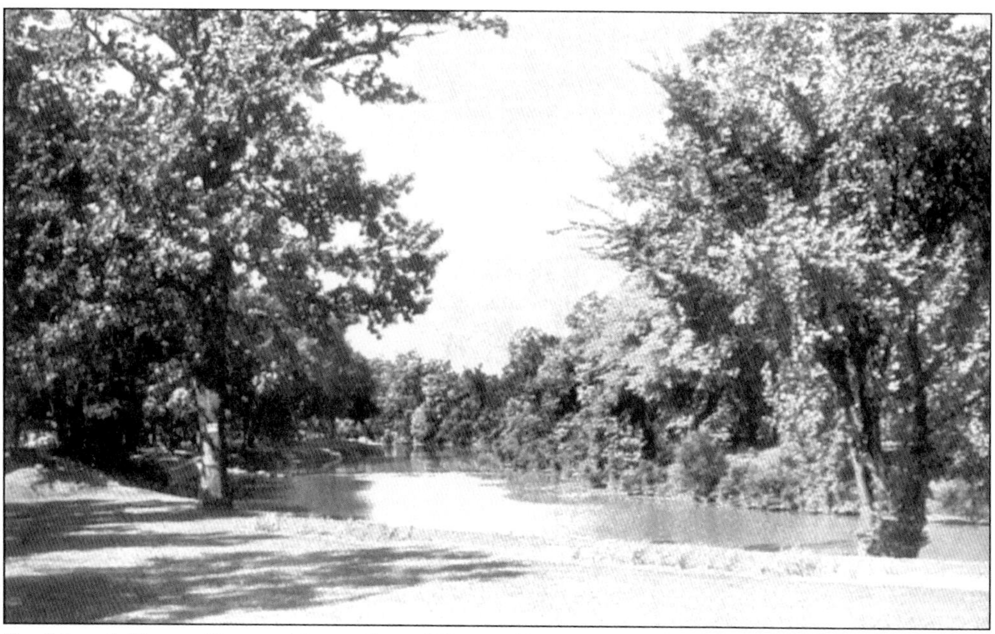

St. Mary's River, Foster Park, Fort Wayne, Indiana.

RAILROADS

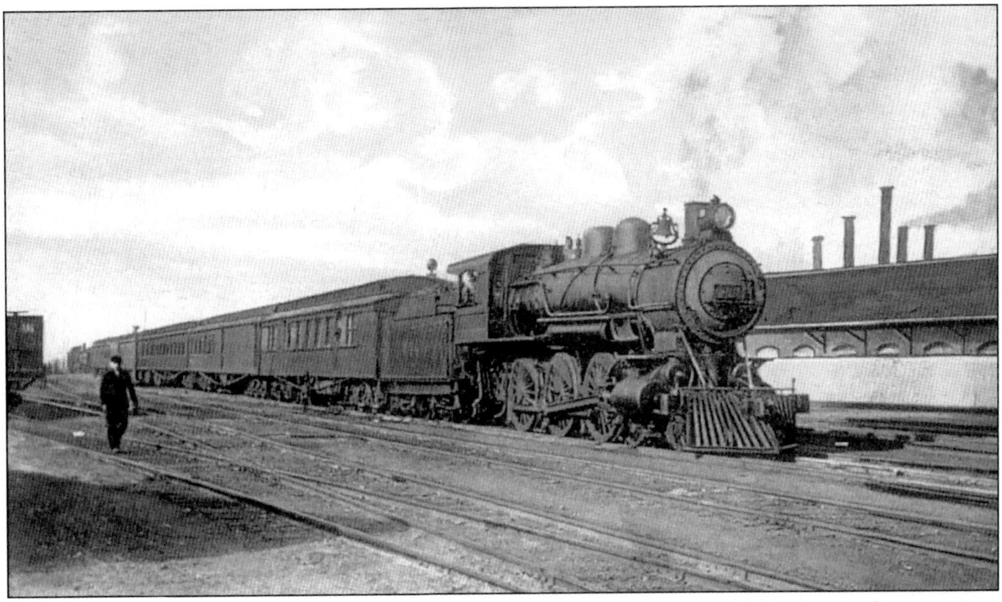

NO. 8 TRAIN, WABASH RAILROAD, AT FORT WAYNE, INDIANA, *C.* 1911. Steam locomotives were used to pull fast passenger trains.

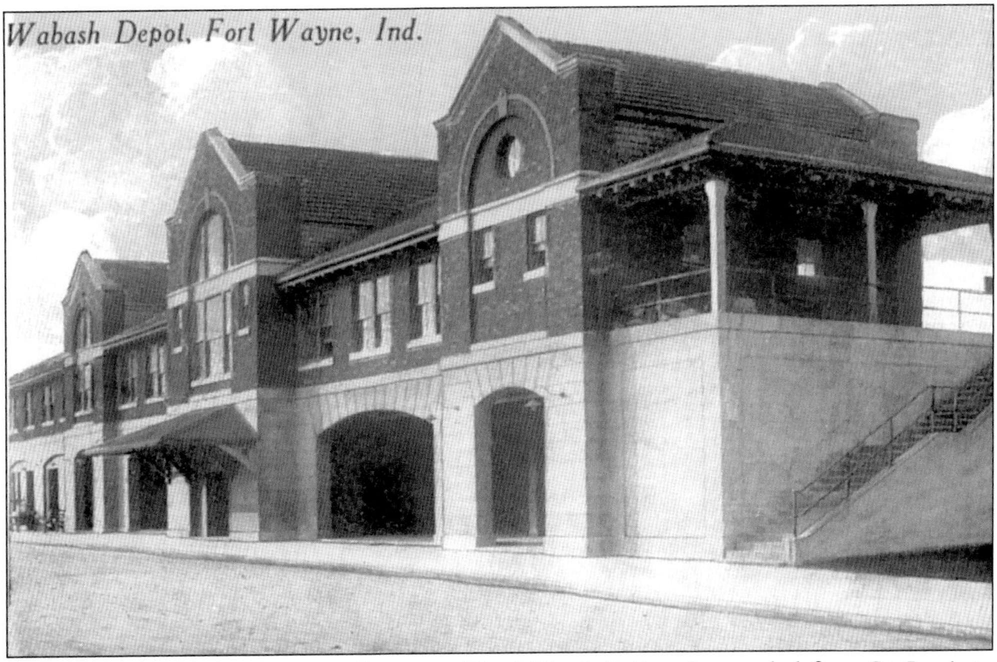

WABASH DEPOT, FORT WAYNE, INDIANA. The Wabash Railroad extended from St. Louis to Detroit and provided a great source of transportation for Fort Wayne persons and industries.

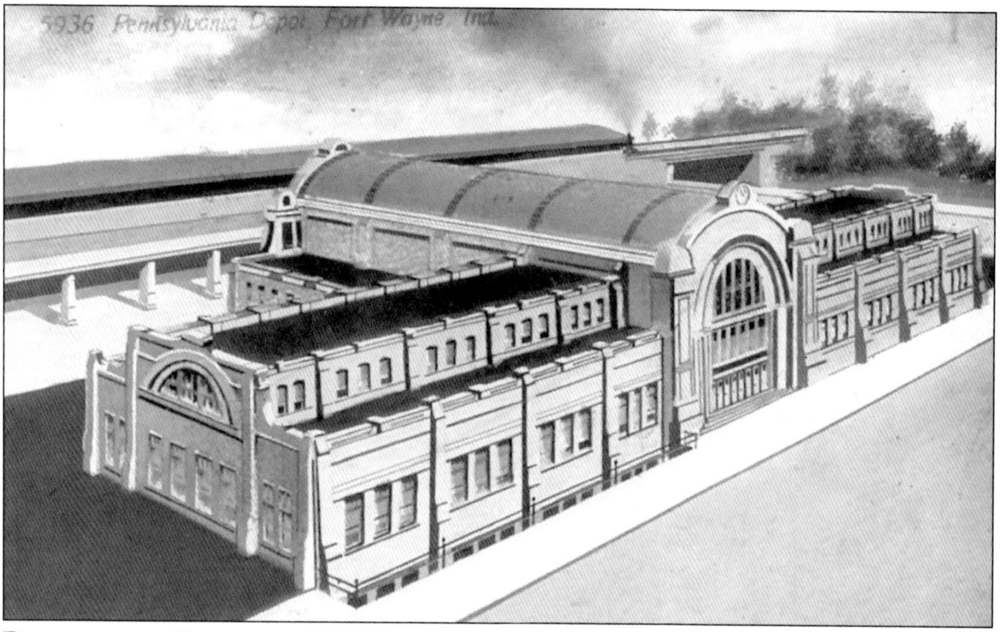

PENNSYLVANIA DEPOT, FORT WAYNE, INDIANA, *c.* 1911. An artist's conception of this handsome structure is shown here. It is also know as the "Baker Street Station."

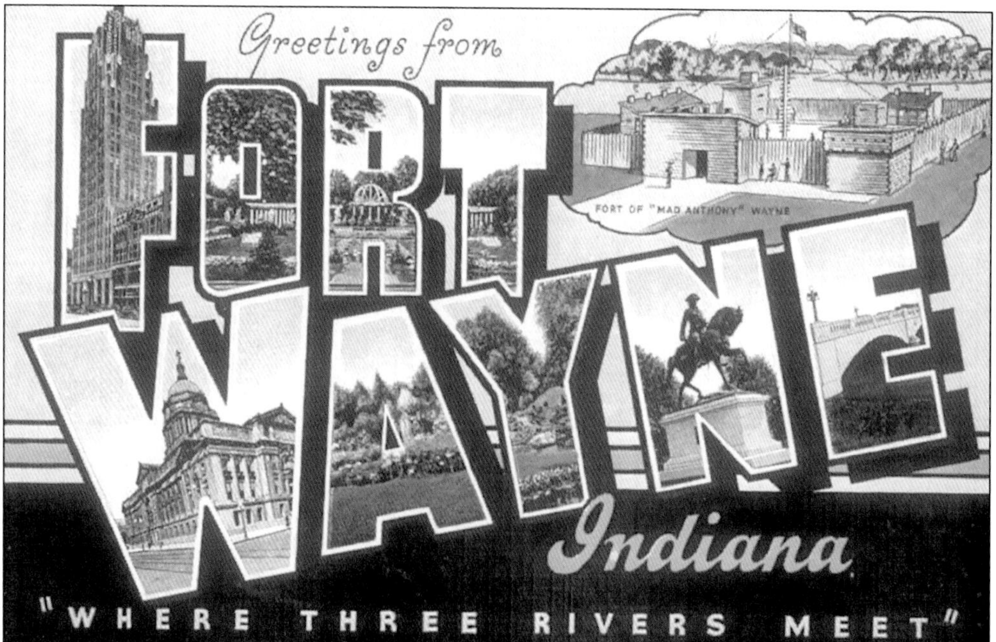

GREETING FROM FORT WAYNE, INDIANA—"WHERE THREE RIVERS MEET." A key to Views on Other Side is as follows: F—Lincoln Bank Tower, O—Sunken Gardens, Lakeside Park, R—Sunken Gardens, Lakeside Park, T—Sunken Gardens, Lakeside Park, W—Allen County Courthouse, A—Memorial Park, Y—Gardens in Swinney Park, N—Anthony Wayne Monument, E—Section of Harrison Street Bridge. This is another example of a "large letter" postcard.

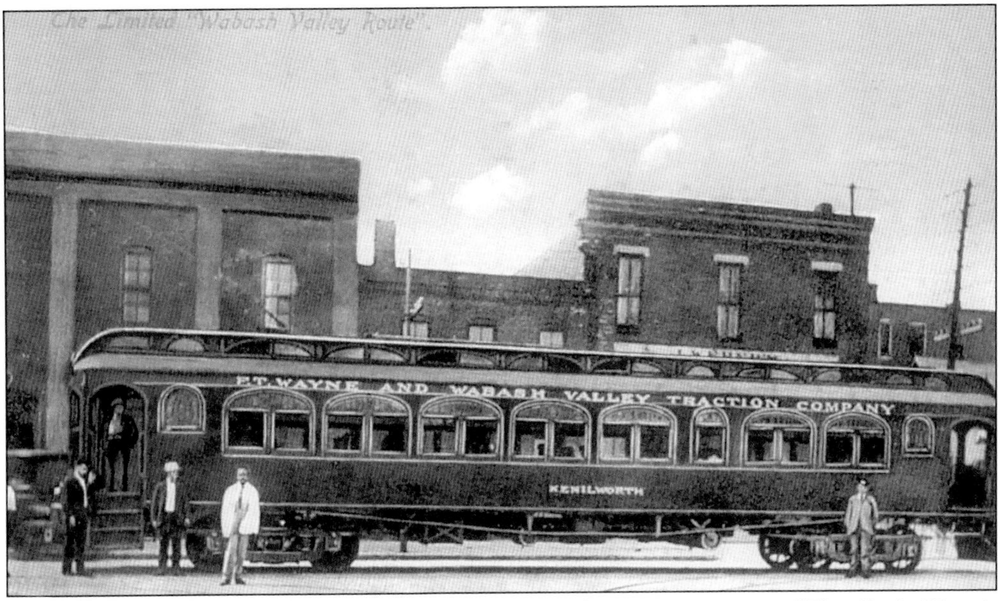

The Limited "Wabash Valley Route," *c.* 1909. This message states: "The Craig Biscuit Co., Fort Wayne, Ind. I will call on you Tuesday. Ed Kynaston, Salesman. Goods of Quality." The Fort Wayne and Wabash Valley Traction Company provided interurban service to and from Fort Wayne.

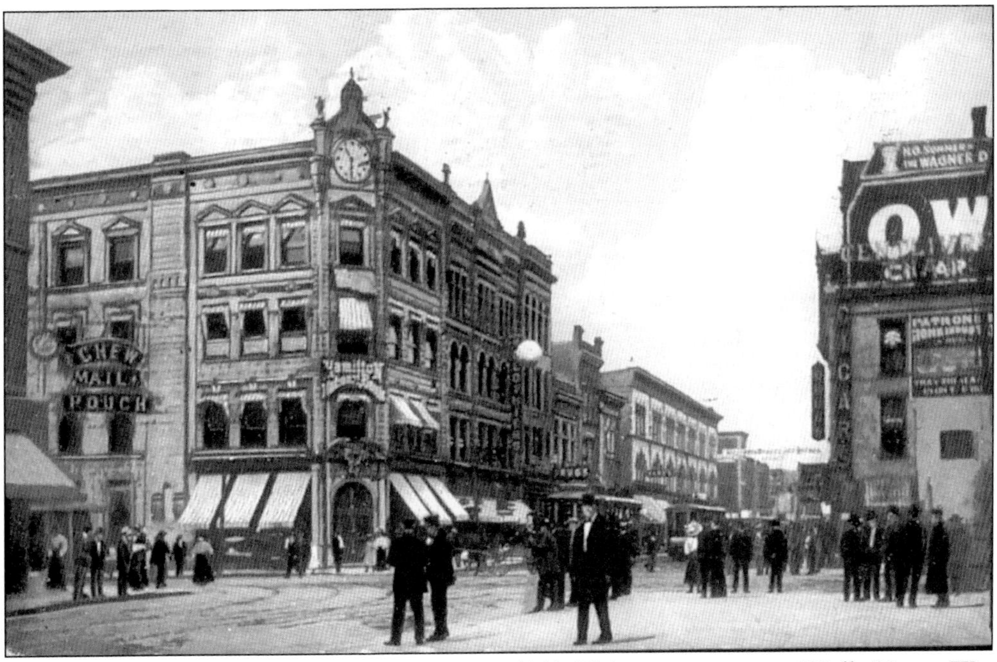

Transfer Corner, Fort Wayne, Indiana, *c.* 1911. This message states: "Hello Henry Was playing ball today about 20 miles from here so came over tonight and saw Mac. He is going good. I am playing Sunday ball with a team South Whitley. Nice money boy. Going good. Give best to the gang. How is your arm?" Many trolley lines converged here so that passengers could transfer to other cars.

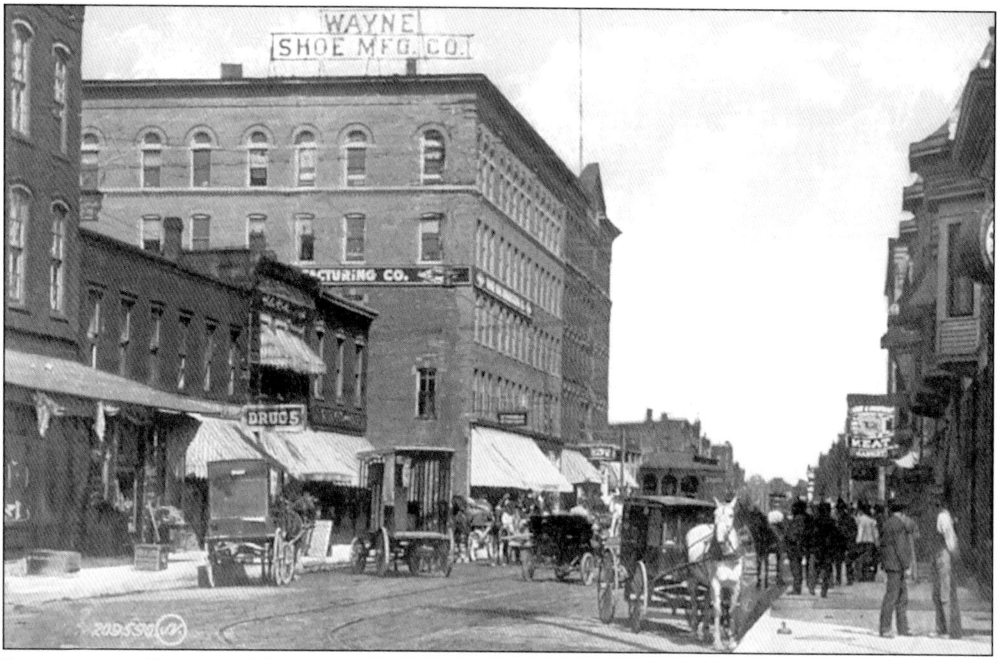

INTERURBAN STATION, HARRISON STREET NEAR MAIN, FORT WAYNE, INDIANA. The station was downtown so that passengers could transfer to Fort Wayne Trolleys to continue their journey within the city.

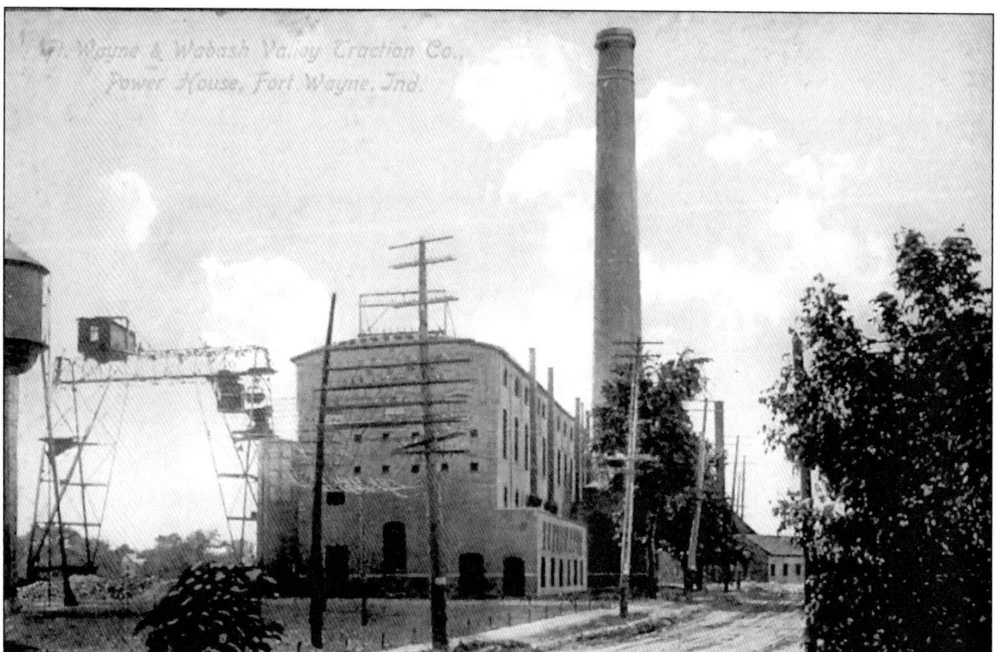

FT. WAYNE & WABASH VALLEY TRACTION CO., POWER HOUSE, FORT WAYNE, INDIANA. Interurban cars were powered by electricity, which was generated in power houses located along its lines.

AIRPORTS

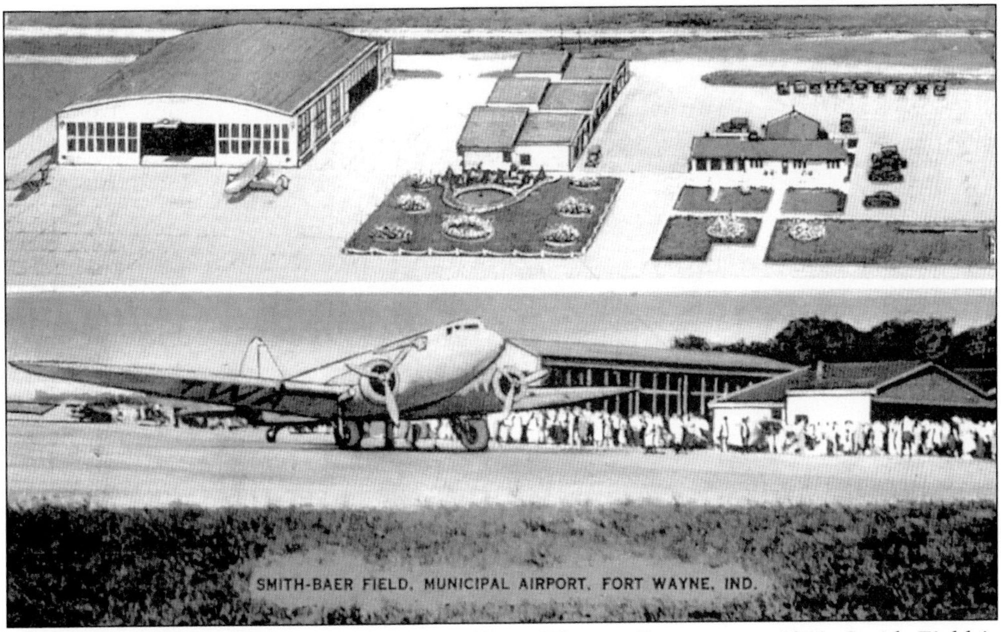

SMITH-BAER FIELD, MUNICIPAL AIRPORT, FORT WAYNE, INDIANA, *C.* 1941. Smith Field is located on the north side of Fort Wayne.

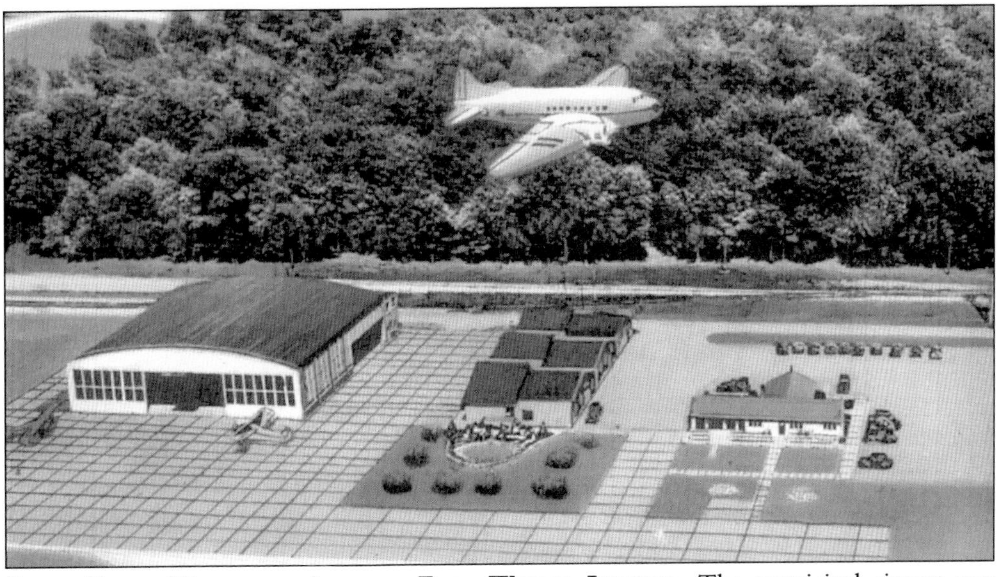

SMITH FIELD, MUNICIPAL AIRPORT, FORT WAYNE, INDIANA. The municipal airport was provided by the City of Fort Wayne. Its operator lived in the building to the right and was on duty 24 hours per day.

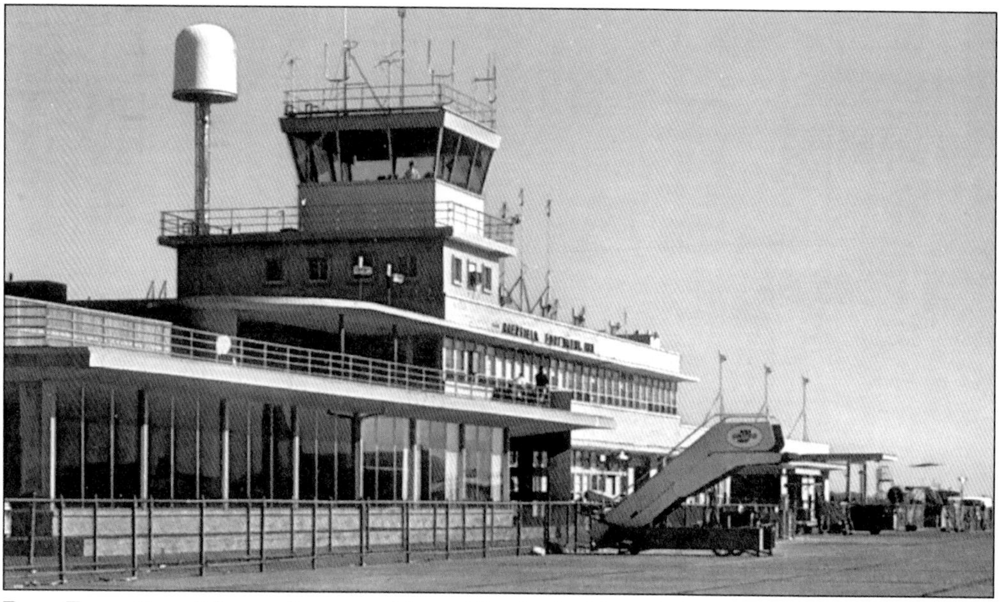

BAER FIELD, FORT WAYNE, INDIANA. Named for Lt. Paul Bear, it is one of the most outstanding airports in the country and is municipally owned, *c.* 1971.

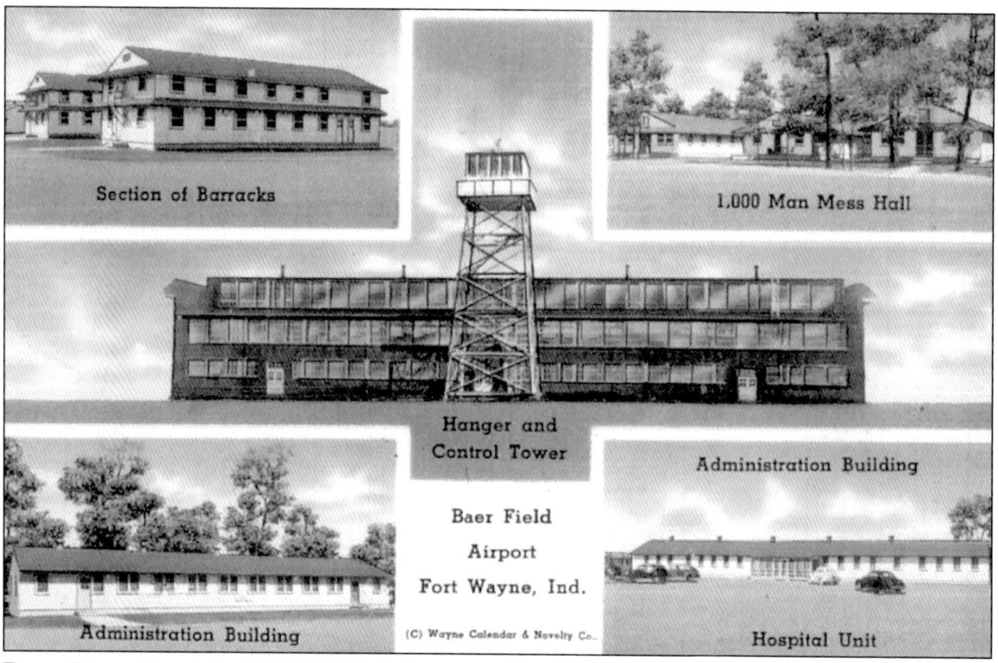

BAER FIELD AIRPORT, FORT WAYNE, INDIANA. Pictured here are as follows: a section of the barracks, the 1,000-man mess hall, the hanger and control tower, the administration building, and the hospital unit. Baer Field was the site of extension military operation during World War II.

INDUSTRY

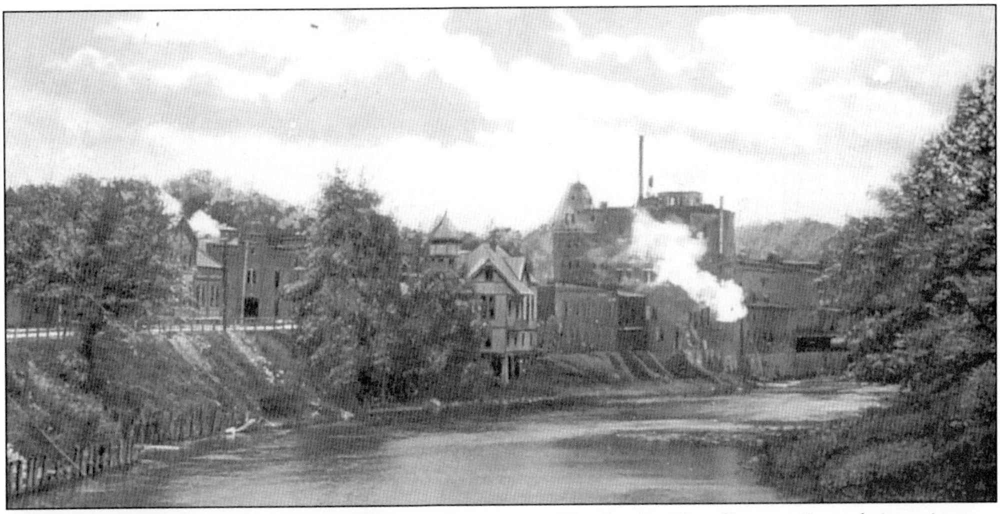

CENTLIVRE BREWERY CO., FORT WAYNE, INDIANA. Charles L. Centlivre, a French immigrant, established the Centlivre Brewery on the St. Joseph River. Fort Wayne became a leading producer of beer.

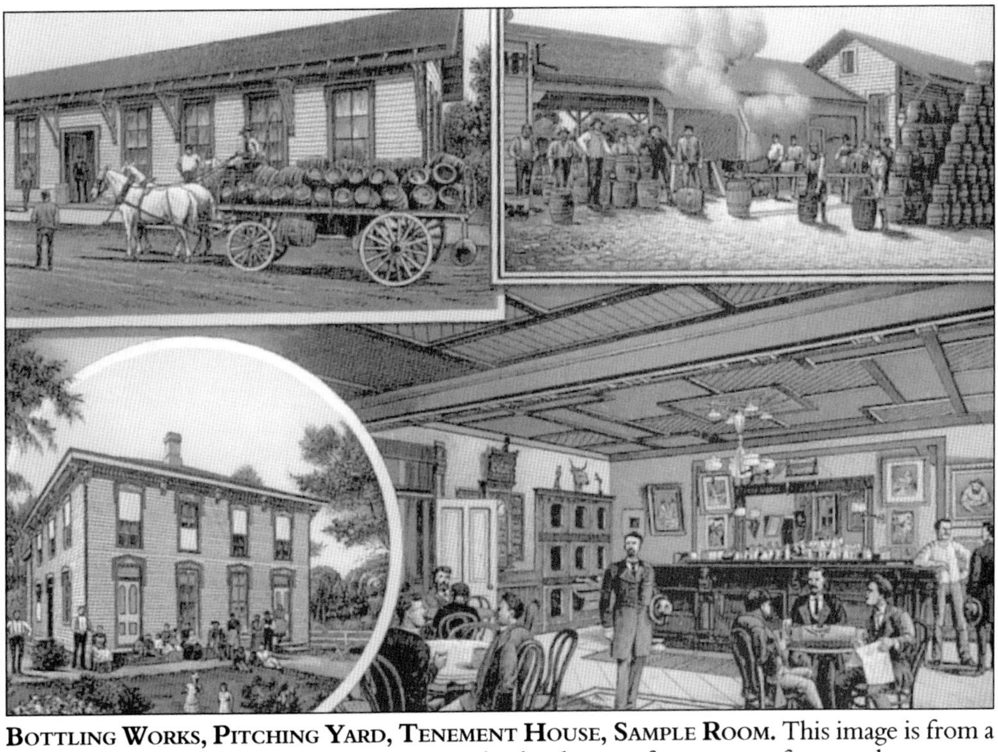

BOTTLING WORKS, PITCHING YARD, TENEMENT HOUSE, SAMPLE ROOM. This image is from a souvenir book of the Centlivre Brewery. Such a book was a forerunner of postcards.

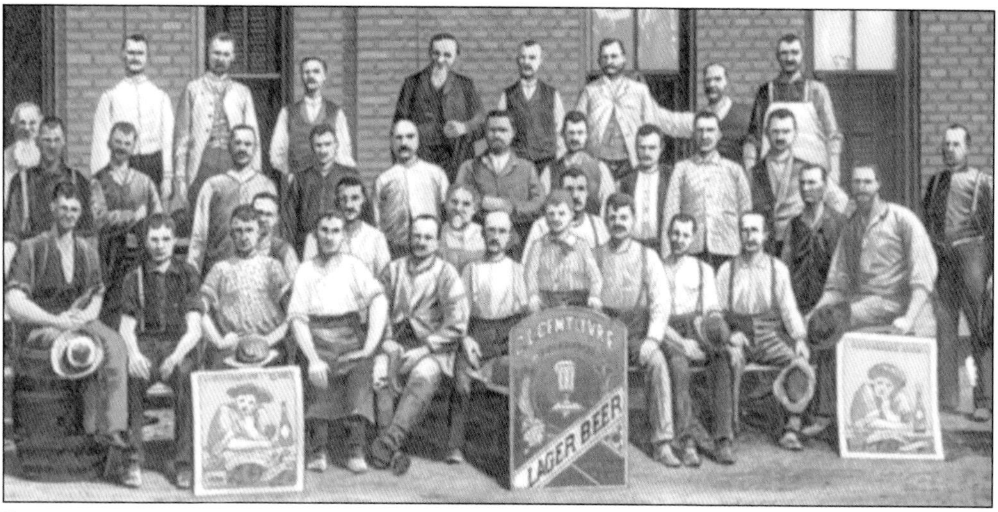

Proprietors and Employers of the Brewery. Charles L. Centlivre was revered by his employees, who honored him by commissioning a statute of him, which was placed on top of the brewery building. It is now located on top of Hall's Gas House Restaurant.

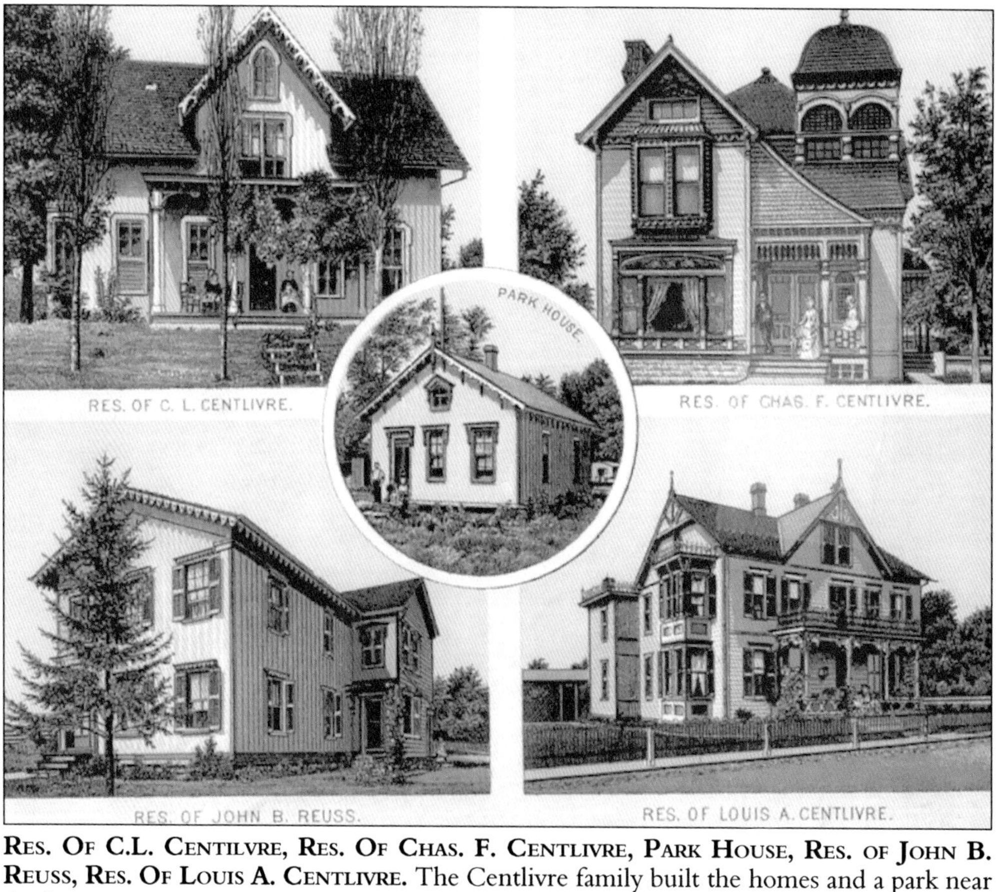

Res. Of C.L. Centilvre, Res. Of Chas. F. Centlivre, Park House, Res. of John B. Reuss, Res. Of Louis A. Centlivre. The Centlivre family built the homes and a park near the brewery.

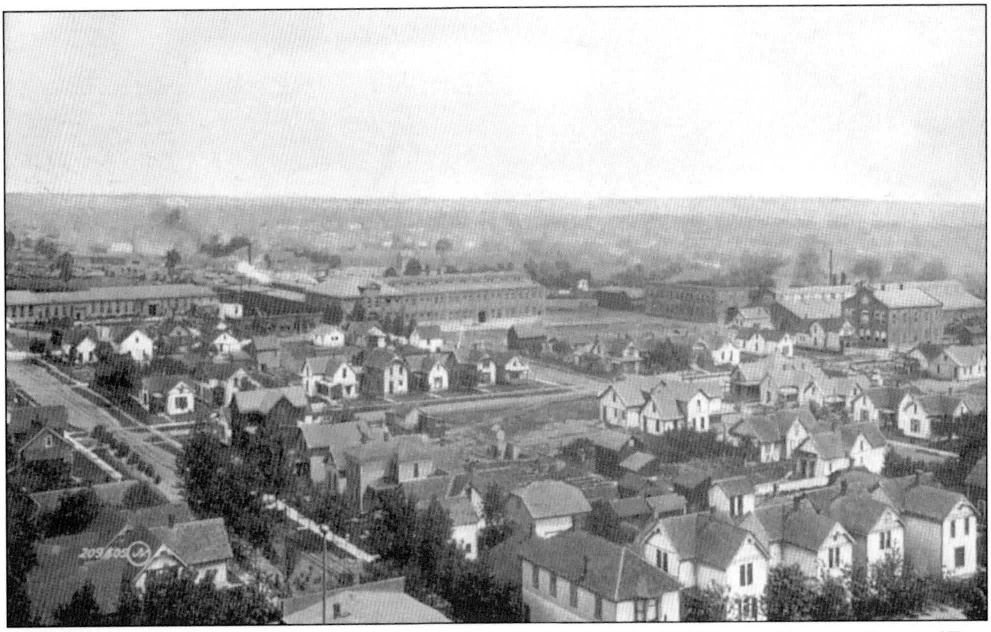

BIRD'S-EYE VIEW OF WESTERN GAS CONSTRUCTION CO.'S PLANT TAKEN FROM TOP OF ELECTRIC LIGHT TOWER, FORT WAYNE, INDIANA, *c. 1909*. This was a major Fort Wayne Industry.

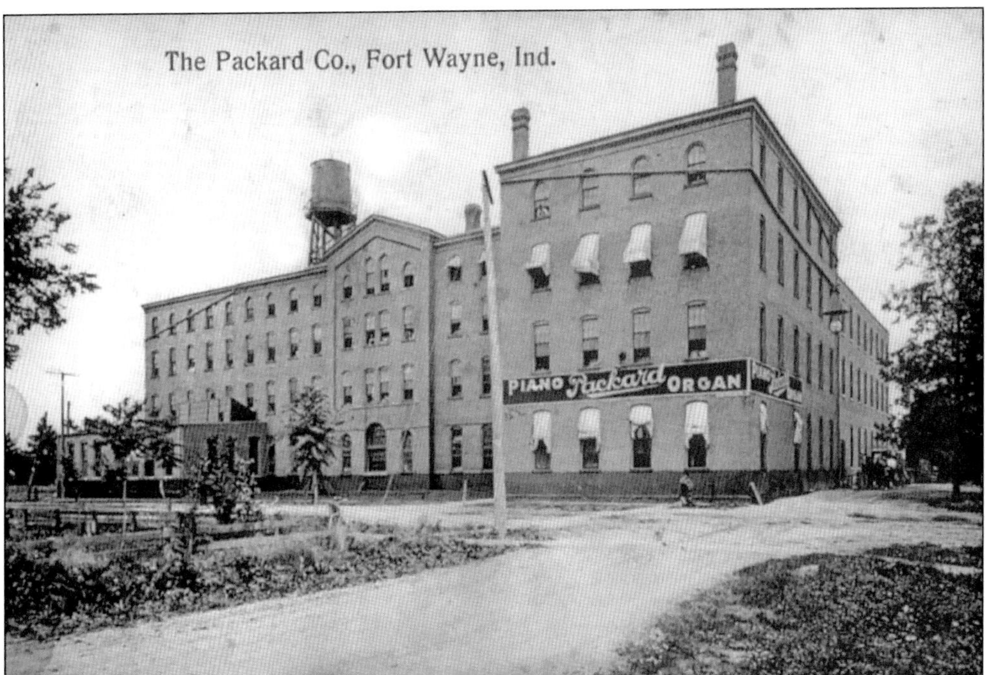

THE PACKARD CO., FORT WAYNE, INDIANA. Packard was a major manufacturer of pianos and organs.

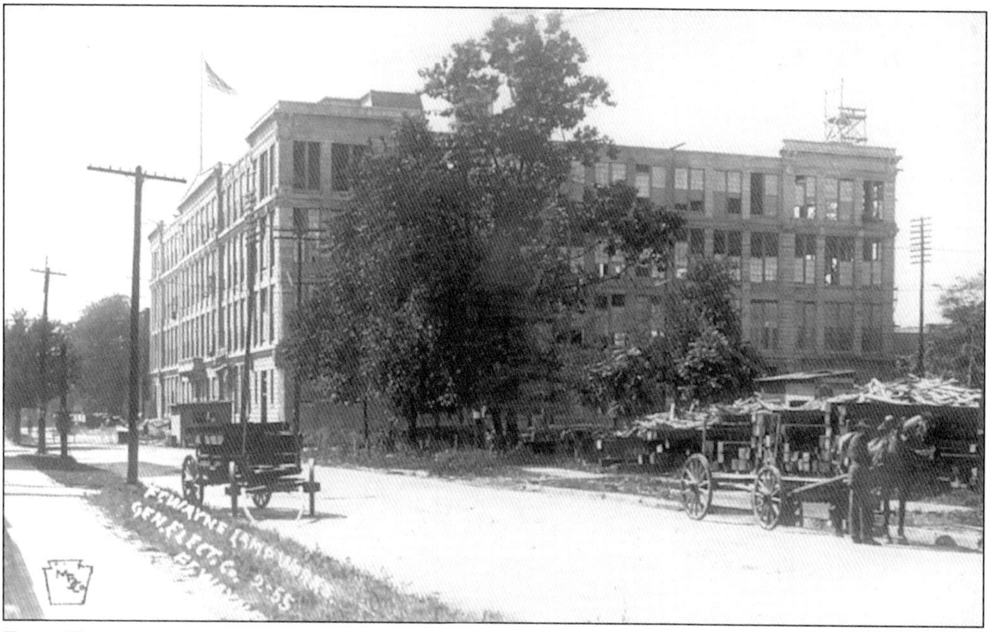

FORT WAYNE LAMP WORKS, GENERAL ELECTRIC COMPANY, FORT WAYNE, INDIANA, *c.* 1908. This is an early view of these factory buildings.

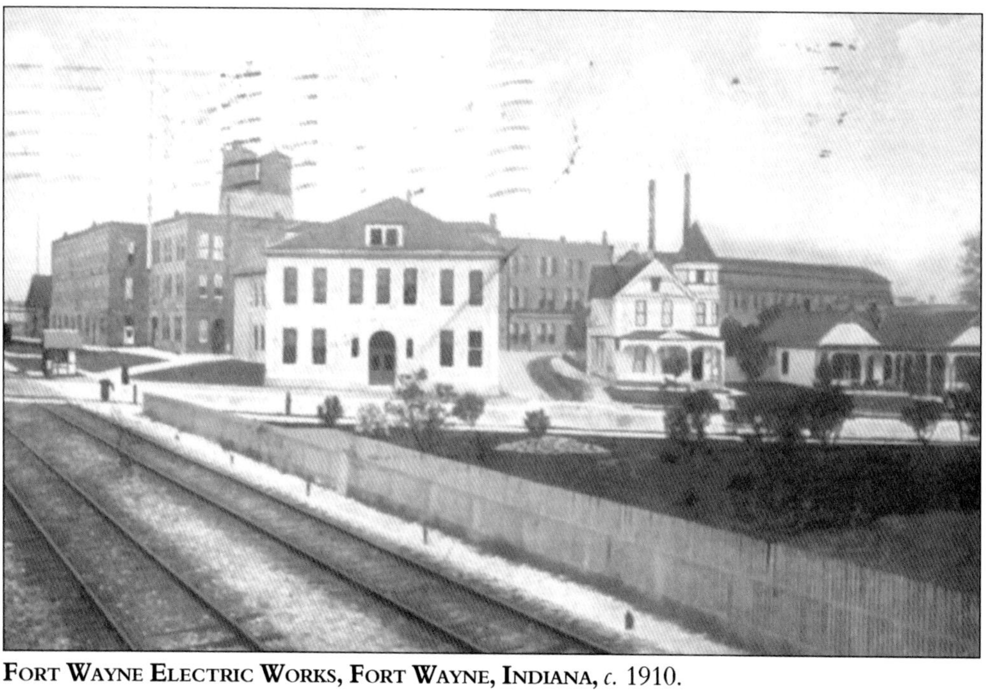

FORT WAYNE ELECTRIC WORKS, FORT WAYNE, INDIANA, *c.* 1910.

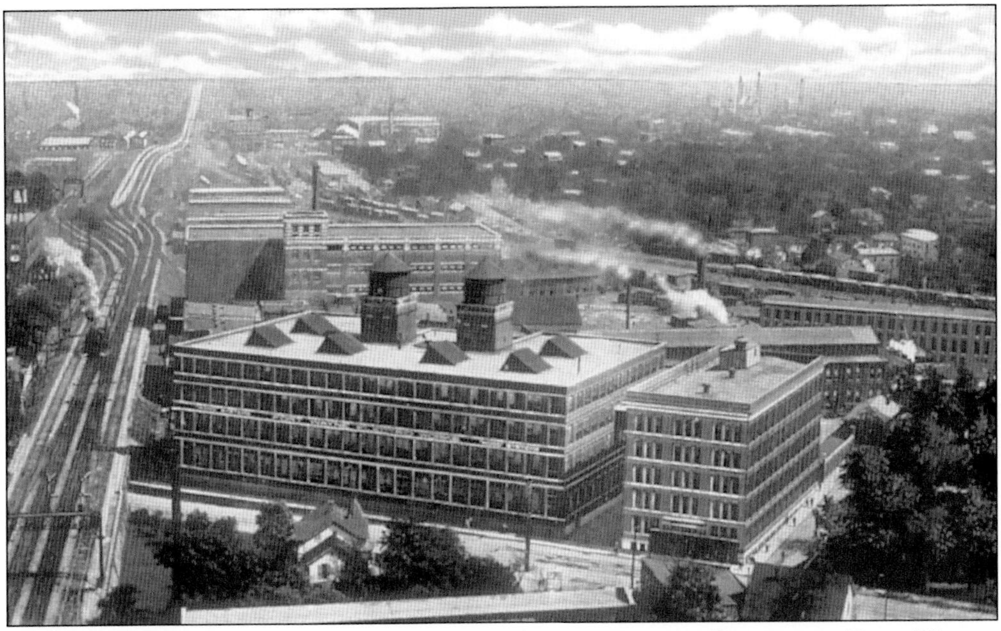

Bird's-Eye View of General Electric Co. Plant, East of Broadway, Fort Wayne, Indiana. GE has been one of Fort Wayne's largest and best employers over the years.

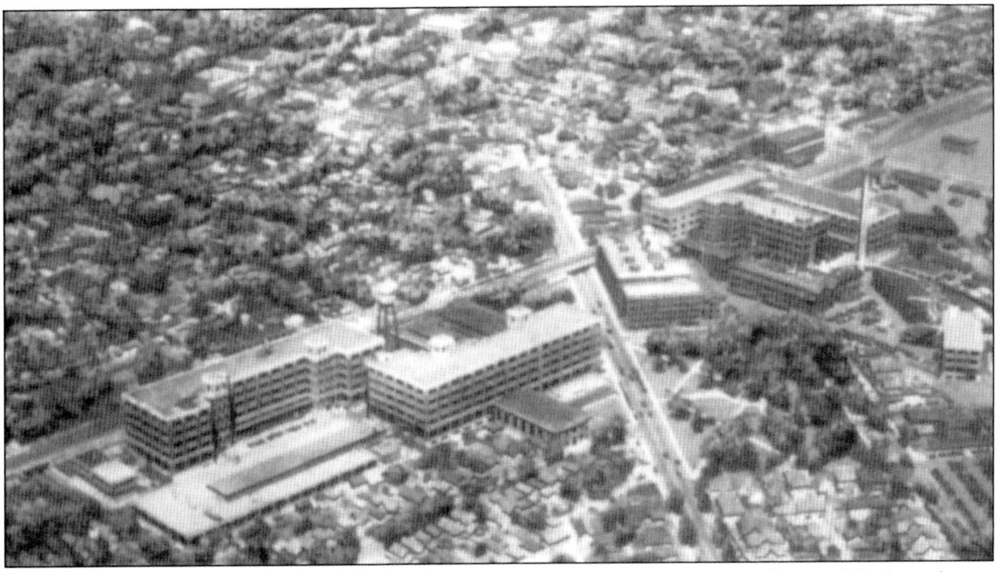

Aerial View of General Electric Works, Fort Wayne, Indiana. This aerial view shows the entire complex.

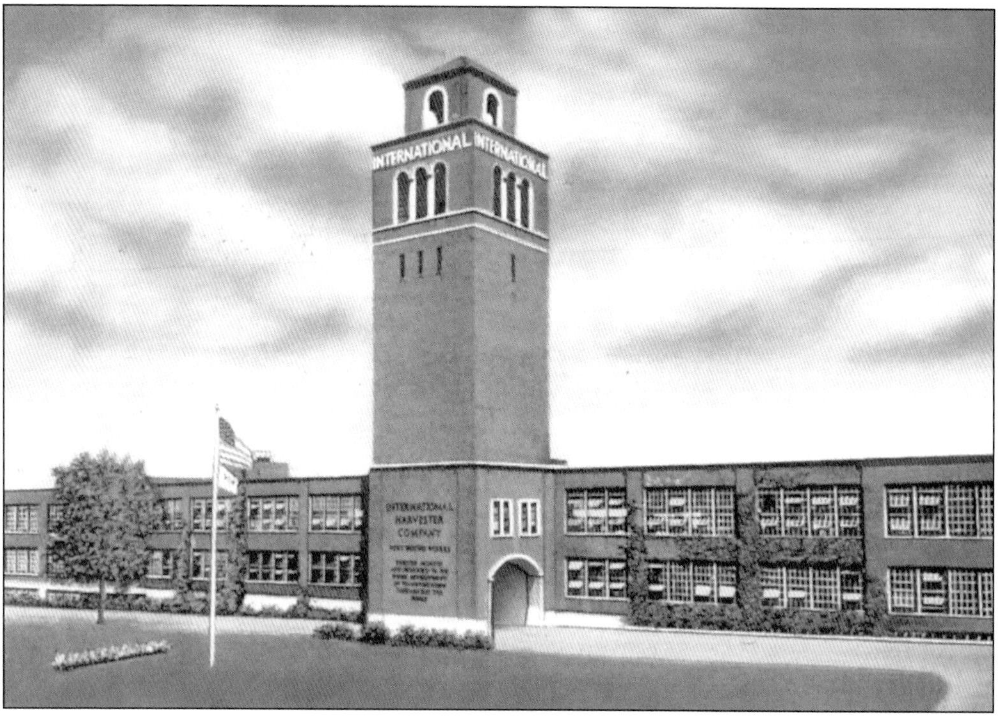

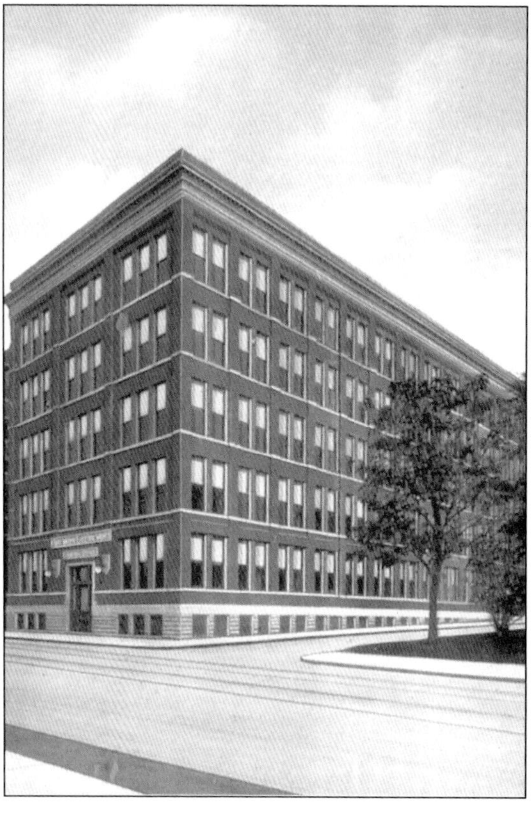

THE INTERNATIONAL HARVESTER CO. TOWER, FORT WAYNE, INDIANA. The International Harvester Tower is a landmark in the eastern part of Fort Wayne. The buildings were erected in 1923. Many large trucks were built at this plant.

OFFICE BUILDING OF FORT WAYNE ELECTRIC WORKS OF GENERAL ELECTRIC COMPANY, FORT WAYNE, INDIANA, *C.* 1912. The message on this card states: "I was to Cedar Pointe last Saturday and got home Sun. morning at 4:00, had a fine time. I think perhaps I will go to Auburn Saturday noon and will come back with you girls Sunday. If I am not in Auburn Sat, you girls be sure to come and call me on phone 3265 Green, 447 Breckenridge St. Jas. Southern, and I will meet you. Haven't heard from Isabelle since last week, but suppose she is better. Bethel."

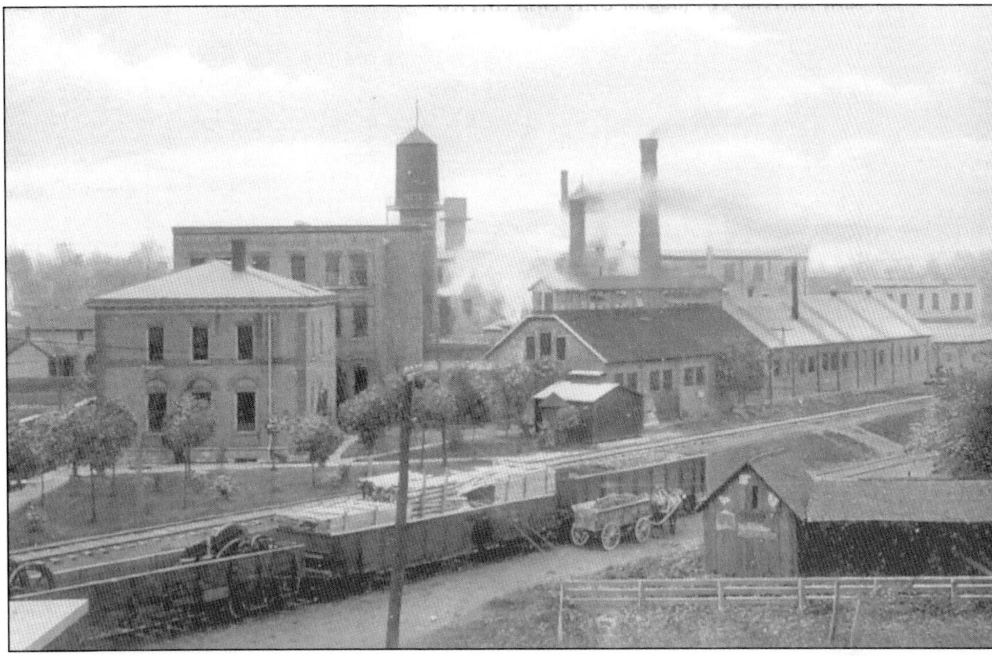

WAYNE KNITTING MILLS, FORT WAYNE, INDIANA. Railroad access was essential to industry.

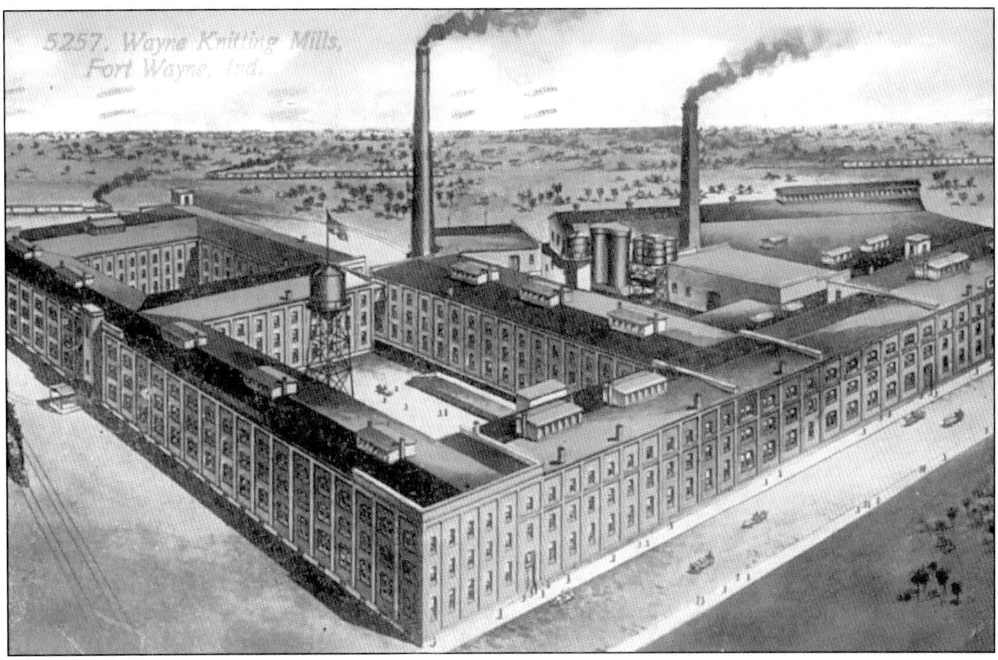

WAYNE KNITTING MILLS, FORT WAYNE, INDIANA, *c.* 1912. Clouds of black smoke belching from chimneys was a symbol of a great industry in the era prior to environmental awareness.

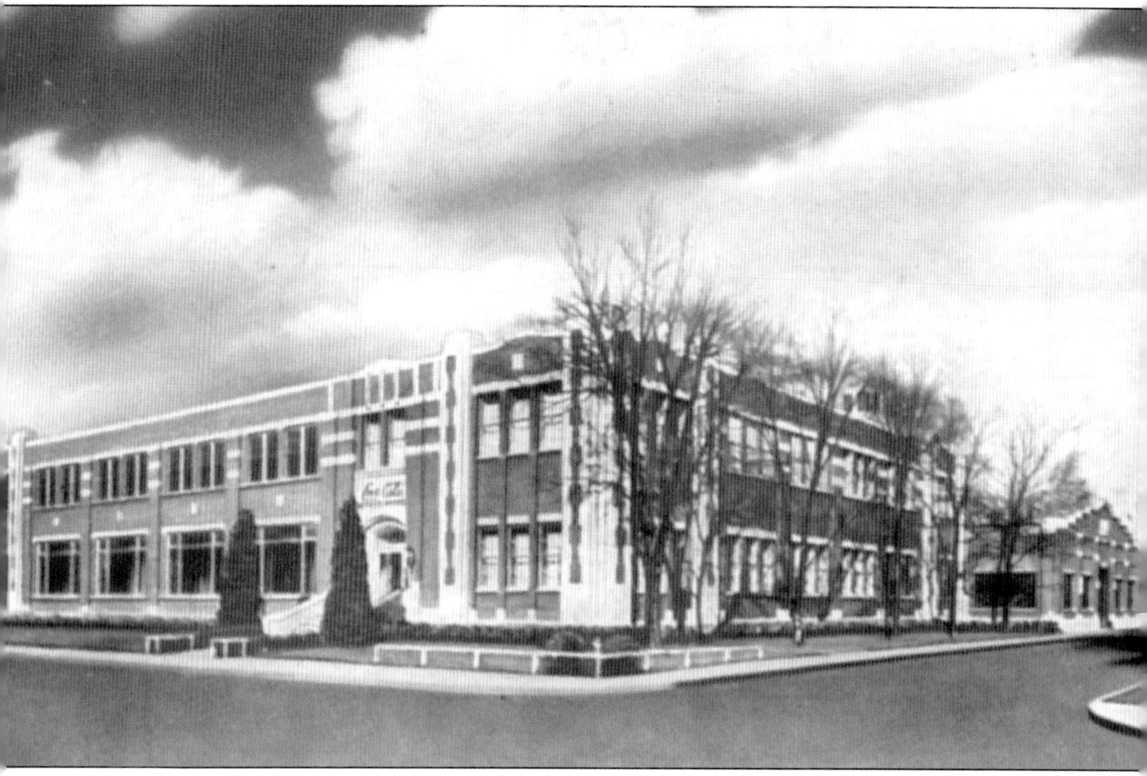

FORT WAYNE COCA-COLA BOTTLING WORKS, INC. This building was constructed in the year 1941. Square footage of floor space was 58,613, and bottling capacity per day was 276,480 bottles.

PARKS

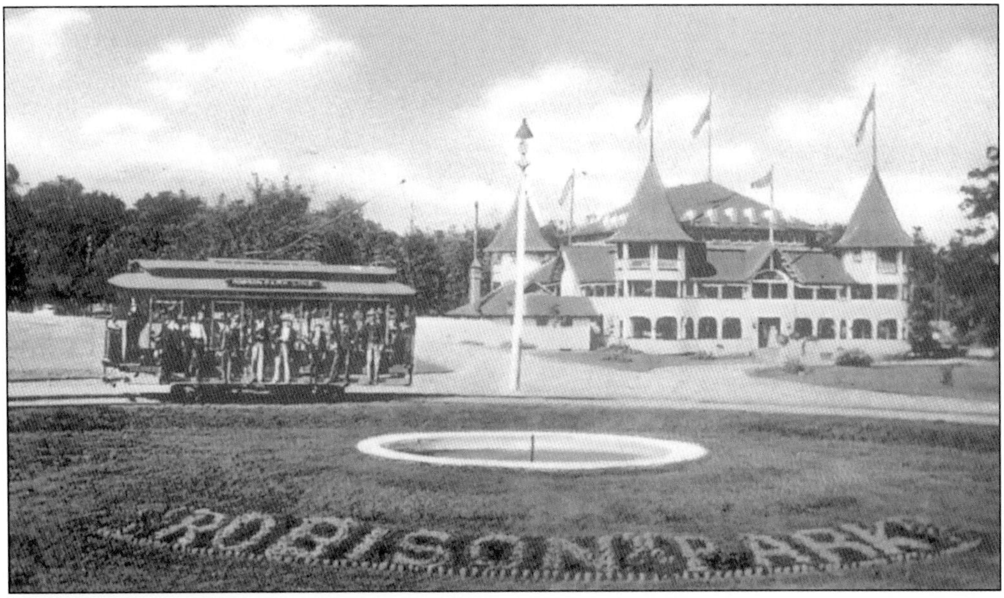

THE PAVILION, ROBISON PARK, FORT WAYNE, INDIANA. Robison Park was constructed in 1896 by the Fort Wayne Consolidated Railway Company as an amusement park to increase demand for travel on its lines. It was located about 7 miles northeast of the center of town.

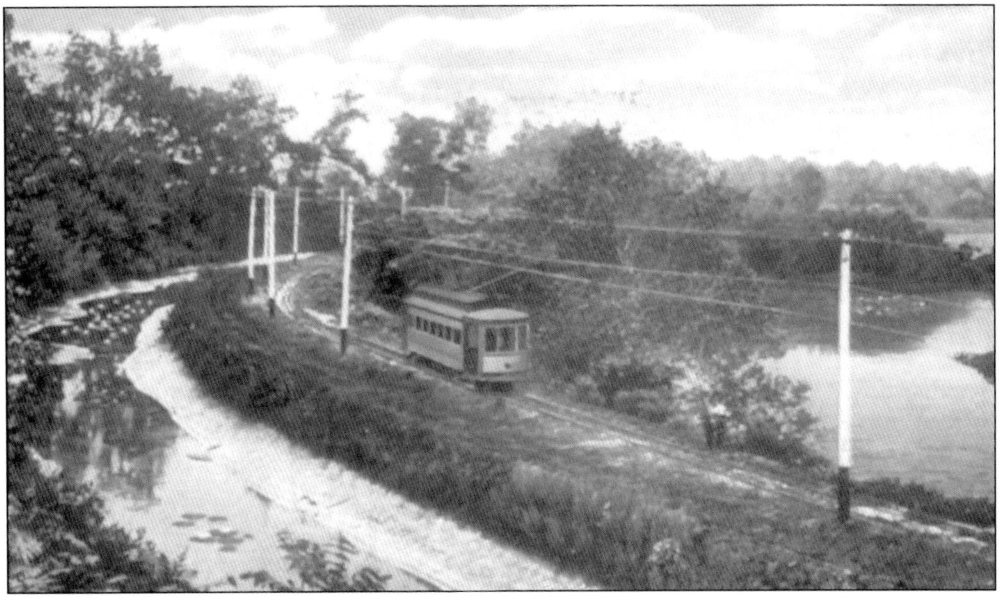

HORSE SHOE BEND ON WAY TO ROBISON PARK, FORT WAYNE, INDIANA, *c.* 1919. This view shows the electrically powered trolley car taking passengers to the park.

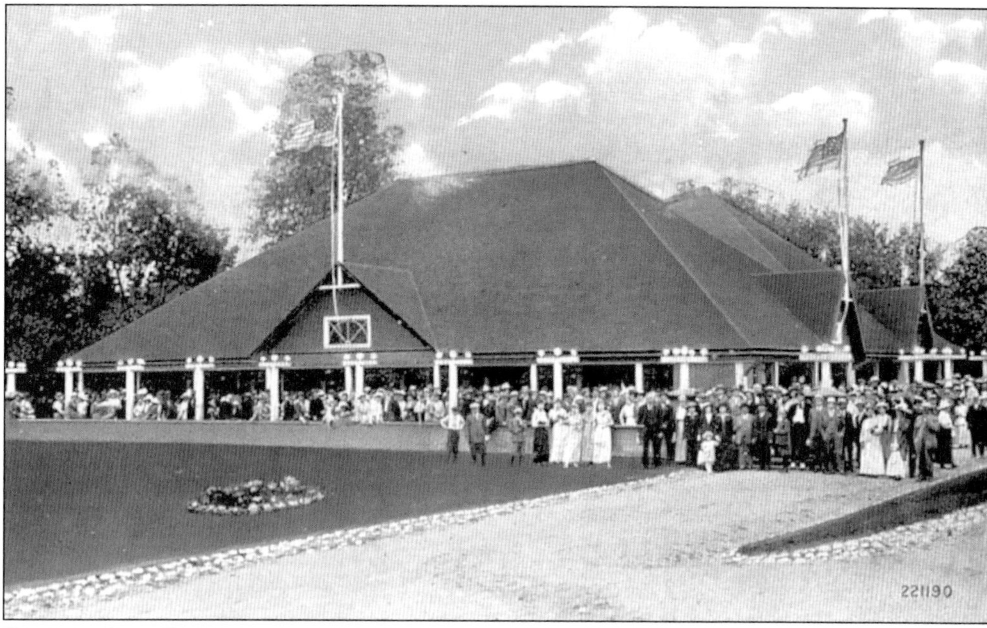

ROBISON PARK DANCING PAVILION, FORT WAYNE, INDIANA, *c.* 1910. Many elaborate structures graced the grounds.

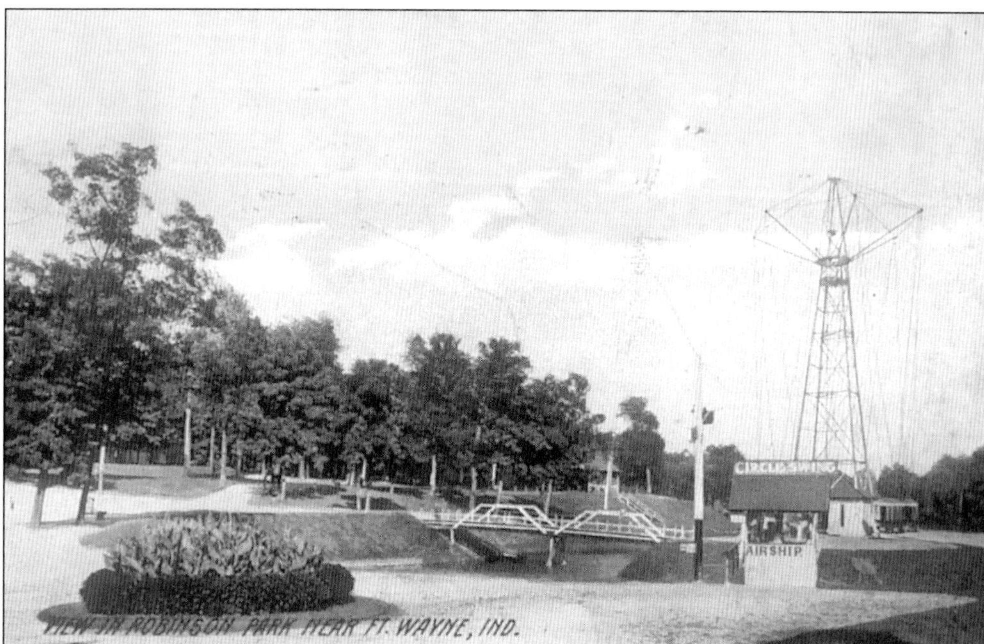

VIEW OF ROBISON PARK NEAR FORT WAYNE, INDIANA, *c.* 1909. The ride shown was the Circle Swing Airship ride.

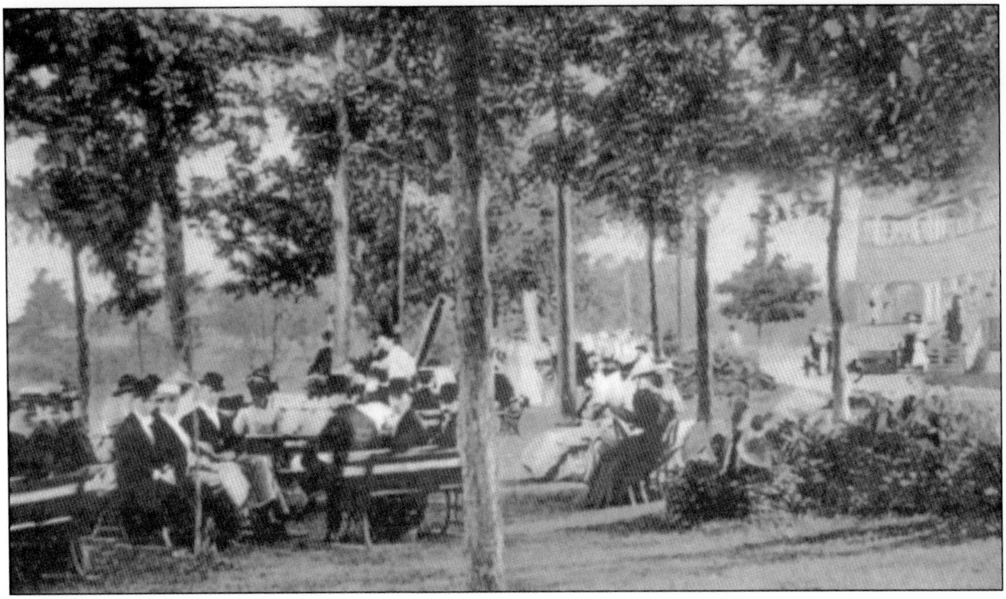

The Rest, Robison Park, Fort Wayne, Indiana. Benches and picnic tables were provided.

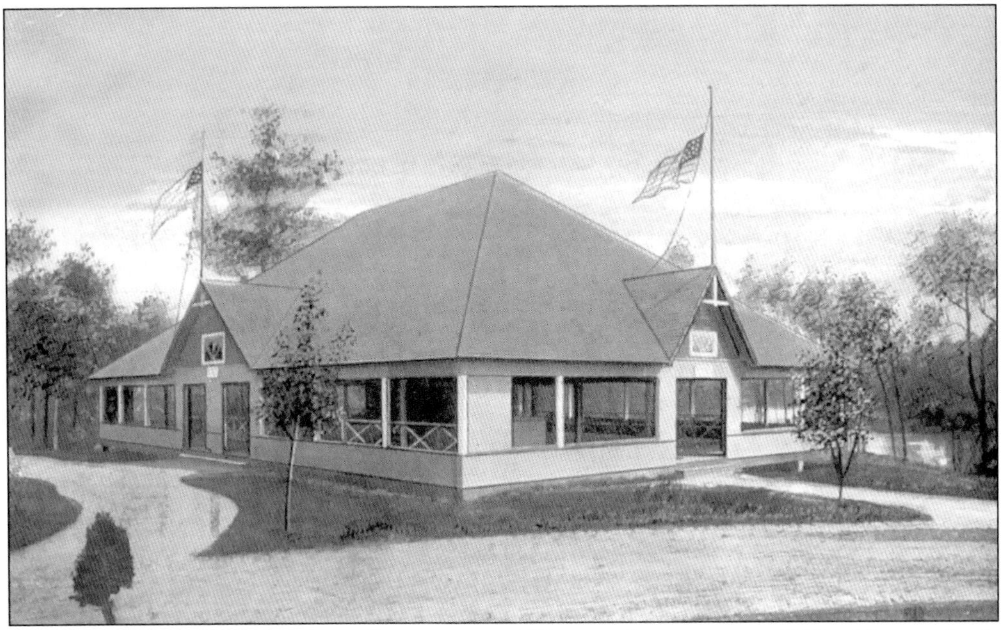

Dancing Pavilion, Robison Park, Fort Wayne, Indiana, c. 1913. The author's grandparents, Carl and Viola Smith, traveled from Butler to Fort Wayne to spend their honeymoon at Robison Park.

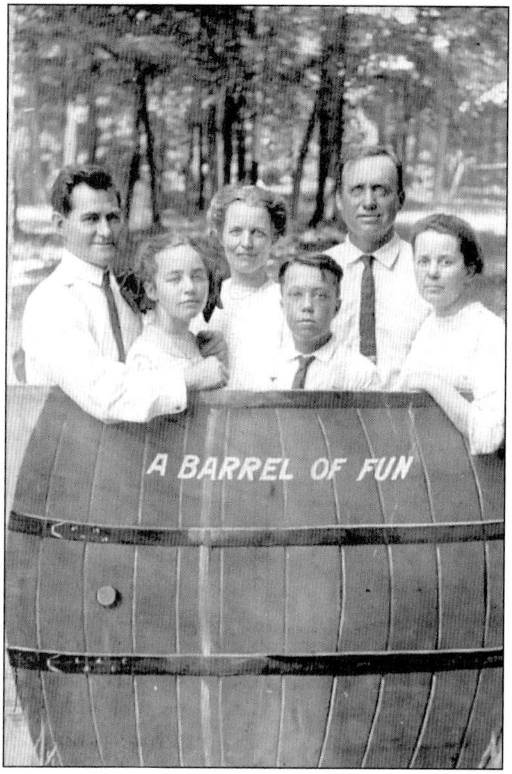

ROBISON PARK, JULY 4, 1911. A BARREL OF FUN. This is an example of a novelty photograph.

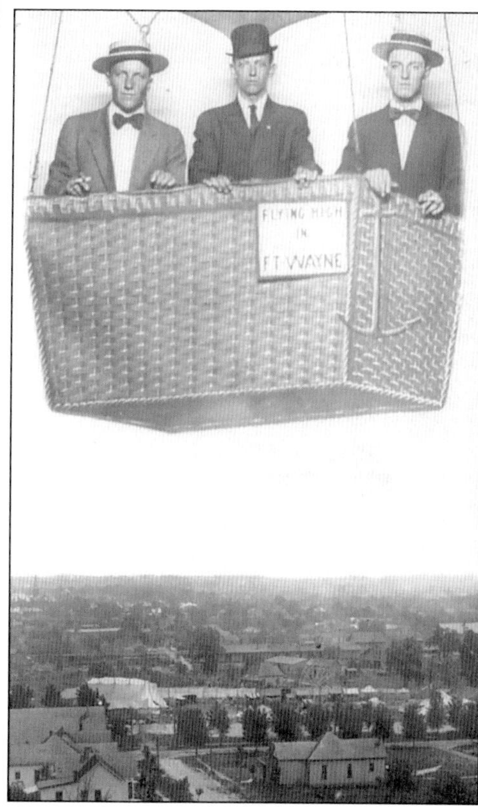

FLYING HIGH IN FORT WAYNE, INDIANA. This novelty photograph was probably taken at Robison Park.

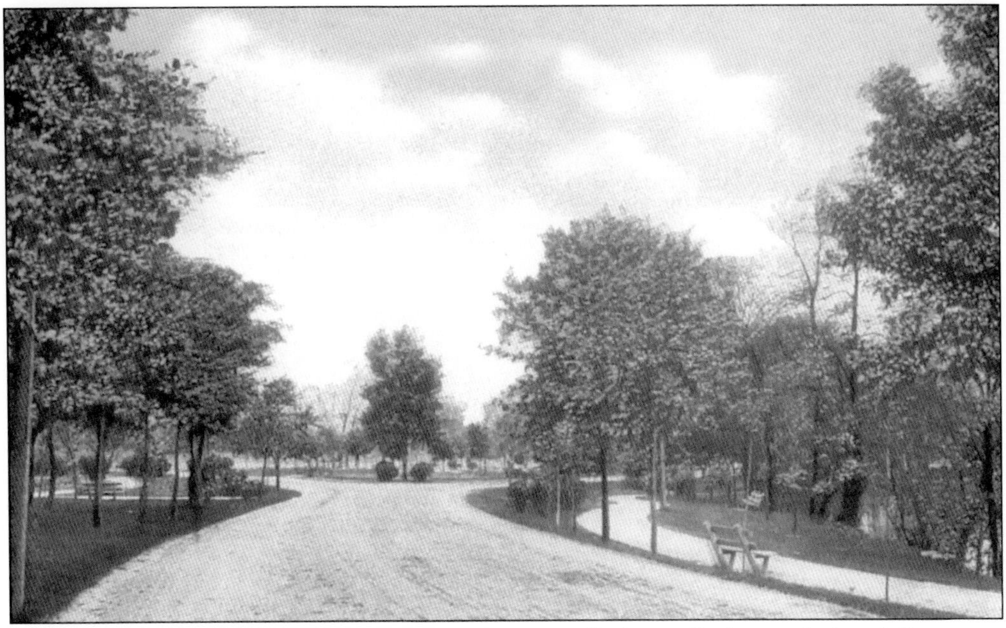

DRIVEWAY, SWINNEY PARK, FORT WAYNE, INDIANA. Swinney Park was designed for access by automobile.

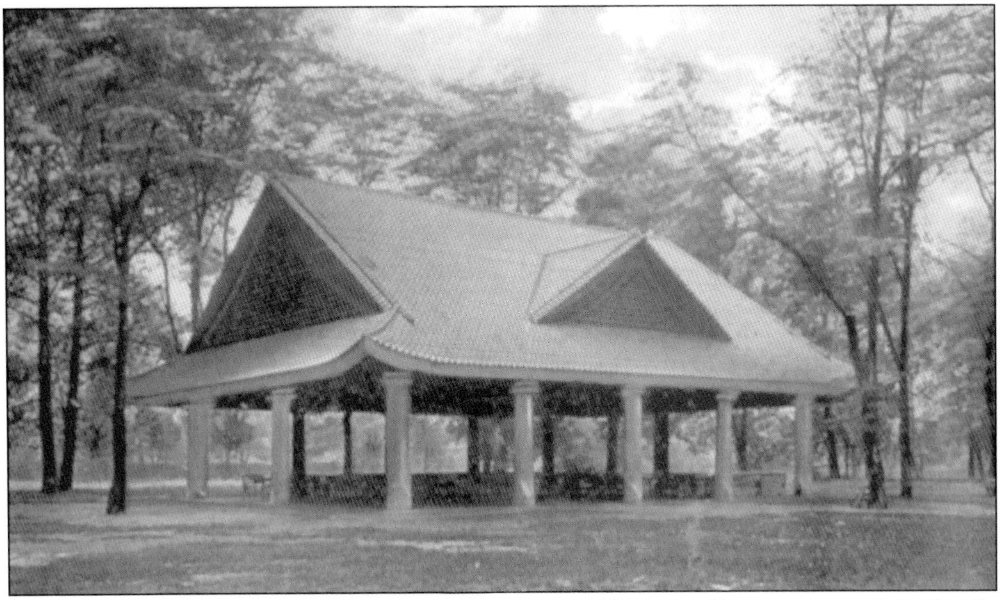

PAVILION, SWINNEY PARK, FORT WAYNE, INDIANA, *c.* 1913. Pavilions were used for family reunions and other large gatherings.

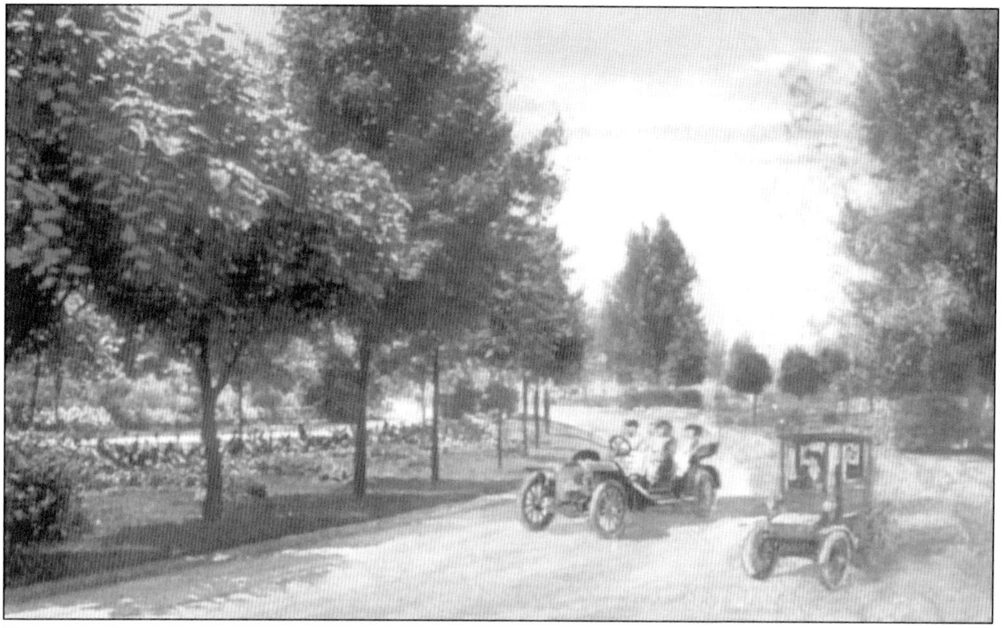

Drive in Swinney Park, Fort Wayne Indiana. Automobiles could be used to view the beauty of Swinney Park.

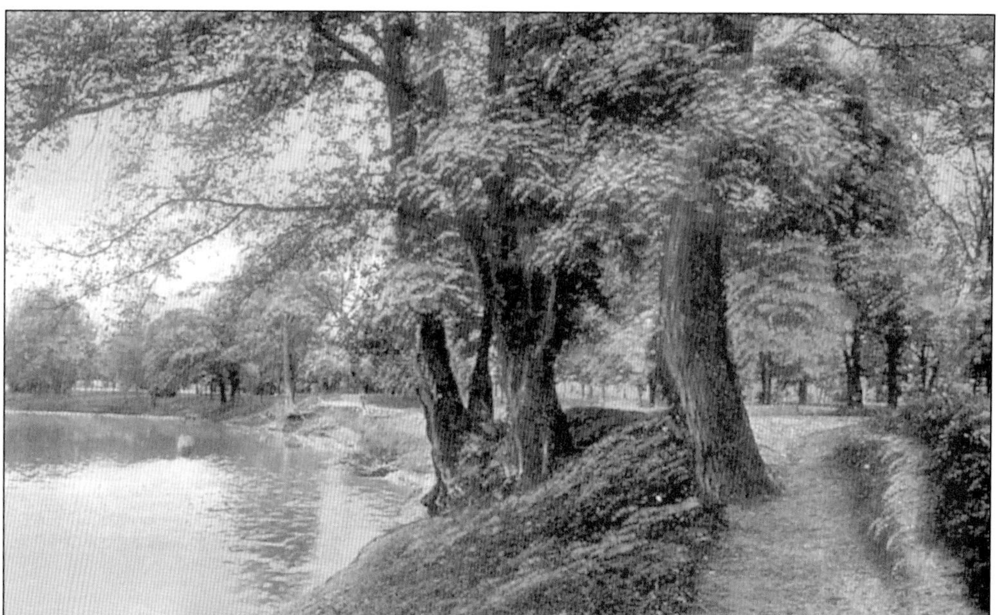

Lovers' Lane, Swinney Park, Fort Wayne, Indiana, *c.* 1913.

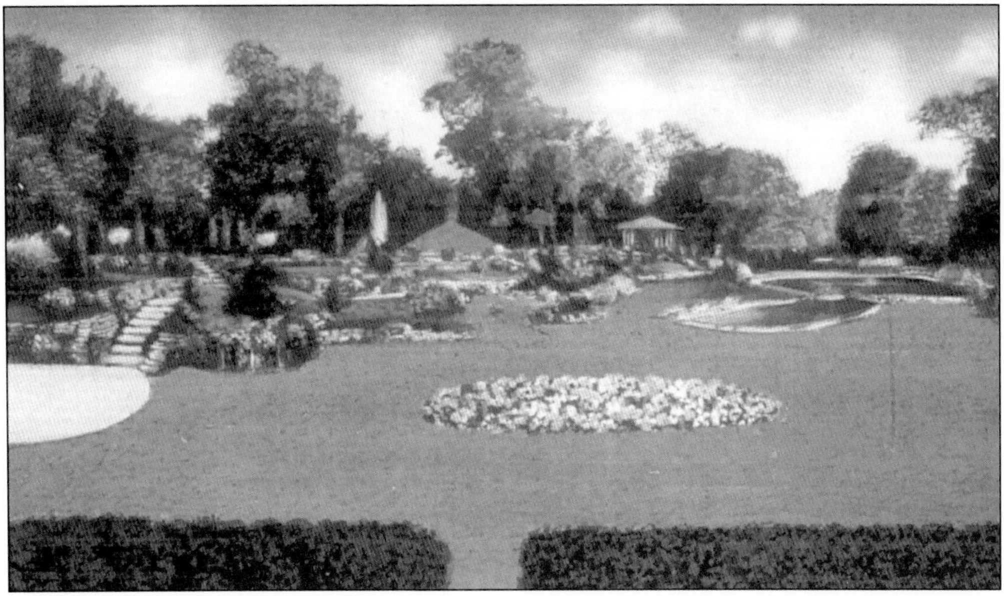

Panoramic View of Adolph Jaenicke Gardens (Swinney Park) Fort Wayne, Indiana, *c.* 1937. Adolph Jaenicke was the Fort Wayne Park Superintendent who established the flower gardens in Fort Wayne Parks.

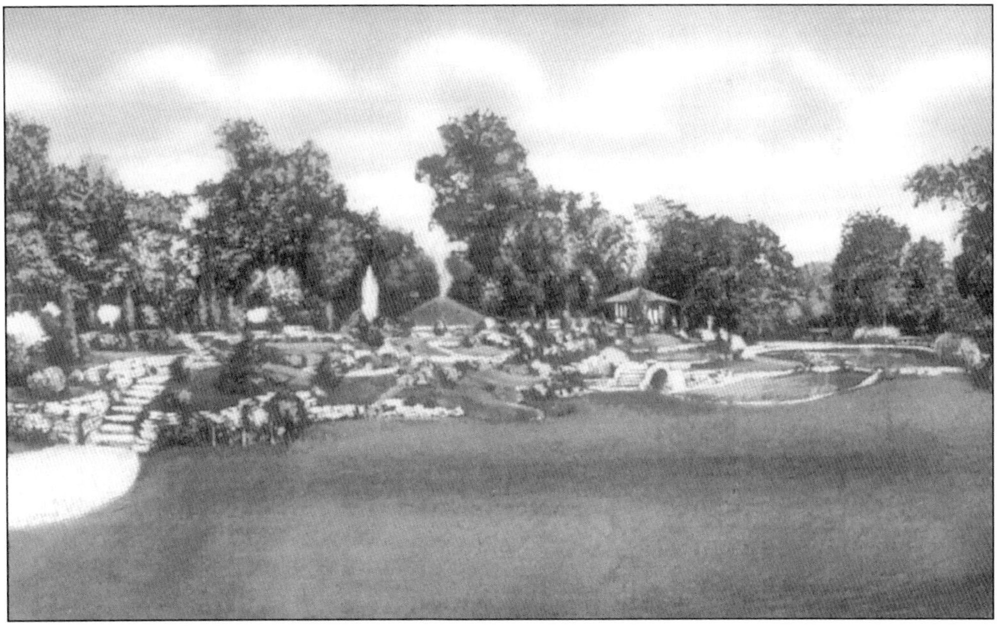

Jaenicke Garden, Swinney Park, Fort Wayne, Indiana.

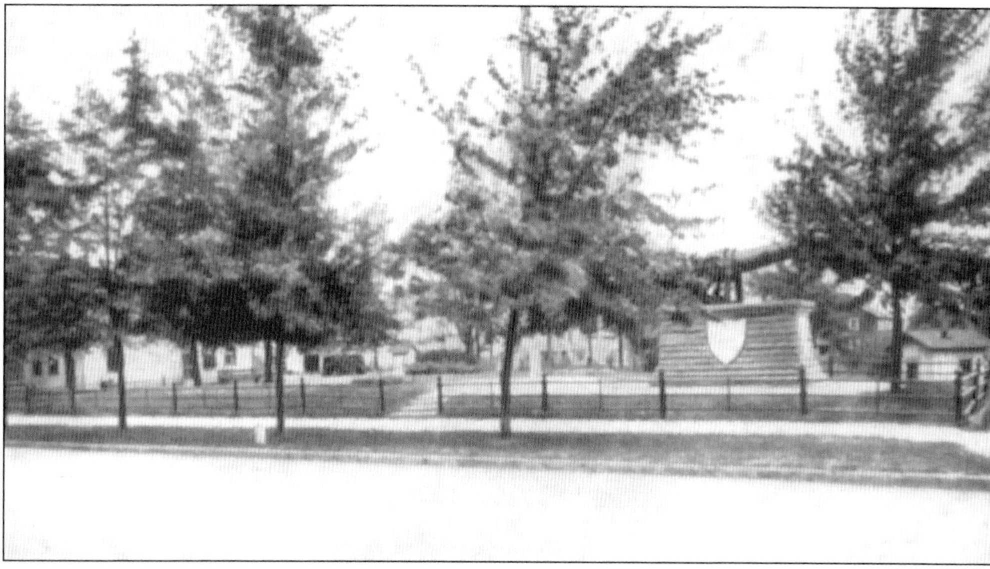

OLD FORT PLACE, FORT WAYNE, INDIANA.

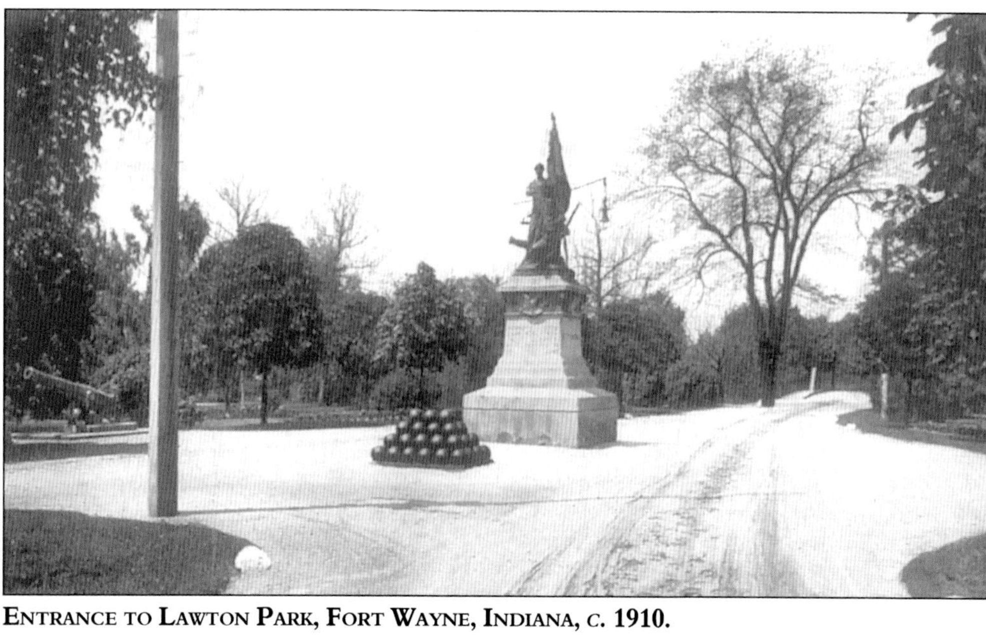

ENTRANCE TO LAWTON PARK, FORT WAYNE, INDIANA, *c.* 1910.

Soldiers' Monument, Lawton Park, Fort Wayne, Indiana.

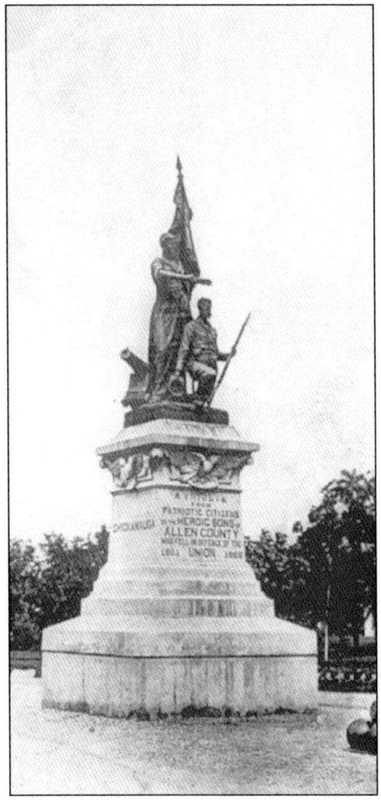

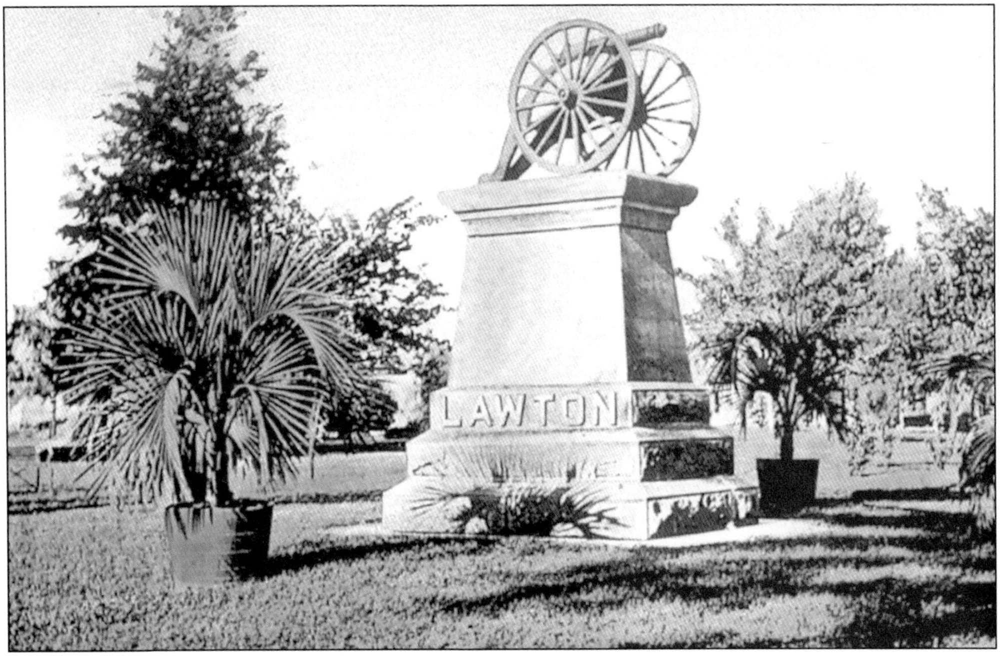

Lawton Park, Fort Wayne, Indiana, *c.* 1910.

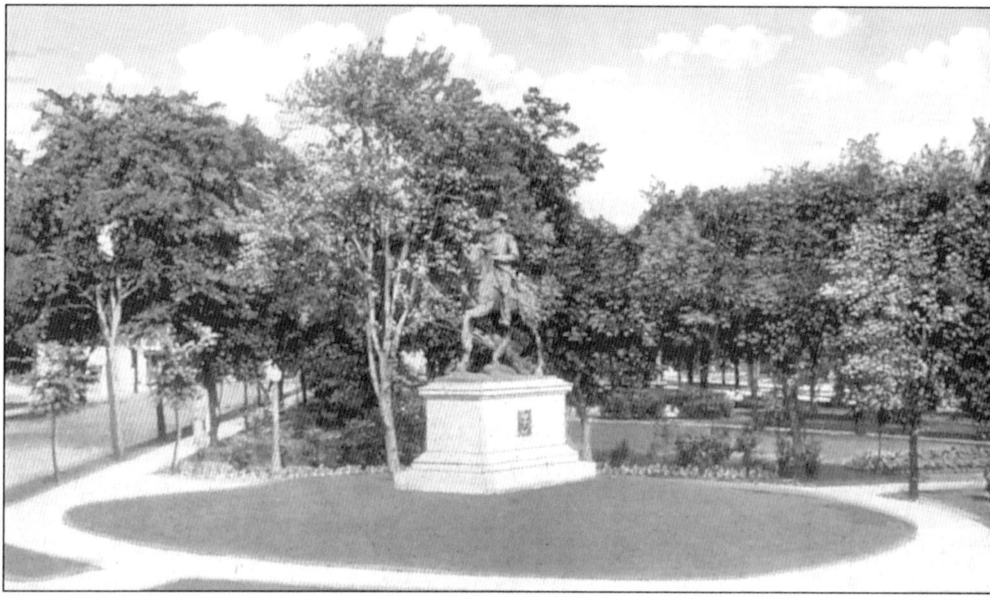

ANTHONY WAYNE MONUMENT, FORT WAYNE, INDIANA, *c.* 1921.

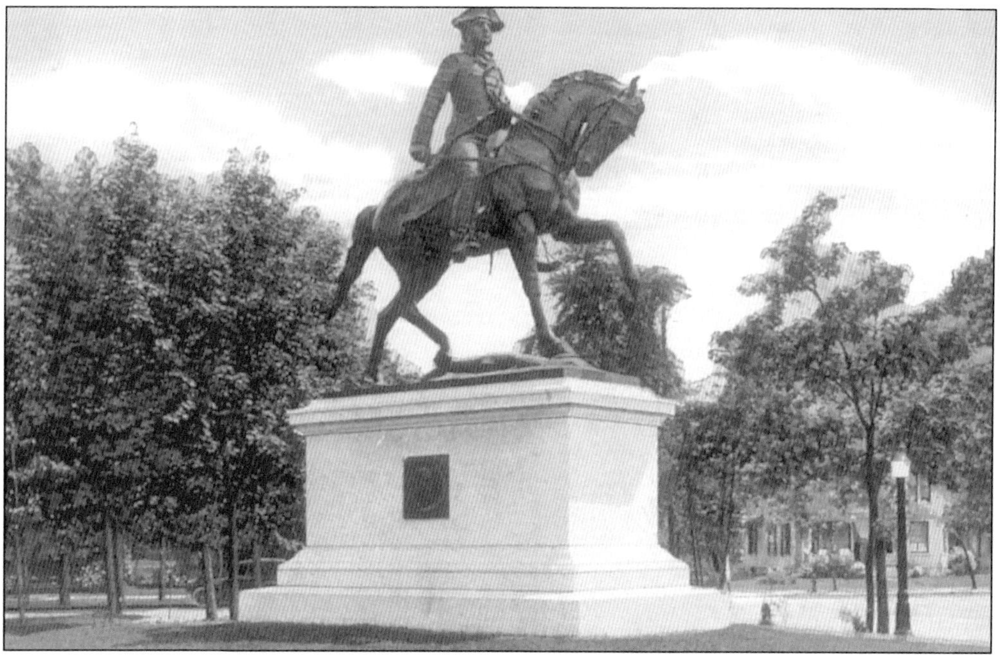

ANTHONY WAYNE MONUMENT, FORT WAYNE, INDIANA. This heroic bronze equestrian statue of Major General Anthony Wayne was erected in Hayden Park by the people of Fort Wayne. Following the defeat of General Josiah Harmar in 1790, and General Arthur St. Clair in 1791, President George Washington selected "Mad Anthony" Wayne to lead a third army against the combined tribes. At the battle of Fallen Timber, on the banks of the Maumee River, Wayne erected Fort Wayne on the site of the present city, marking the end of the Indian wars. The monument is now located at Frieman Square in downtown Fort Wayne.

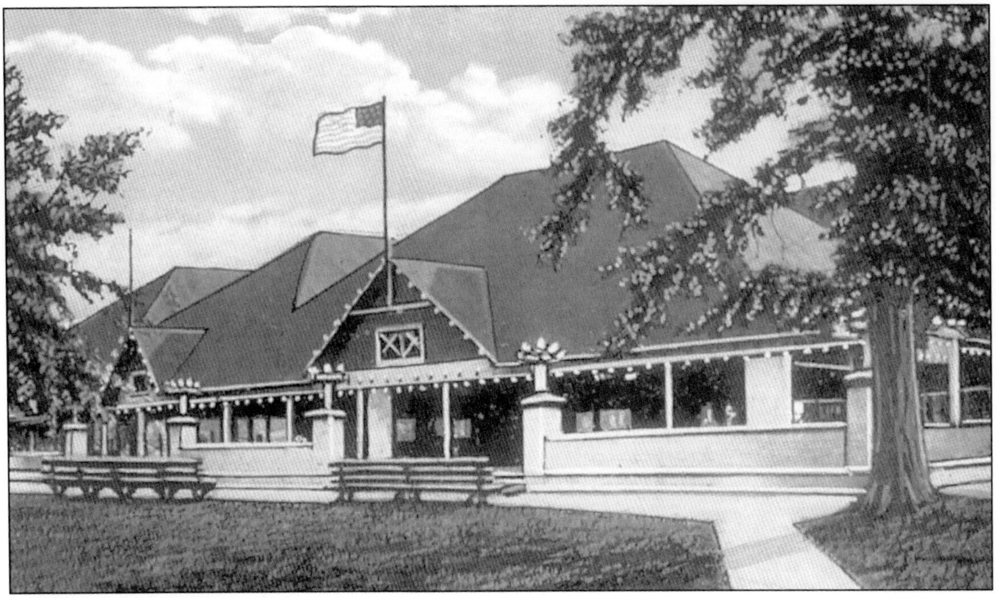

DANCING PAVILION AT TRIER'S PARK, FORT WAYNE, INDIANA. Another popular park in Fort Wayne is pictured above.

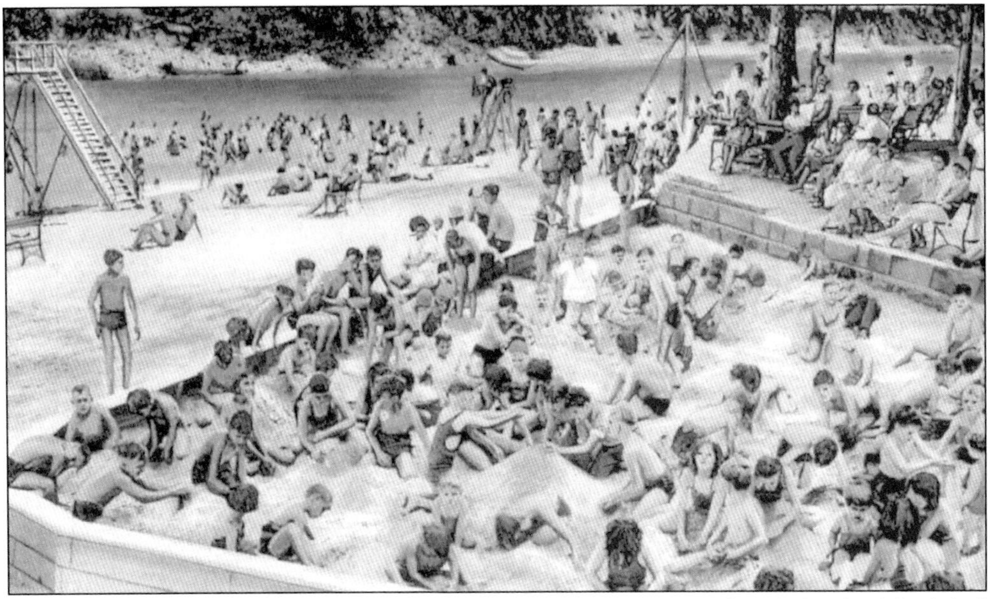

MUNICIPAL BATHING BEACH, FORT WAYNE, INDIANA, *c.* 1947. In the 1940s, the Municipal Bathing Beach was located above the St. Joseph River Dam in what is now called Johnny Appleseed Park. Pollution concerns closed the beach in the 1950s.

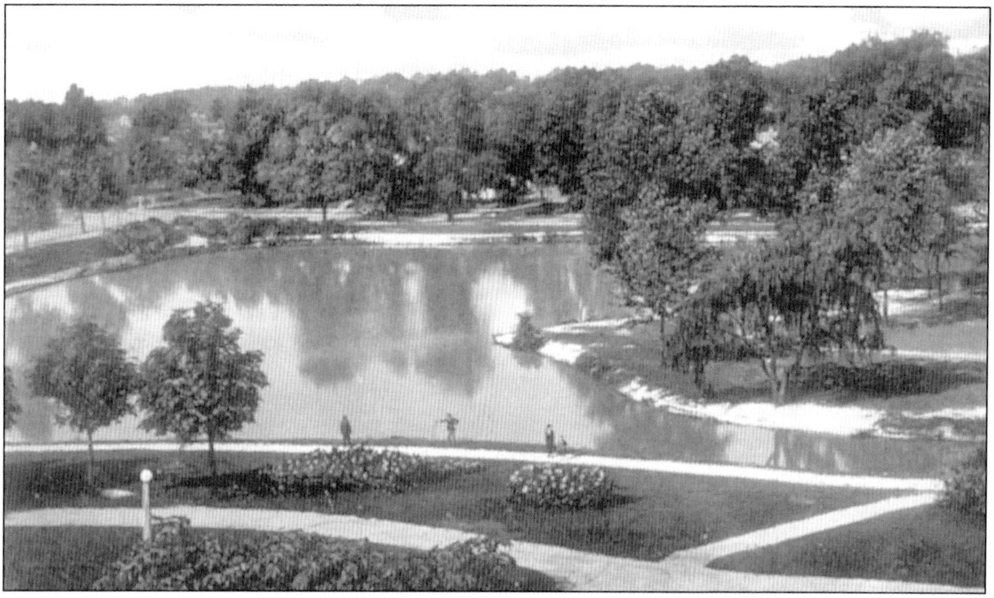

SECTION VIEW RESERVOIR PARK, FORT WAYNE, INDIANA. In 1880, the reservoir was built by the City of Fort Wayne to provide a storage space for water drawn out of dug wells. The area surrounding the reservoir developed as a park area. The reservoir was filled in 1959. Sledding and ice skating are popular in the winter.

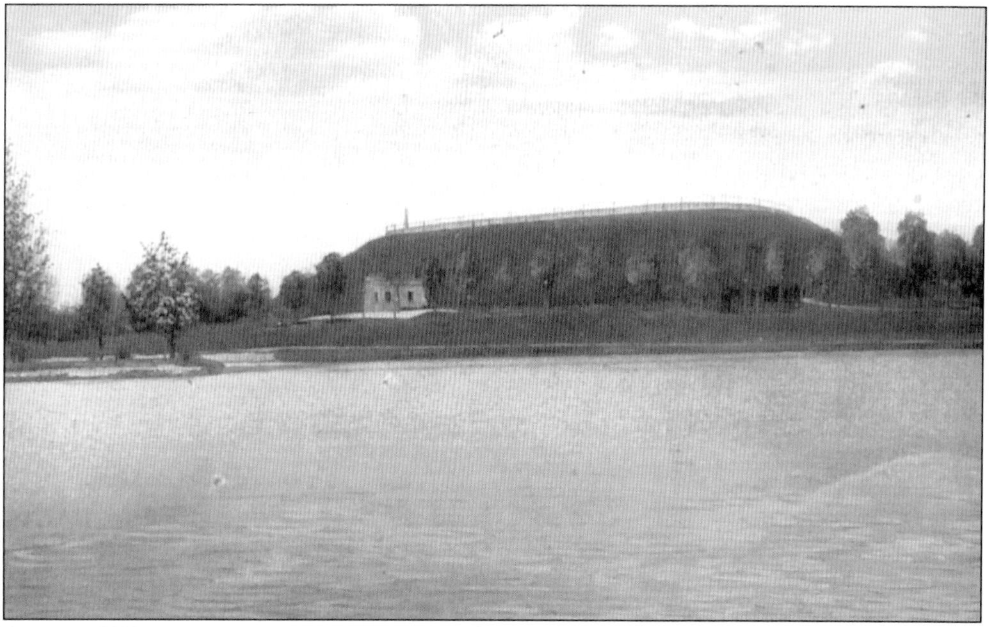

RESERVOIR PARK, FORT WAYNE, INDIANA. This message states: "Dear Friend. We arrived in the city about noon and have just begun to look around. The wind was so strong that we had to keep our mouths shut to keep our teeth from blowing away. Believe all you want to of this. Ralph."

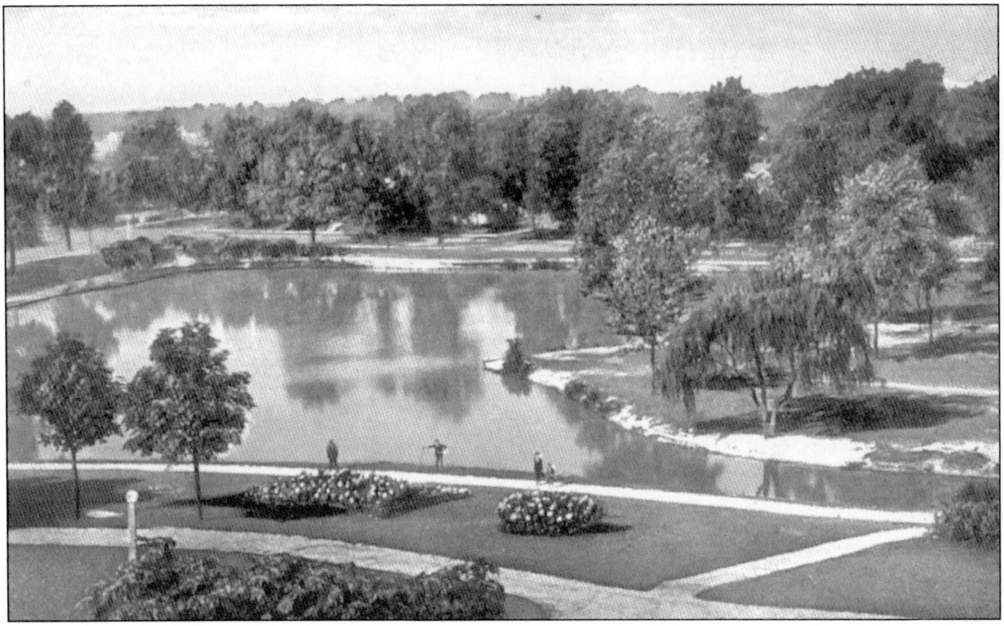

S.W. Section "Reservoir Park" Fort Wayne, Indiana. This is a beautiful setting enjoyed by residents of South Fort Wayne.

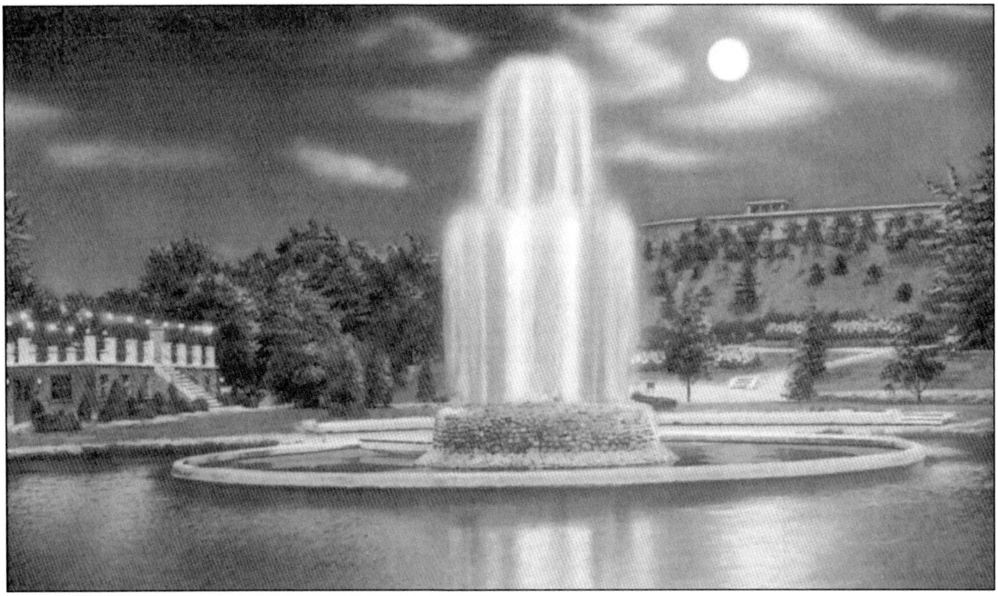

Electric Fountain in Reservoir Park, Fort Wayne, Indiana. This fountain is equipped to throw water 25 feet into the air. The color effects are secured by a battery of 30 multicolored floodlights. This fountain was donated to the City of Fort Wayne by General Electric Company.

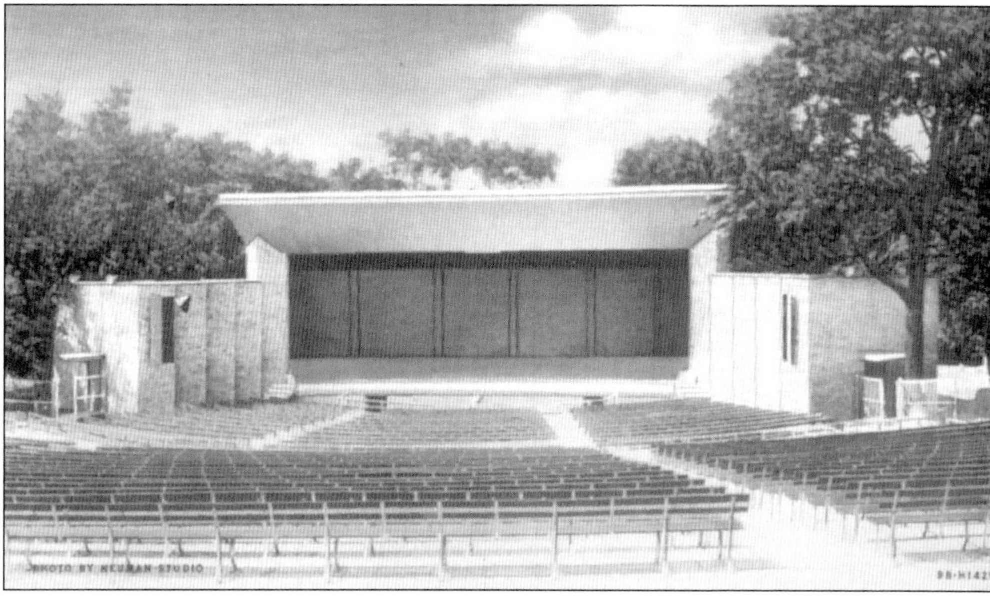

News-Sentinel Outdoor Theater, Franke Park, Fort Wayne, Indiana. This was the original configuration of the theater.

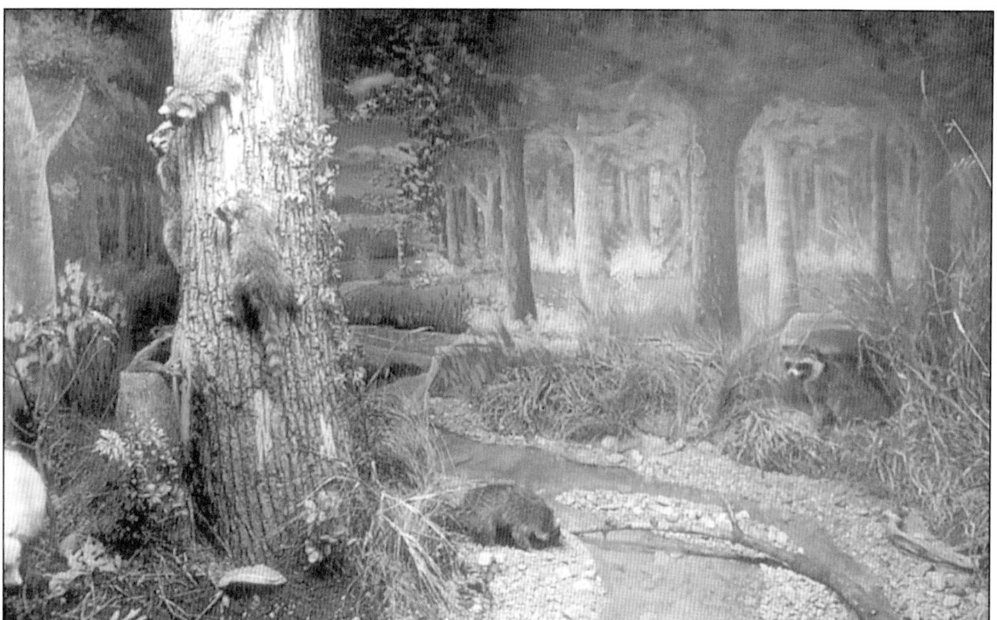

The Jack D. Diehm Memorial Museum of Natural History Franke Park/Fort Wayne, Indiana. Since destroyed by fire, the museum had provided an outstanding exhibit of mounted creatures.

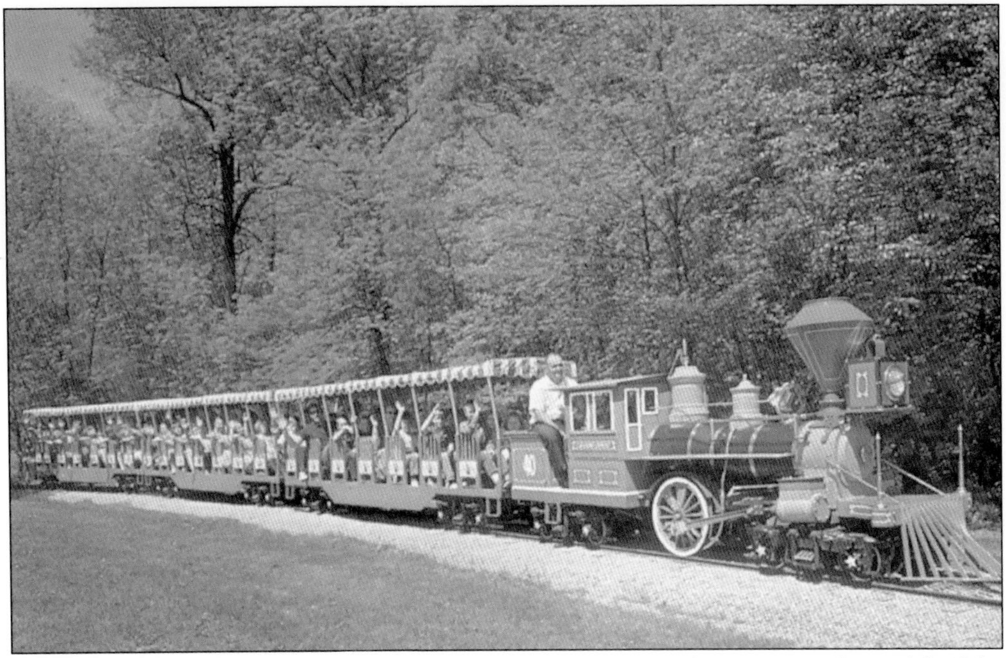

Children's Zoo, Fort Wayne, Indiana. This train is an authentic 1/3 scale model of the famous 1863 C.P. Huntington traveling over nearly 1 mile of track through the zoo and along the shore of beautiful Shoaff Lake in Franke Park.

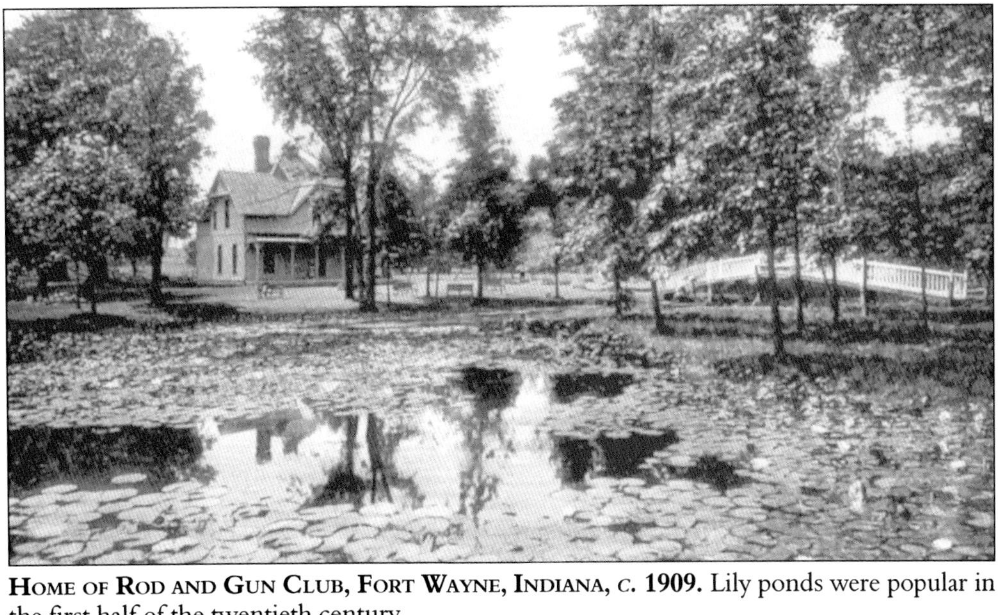

Home of Rod and Gun Club, Fort Wayne, Indiana, *c.* 1909. Lily ponds were popular in the first half of the twentieth century.

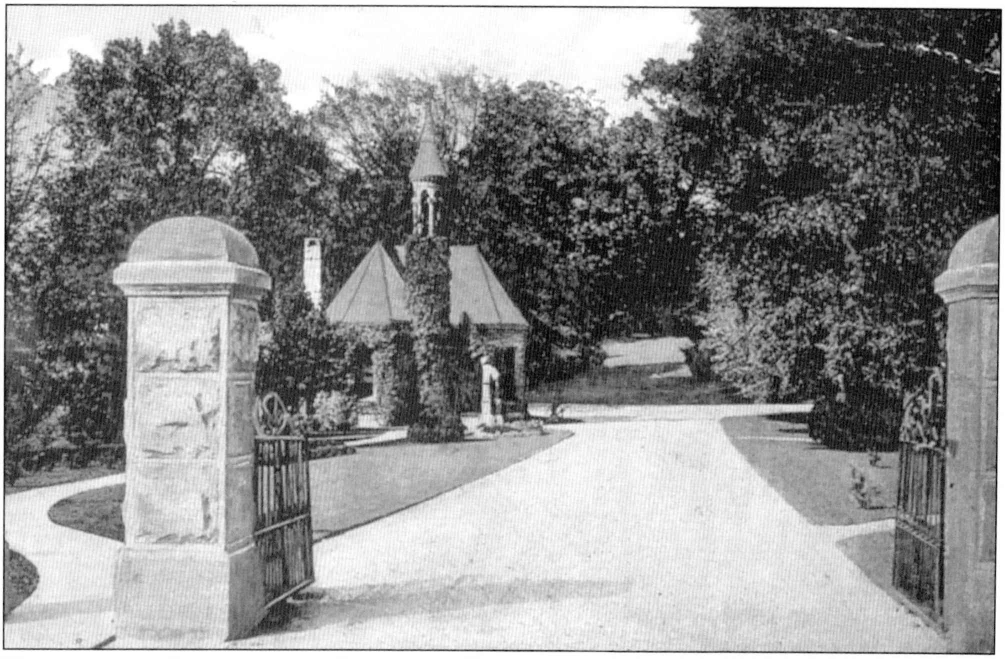

Entrance to Lindenwood Cemetery, Fort Wayne, Indiana, *c.* 1913. Fort Wayne's premier cemetery is the final resting place of many Fort Wayne residents.

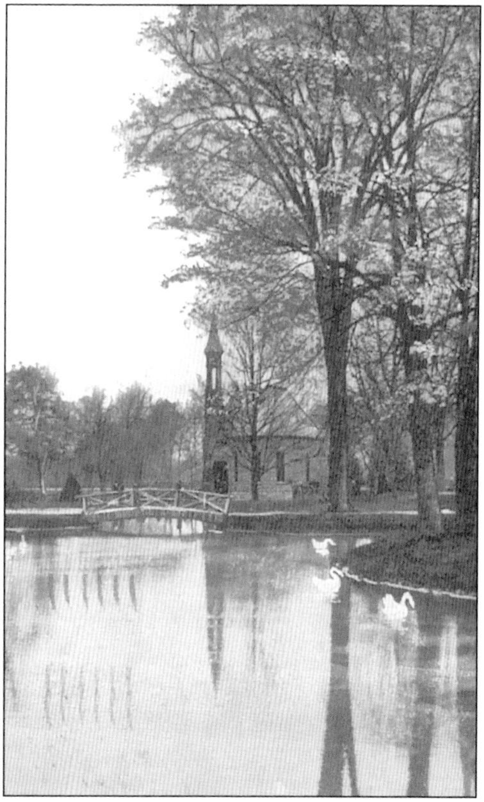

Lake at Lindenwood Cemetery, Fort Wayne, Indiana, *c.* 1911. The chapel is in the background.

RESIDENTIAL

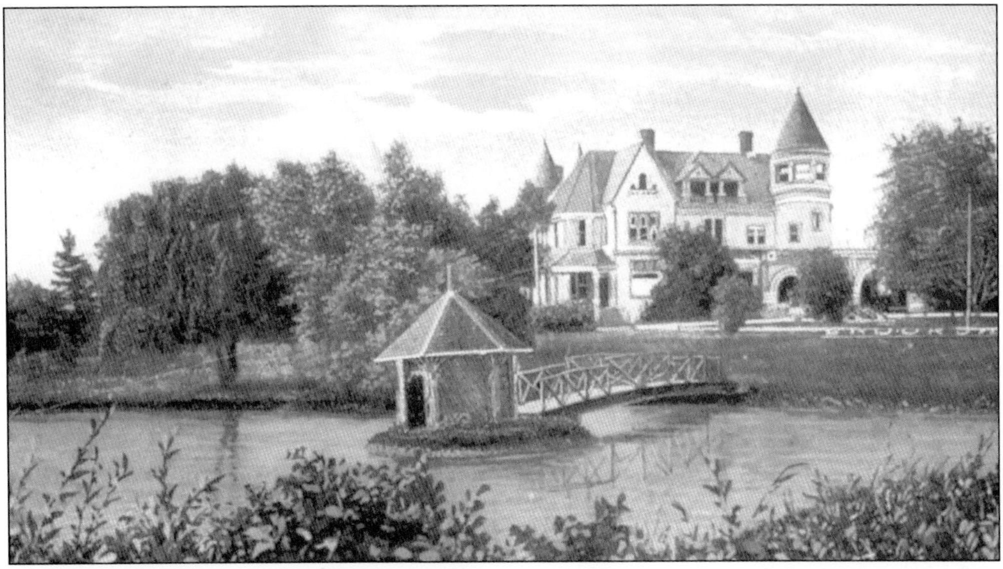

THE BASS RESIDENCE, FORT WAYNE, INDIANA, *c.* 1909. Now part of the University of St. Francis, the mansion of Fort Wayne industrial John Bass was also known as "Brookside."

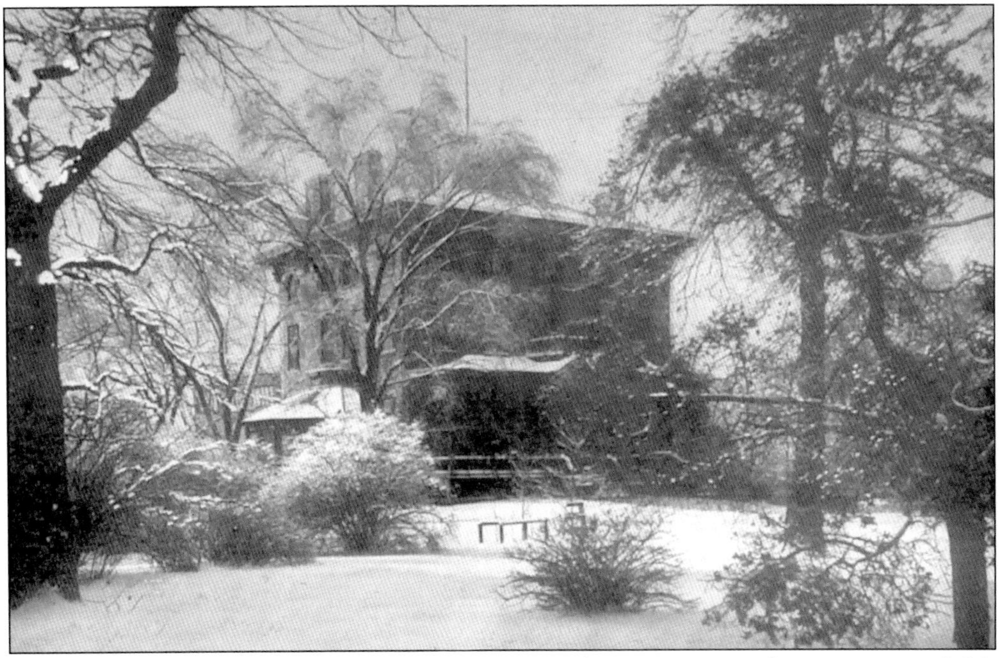

HAMILTON HOMESTEAD, FORT WAYNE, INDIANA. This is an unusual snow scene of this fine mansion.

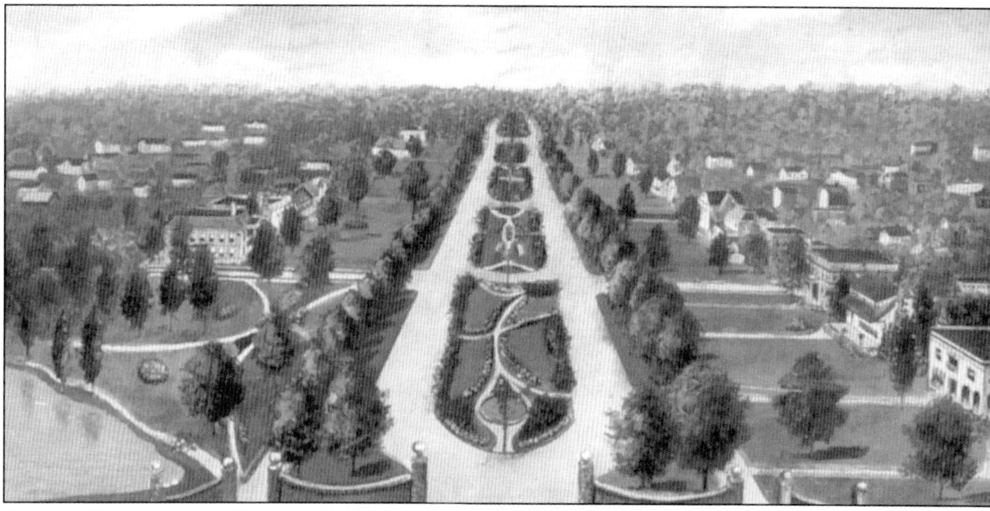

FOREST PARK, FORT WAYNE, INDIANA, *C.* 1915. One of Fort Wayne's finest neighborhoods was developed with wide boulevards to accommodate the automobile.

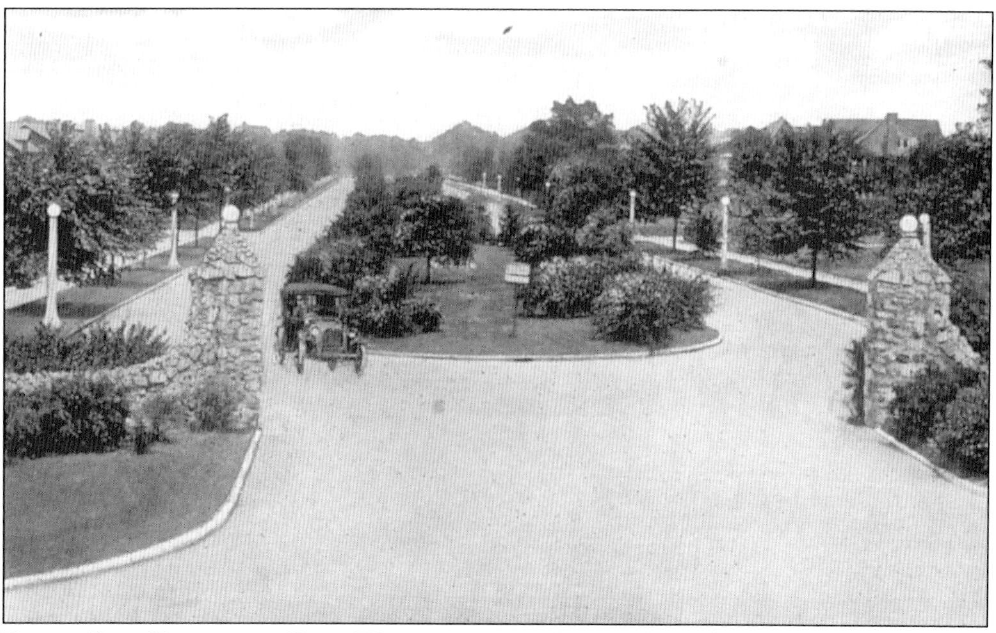

FOREST PARK BOULEVARD, FORT WAYNE, INDIANA. A car is shown leaving Forest Park.

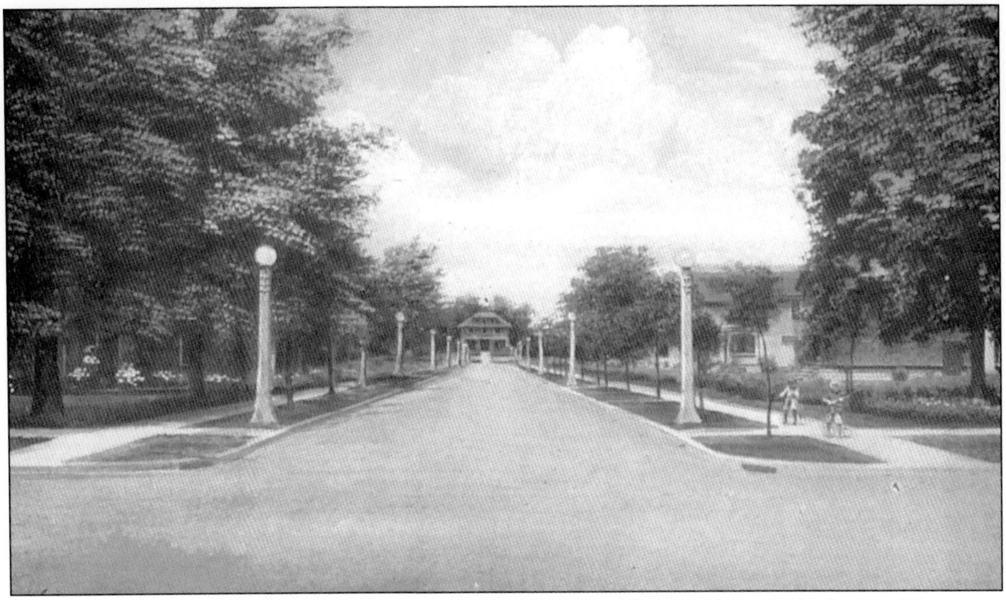

WILDWOOD AVENUE, FORT WAYNE, INDIANA. A fine neighborhood scene is depicted here.

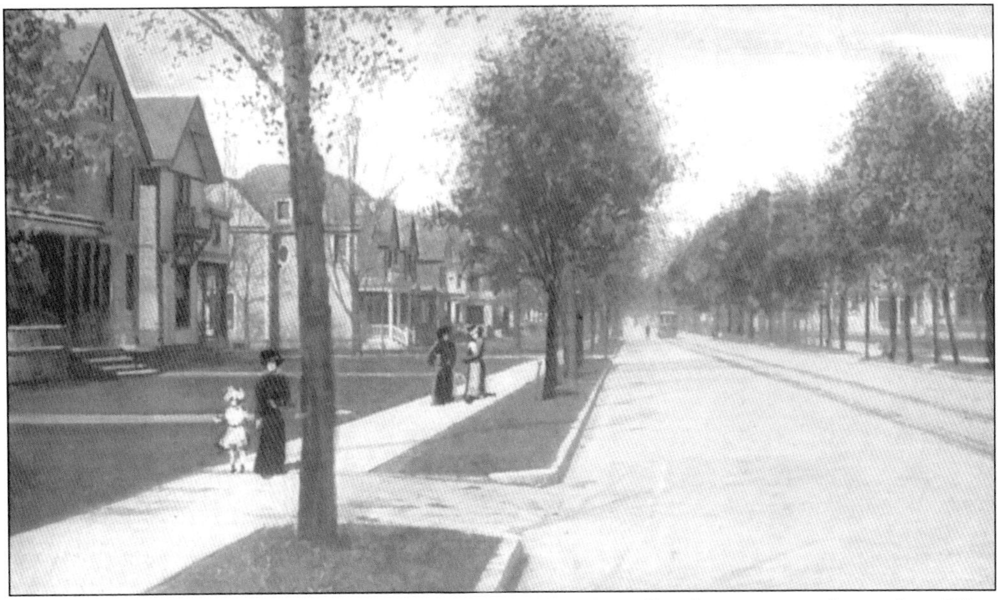

WEST CREIGHTON AVENUE, FORT WAYNE, INDIANA. Many fine homes were located on West Creighton Avenue.

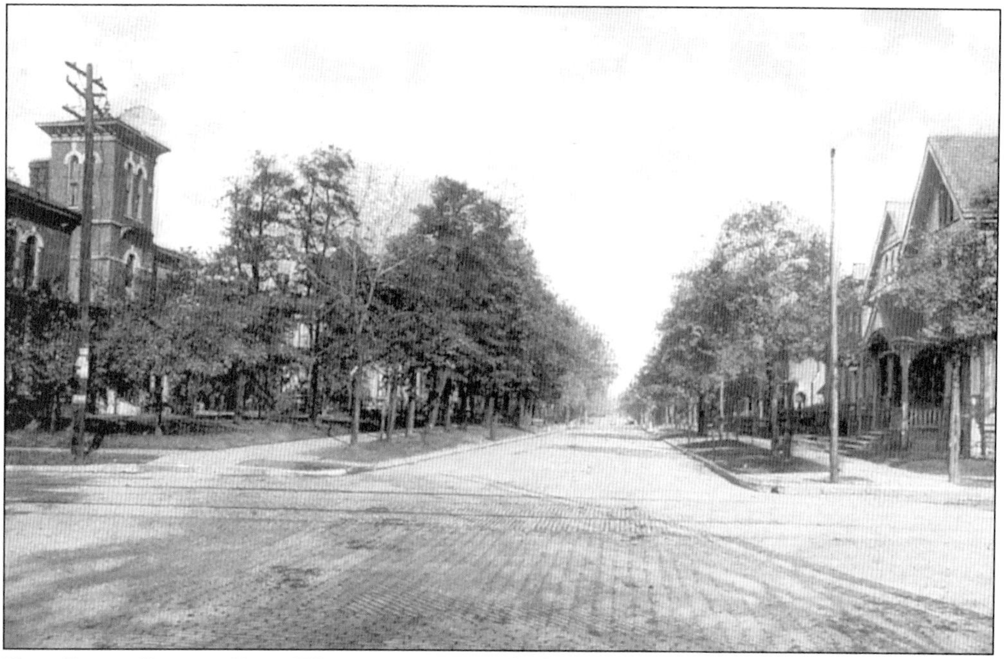

East Berry Street, Fort Wayne, Indiana. The brick street and trolley tracks are shown in the foreground.

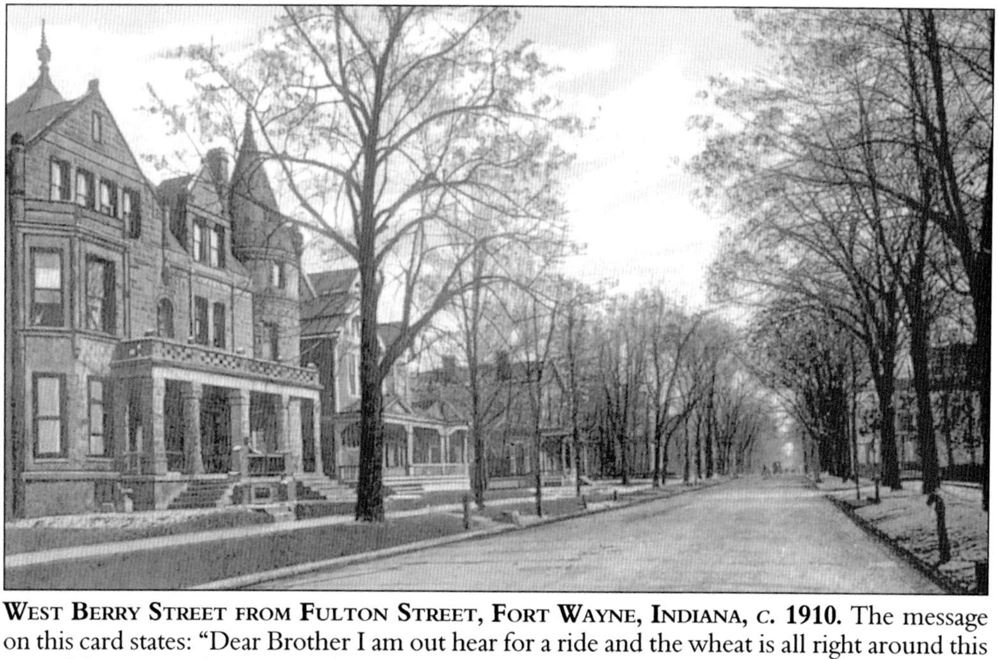

West Berry Street from Fulton Street, Fort Wayne, Indiana, c. 1910. The message on this card states: "Dear Brother I am out hear for a ride and the wheat is all right around this part of the country but corn and oats are poor."

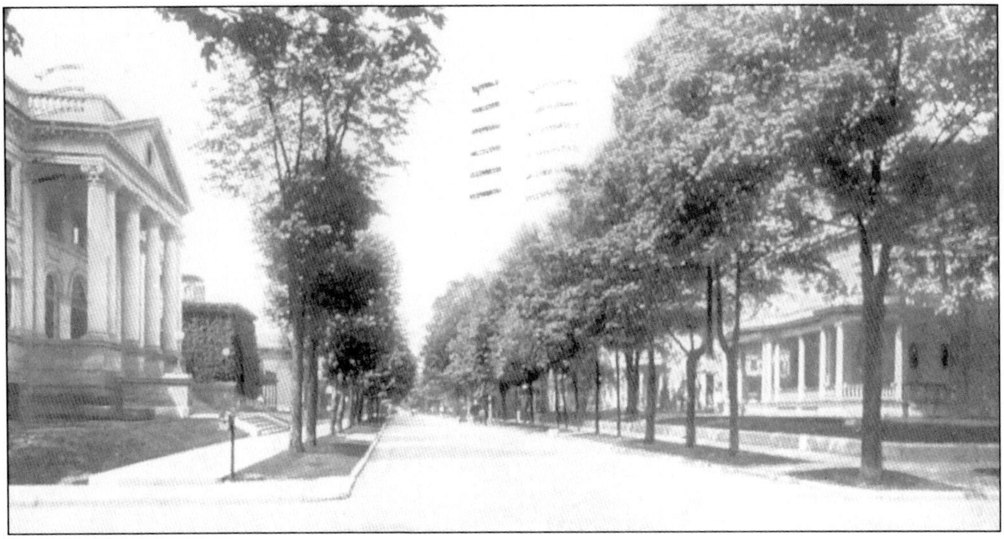

WEST BERRY STREET, FORT WAYNE, INDIANA. *c.* 1909. The Fort Wayne Public Library is on the left.

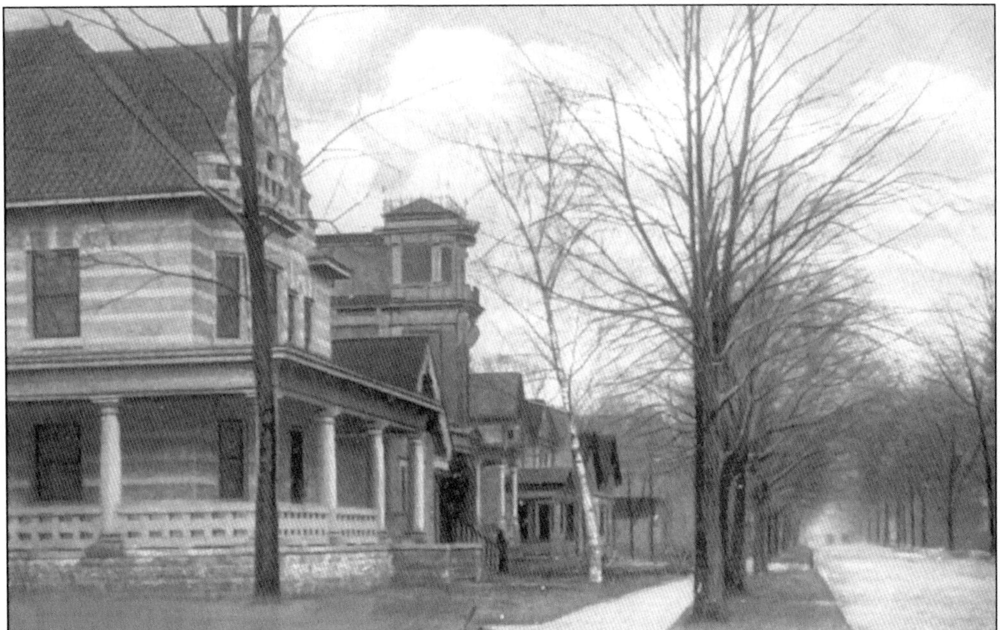

WEST WAYNE STREET, WAYNE, INDIANA. This is now a part of the West Central neighborhood.

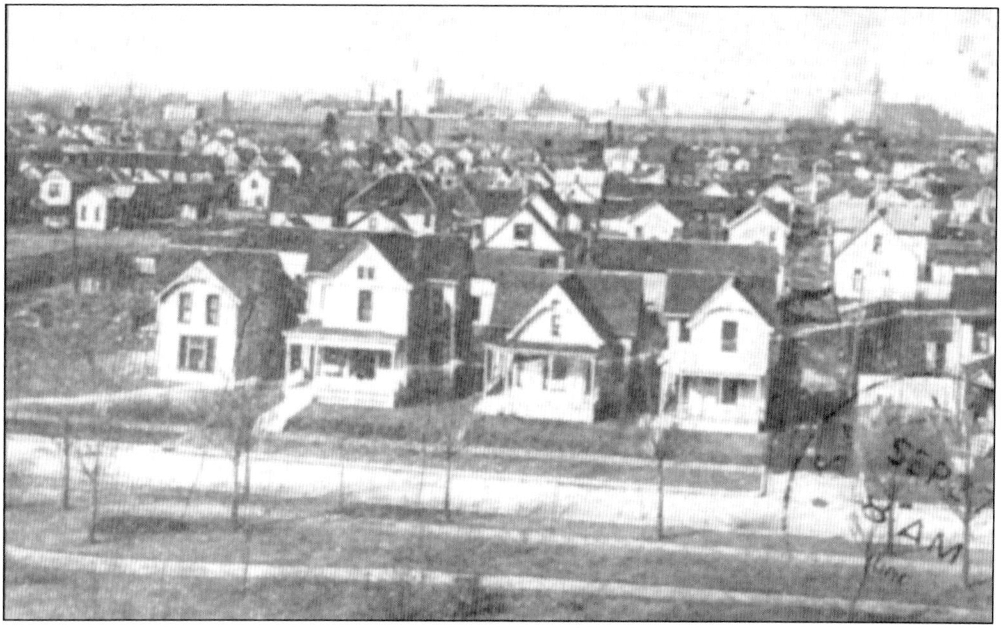

"Greetings from Fort Wayne, Indiana," Bird's-Eye View North of Reservoir Park, c. 1906. Worker's homes were not as large and elaborate as the mansions and fine homes shown on previous pages.

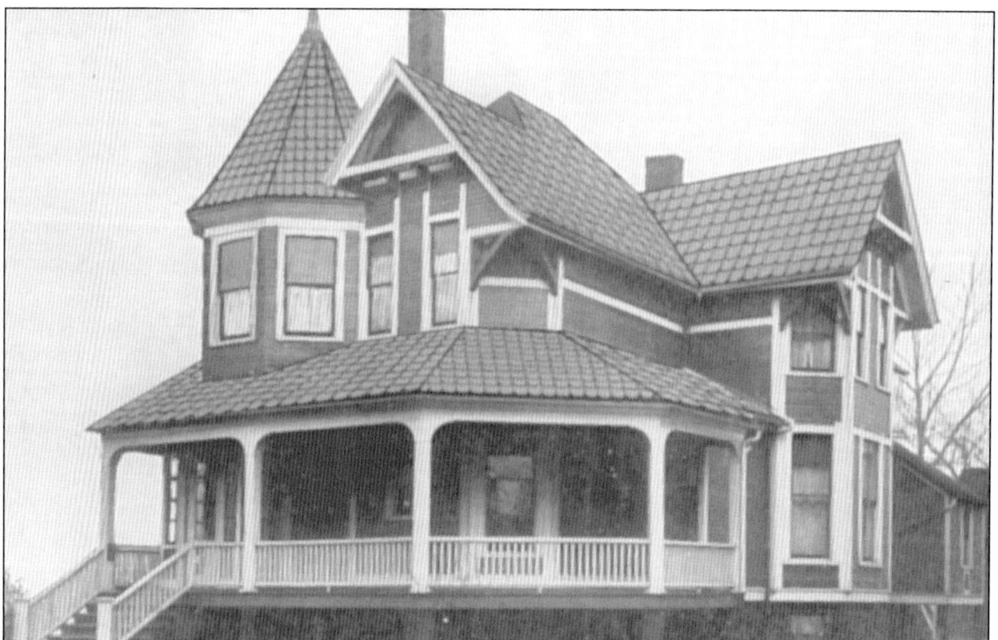

Inlade Design Roofing. This message states: "Inlade Design Roofing. We would like to tell you about Inlade Roofing; it is cheaper than wooden shingles. Looks like Tile. Is extremely durable and fire resisting. Fort Wayne Ready Roofing Co., 1914 South Calhoun Street, Ft. Wayne, Ind."

Downtown Street Scenes

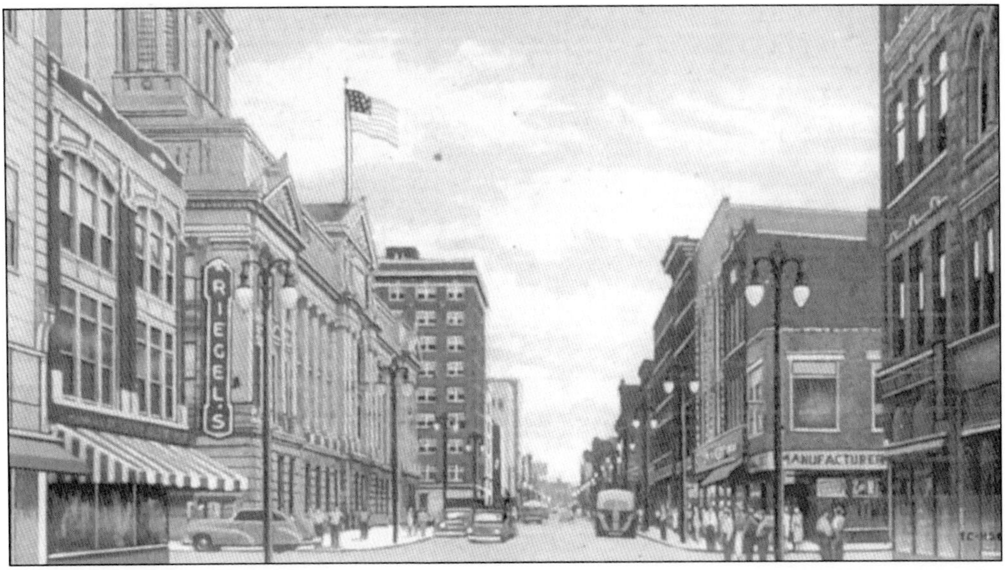

Calhoun Street, Main Business Section, Fort Wayne, Indiana. Calhoun Street was the "Main Street" of Fort Wayne. Riegel's Tobacco Store is on the left. A city bus is on the right.

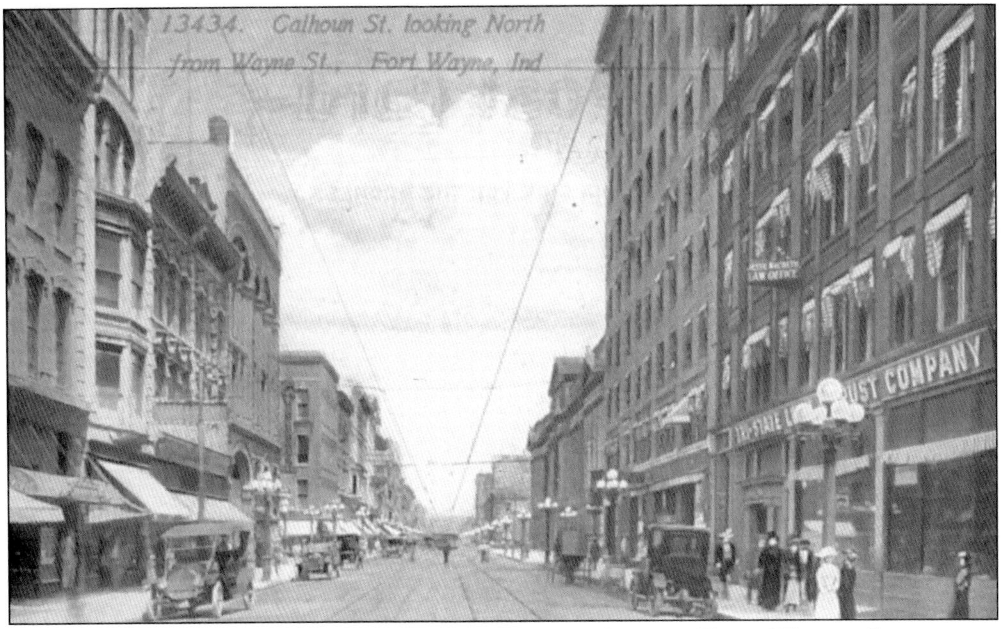

Calhoun Street Looking North From Wayne Street, Fort Wayne, Indiana, c. 1915. This message states: "Compliments of Gary Rundles Atty-at-Law Ft. Wayne." The large building on the right is the Tri-State Loan and Trust Company with the office of Jesse MacBeth on the third floor.

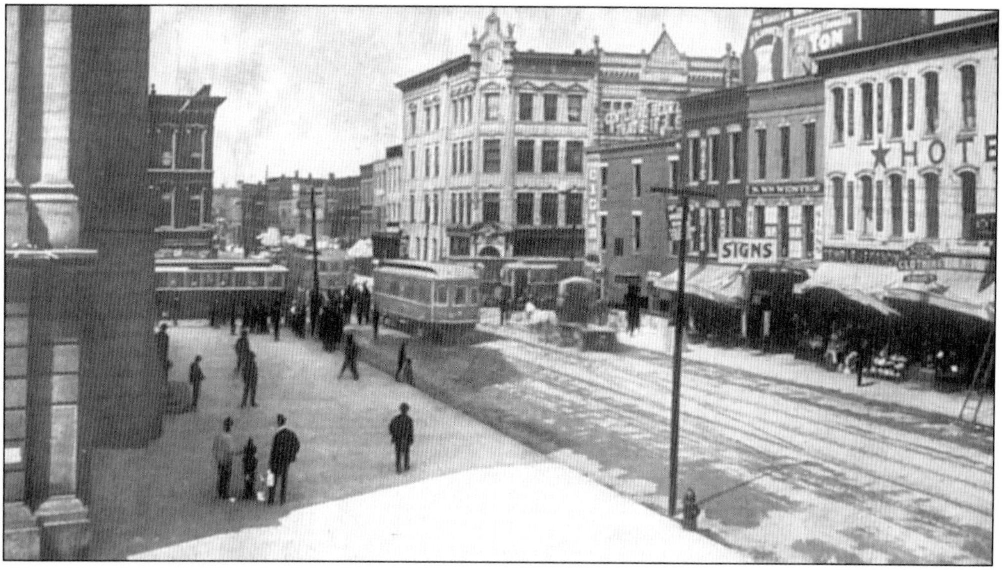

Calhoun and Main Streets, Fort Wayne, Indiana. Trolleys converge at this corner. Visible signs include "Centlivre Beer—That's It"—"WM Wester—Signs"—"Temple Economy Clothes."

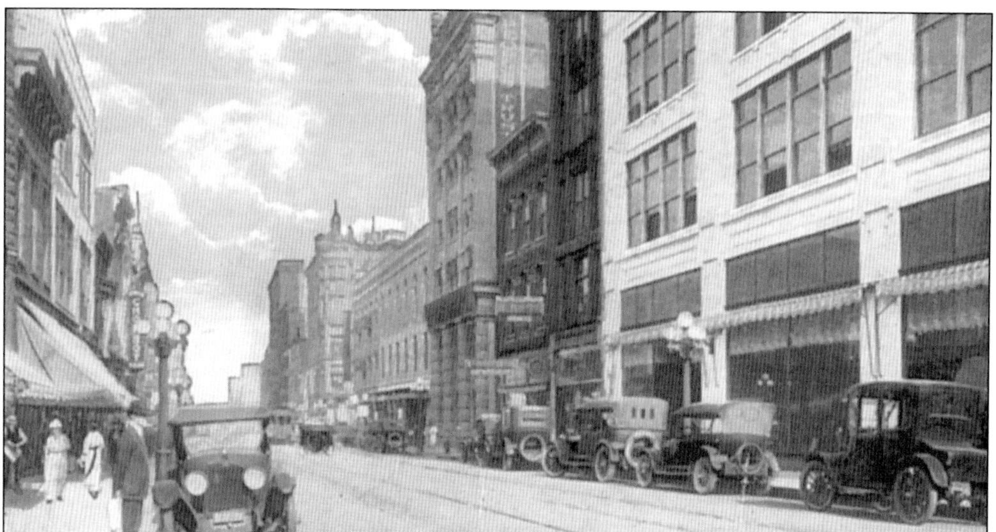

Calhoun Street Looking North, Fort Wayne, Indiana. Several 1920s-era automobiles line the street.

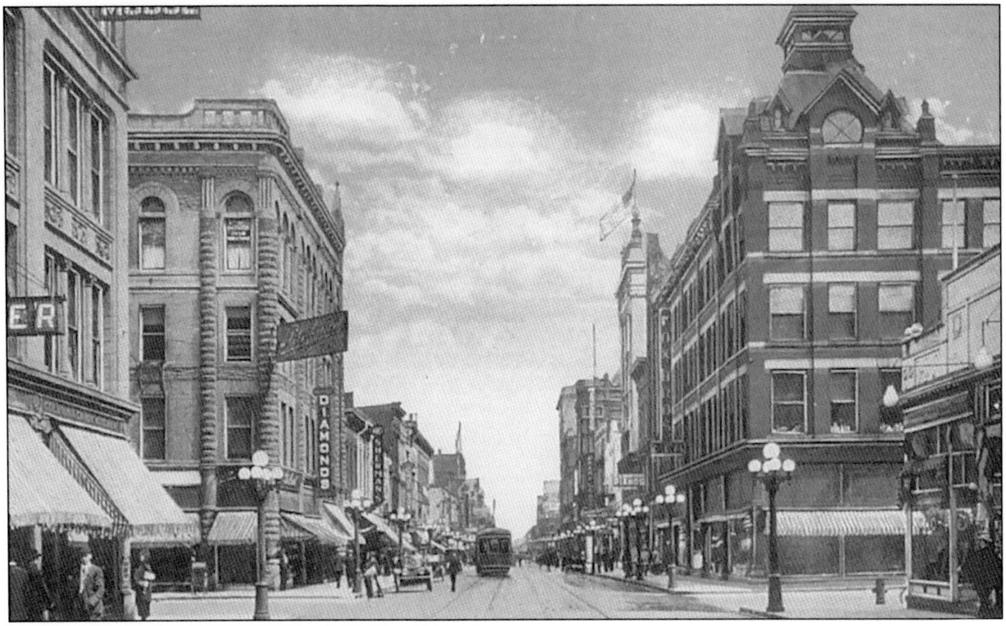

Calhoun Street, North From Washington Street, Fort Wayne, Indiana. Visible signs include "Moose"—"Packard Pianos"—"Diamonds"— "Shermans"—"Fox Bros."

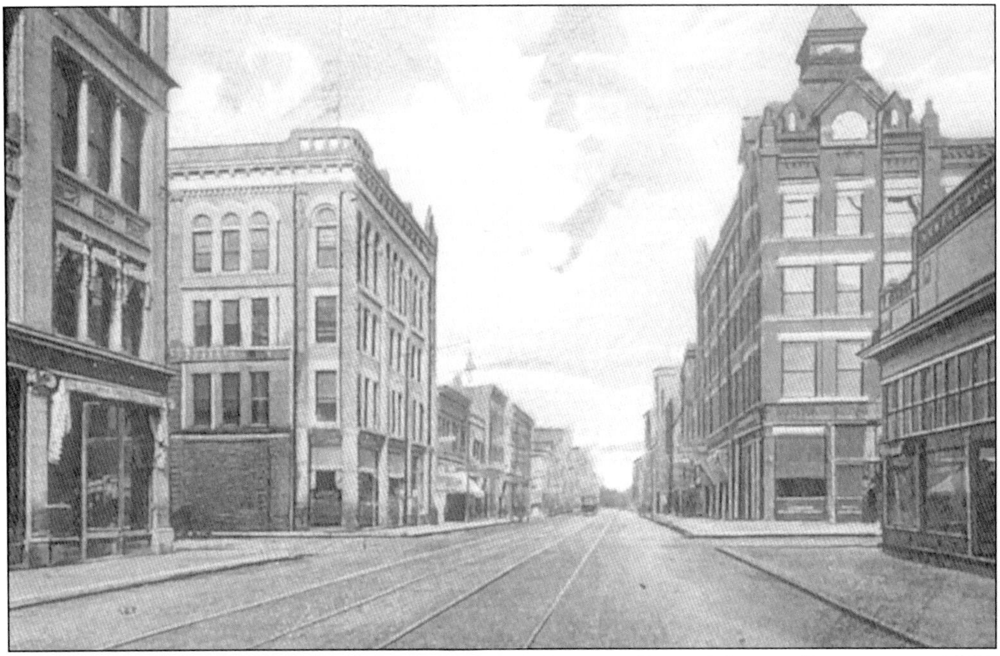

Calhoun Street, North from Washington Street, Fort Wayne, Indiana, *c.* 1908. Empty streets indicated the photograph was probably taken on an early Sunday morning.

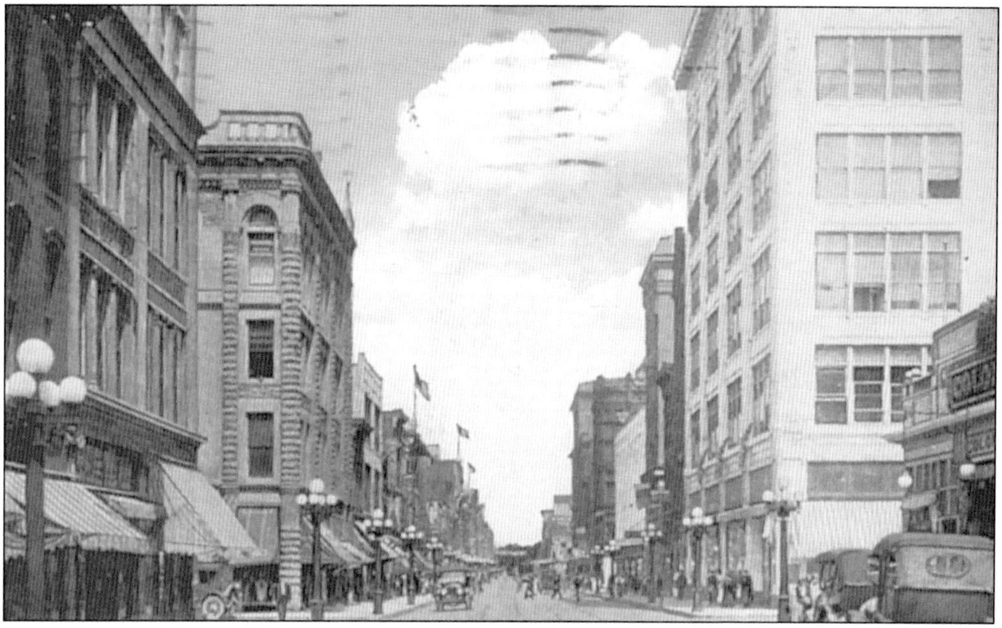

Calhoun Street, Looking North, Fort Wayne, Indiana, *c.* 1923. The Colonial Restaurant is on the right.

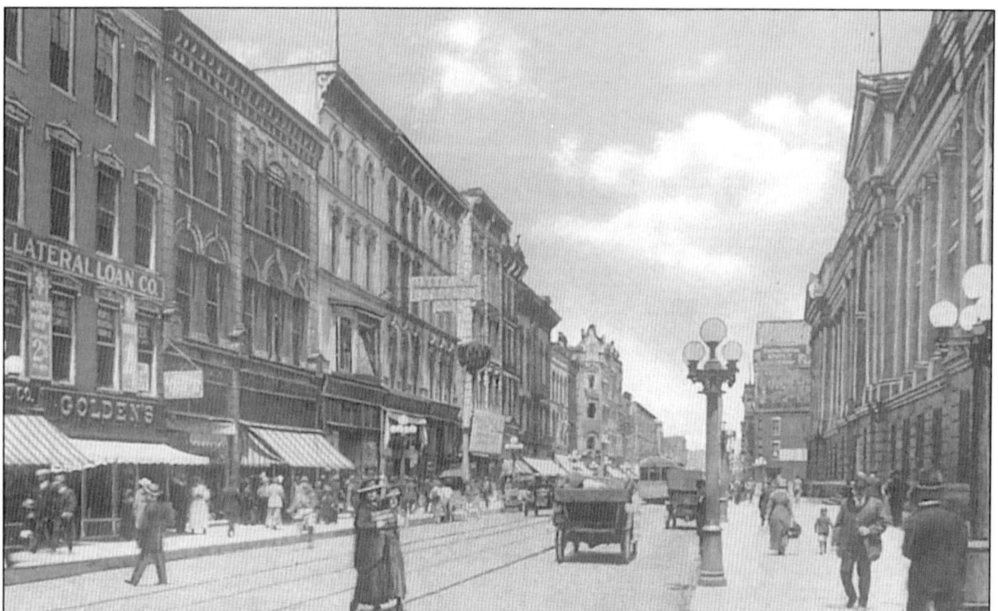

Calhoun Street, Fort Wayne, Indiana, *c.* 1919. Visible signs include "Collateral Loan Co." and "Golden's." The courthouse is on the right.

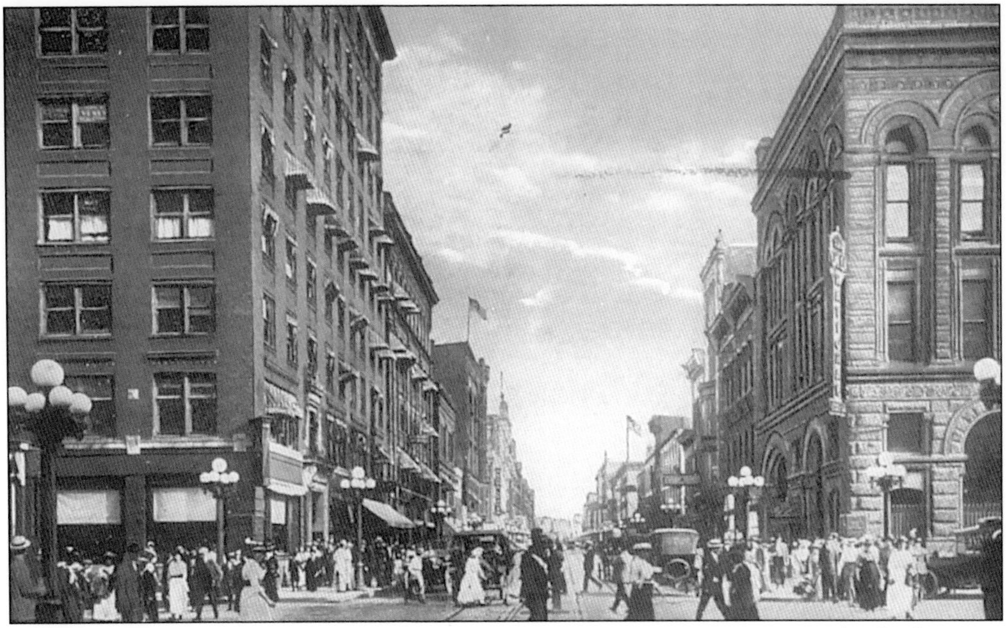

Calhoun Street, South from Berry, Fort Wayne, Indiana, *c.* 1917. Crowds of pedestrians are shown in downtown Fort Wayne.

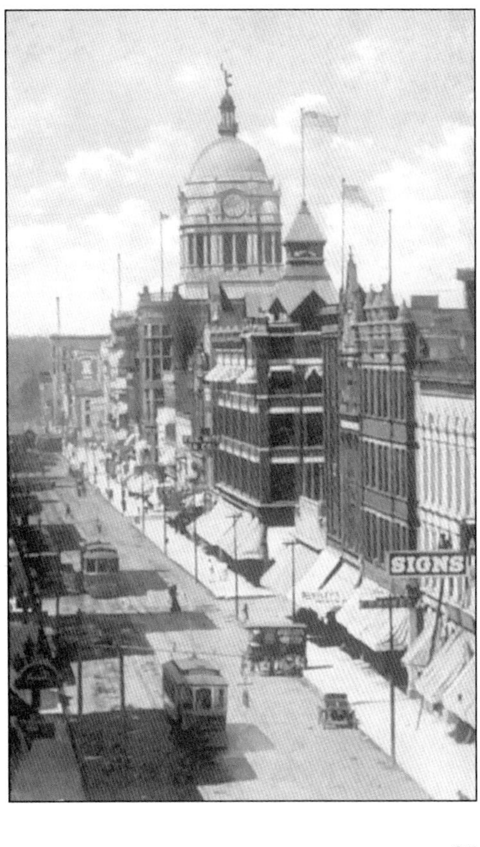

Calhoun Street, Fort Wayne, Indiana. Trolleys are on the street. Visible signs include—"Fox Hite & Co."—"Bursley Premium Coffee"—"Arcade."

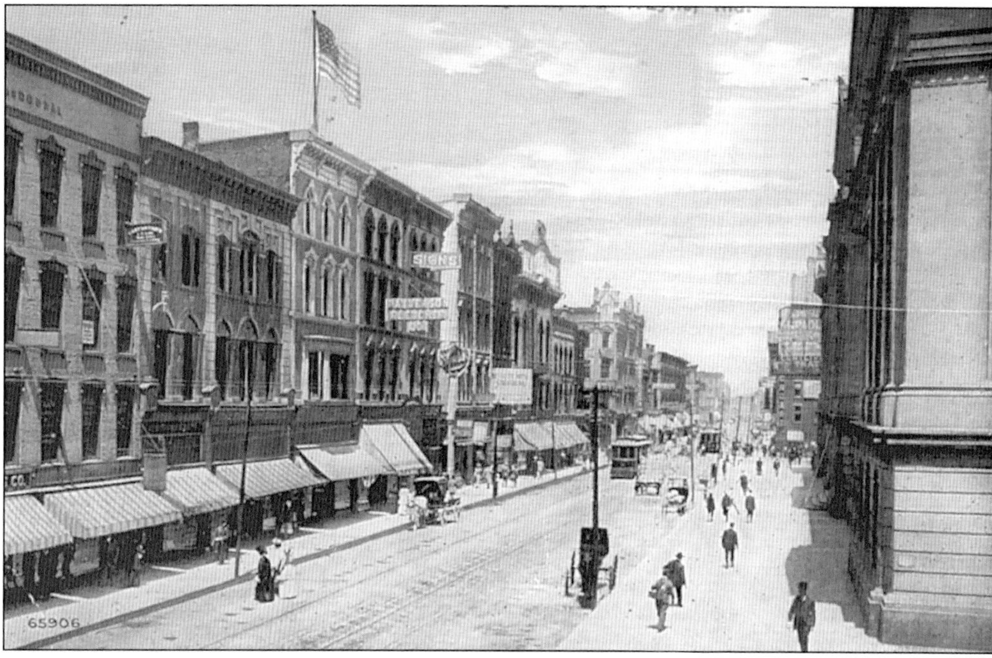

CALHOUN STREET, NORTH FROM BERRY STREET, FORT WAYNE, INDIANA, *c.* 1911. The courthouse is on the right.

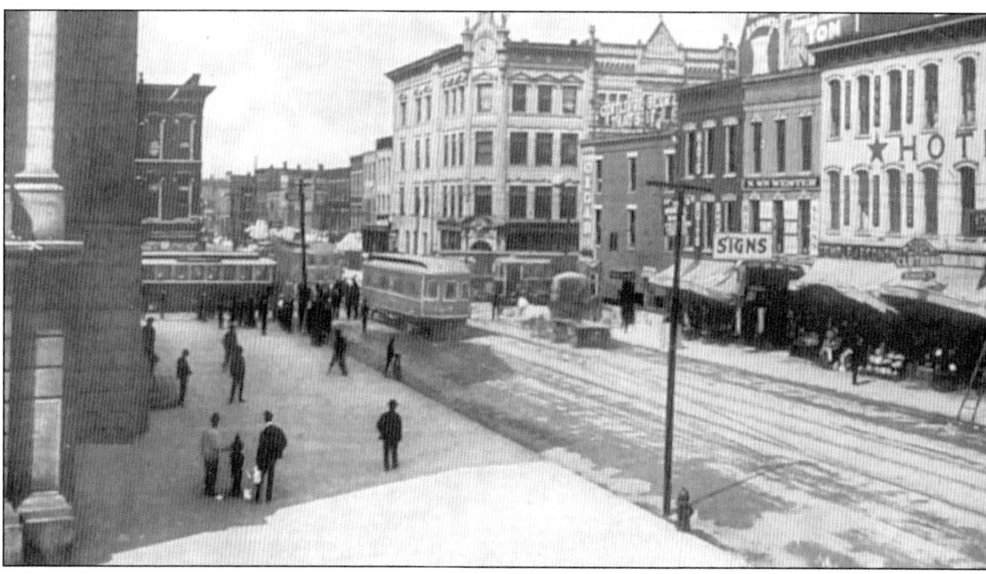

CALHOUN AND MAIN STREETS, FORT WAYNE, INDIANA. An unusual snow scene is shown here.

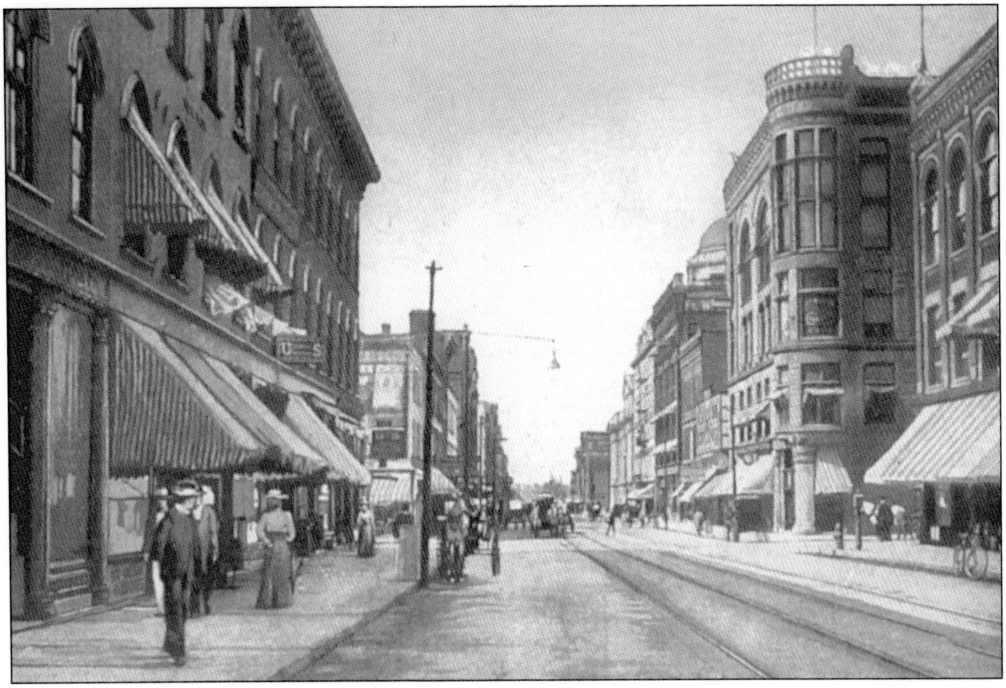

CALHOUN STREET NORTH FROM WAYNE, FORT WAYNE, INDIANA. Long dresses and hats were the standard dress for women shopping in downtown Fort Wayne.

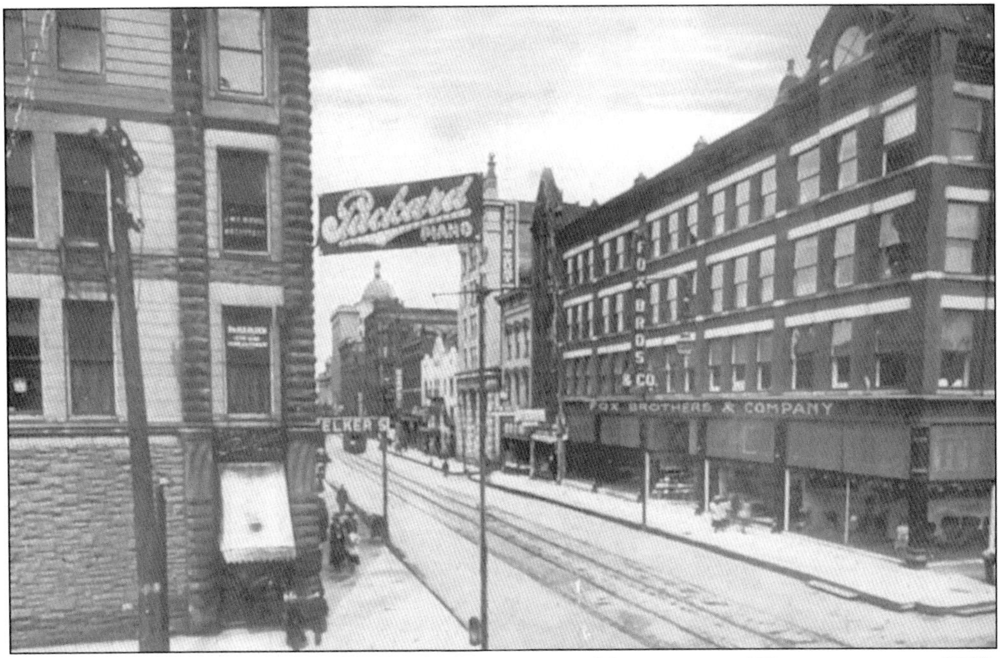

CALHOUN STREET, FORT WAYNE, INDIANA, LOOKING NORTH FROM WASHINGTON, *c.* 1912. Packard Piano is on the left, and Fox Bros. Co. is on the right.

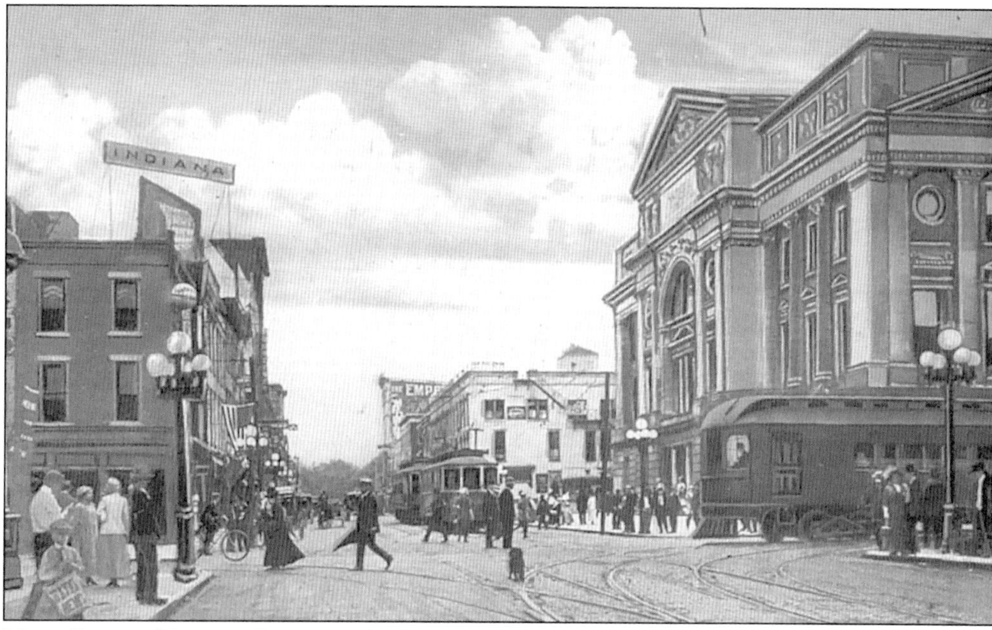

MAIN STREET EAST OF CALHOUN STREET, FORT WAYNE, INDIANA, *C.* 1914. Trolley tracks are laid in the dirt streets.

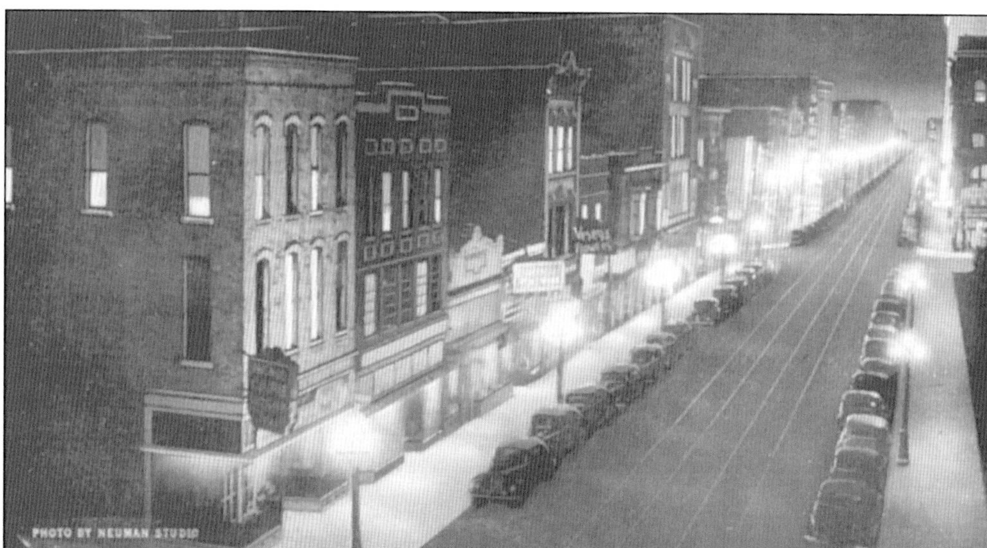

CALHOUN STREET, FORT WAYNE'S MAIN BUSINESS THOROUGHFARE AT NIGHT, FORT WAYNE, INDIANA. An unusual night scene is depicted here.

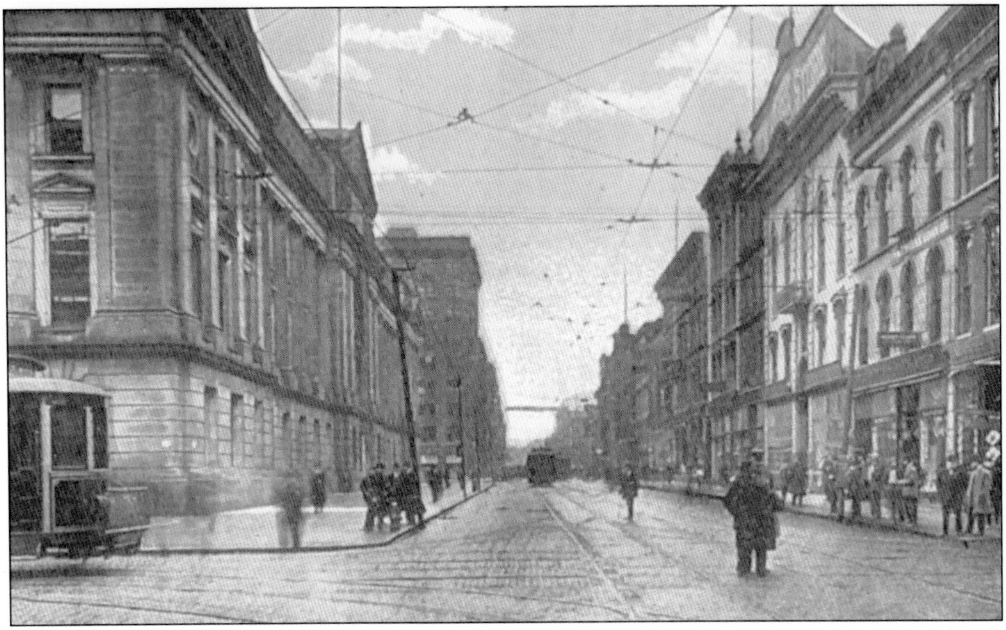

Calhoun Street, South from Transfer Corner, Fort Wayne, Indiana. Streets are brick in this scene.

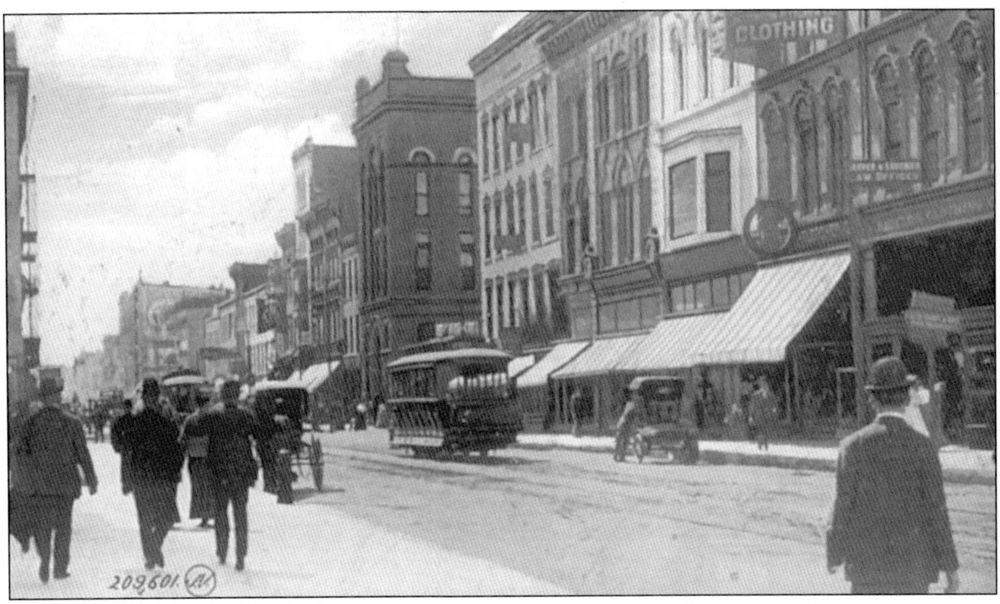

Calhoun Street South from Main Street, Fort Wayne, Indiana. This scene includes a trolley, a horse and buggy, and a person who appears to be cranking the car. Visible signs include "Patterson Fletcher Co.—Clothing" and "Sheilds Clothing Co."

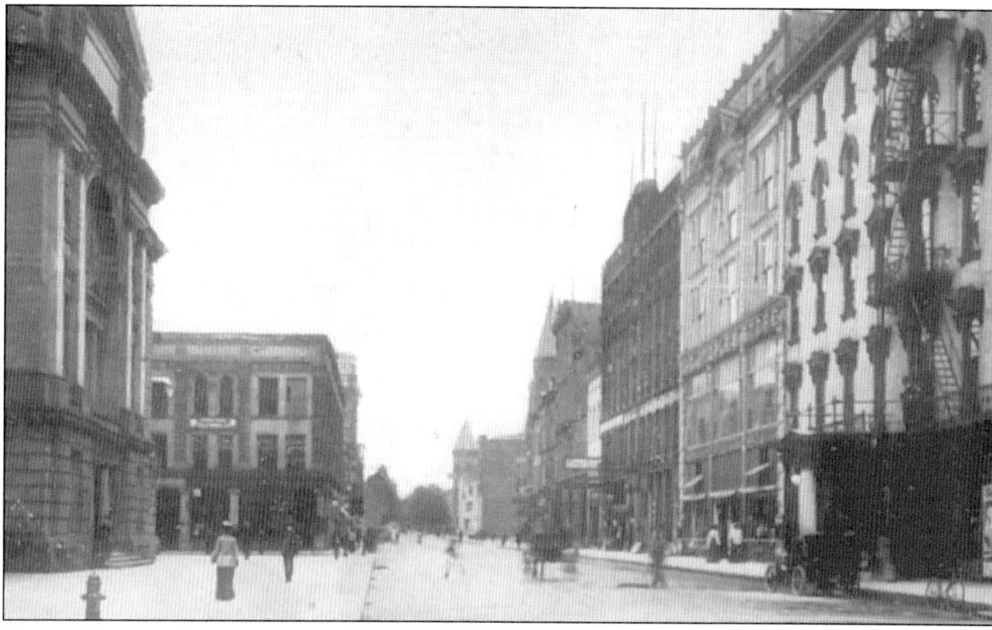

BERRY STREET, LOOKING EAST, FORT WAYNE, INDIANA. This message states: "Dear Edna I guess I will not have time to take my lesson Friday for I am helping to husk corn and have not got time to practice my lesson but will try to take a week from Friday. Very Truly Yours, Maud Bender."

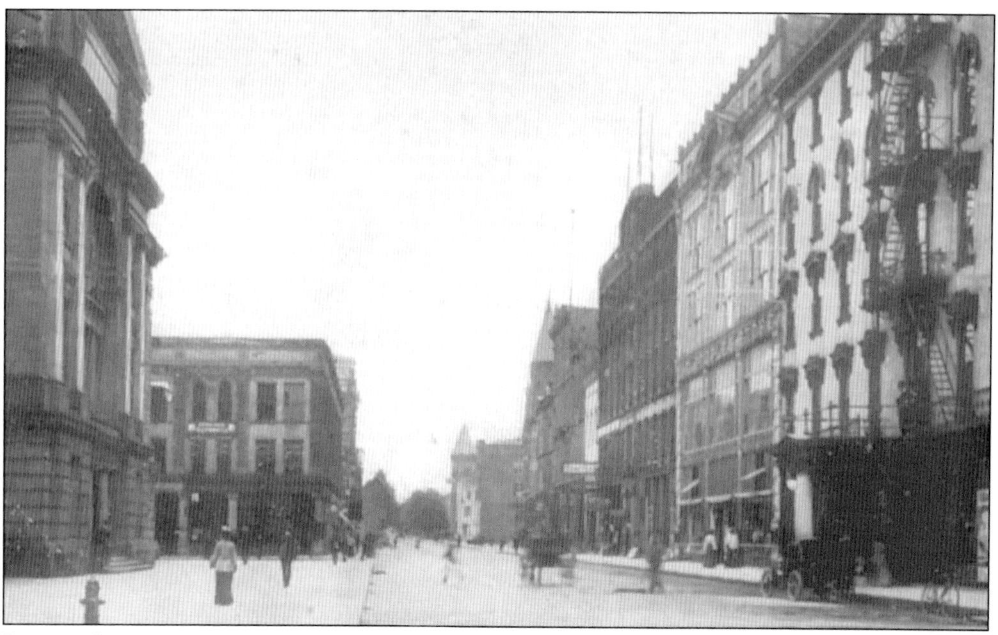

BERRY STREET LOOKING WEST, FORT WAYNE, INDIANA, *c.* 1919. Automobiles are more prevalent.

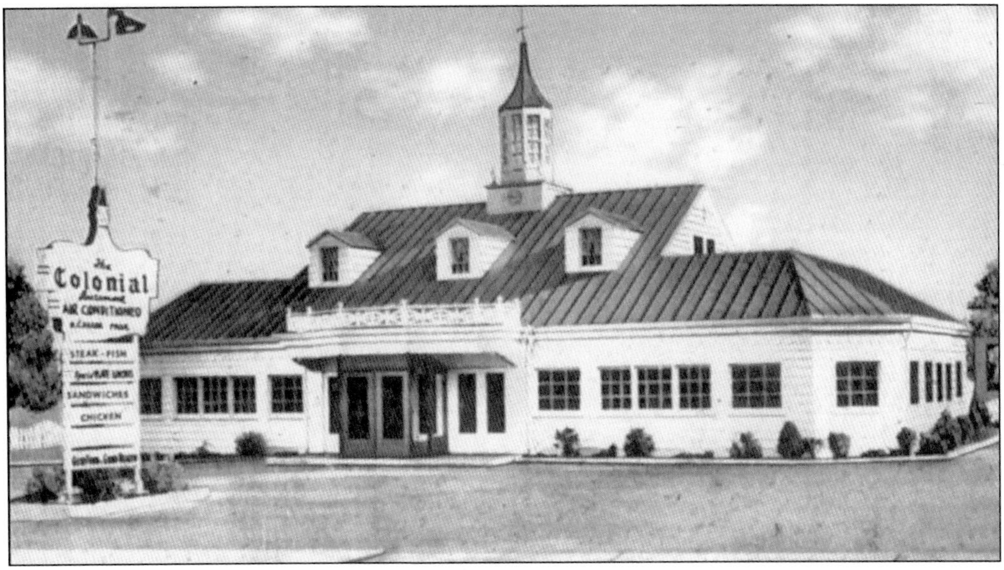

The Colonial Restaurant, Fort Wayne, Indiana. This is a popular Fort Wayne eatery.

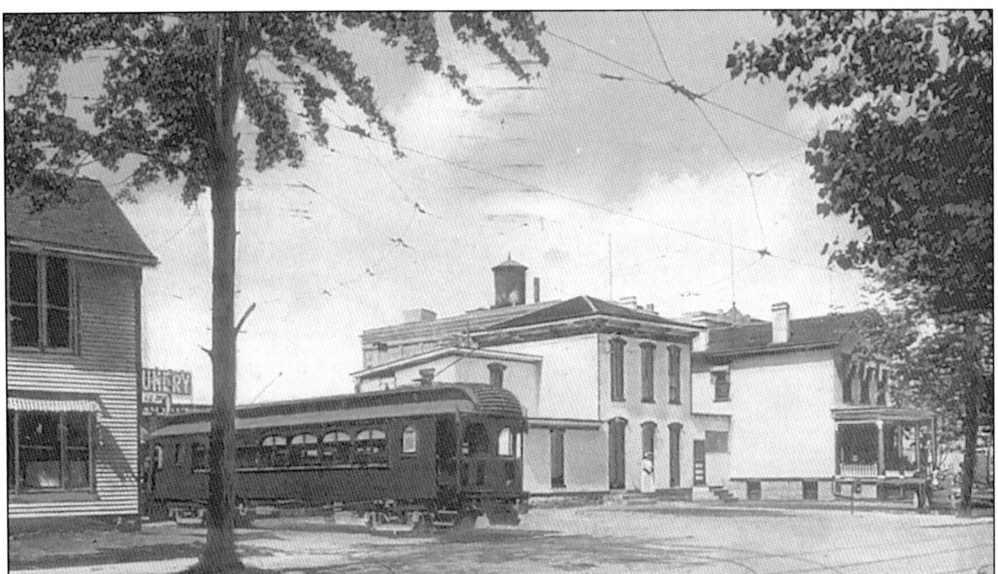

Interurban Station, Fort Wayne, Indiana, *c.* 1915. The larger cars were used between cities.

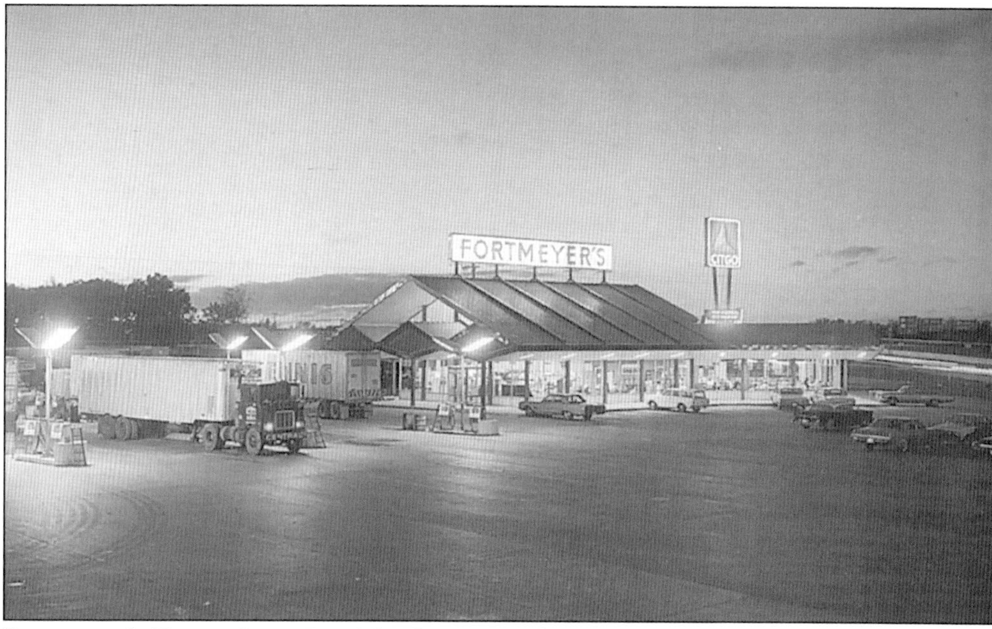

Fortmeyer's Truck Stop, Inc. This business is located at the junction of U.S. 30–33 West and Interstate 69. It is a popular spot for trucks to stop.

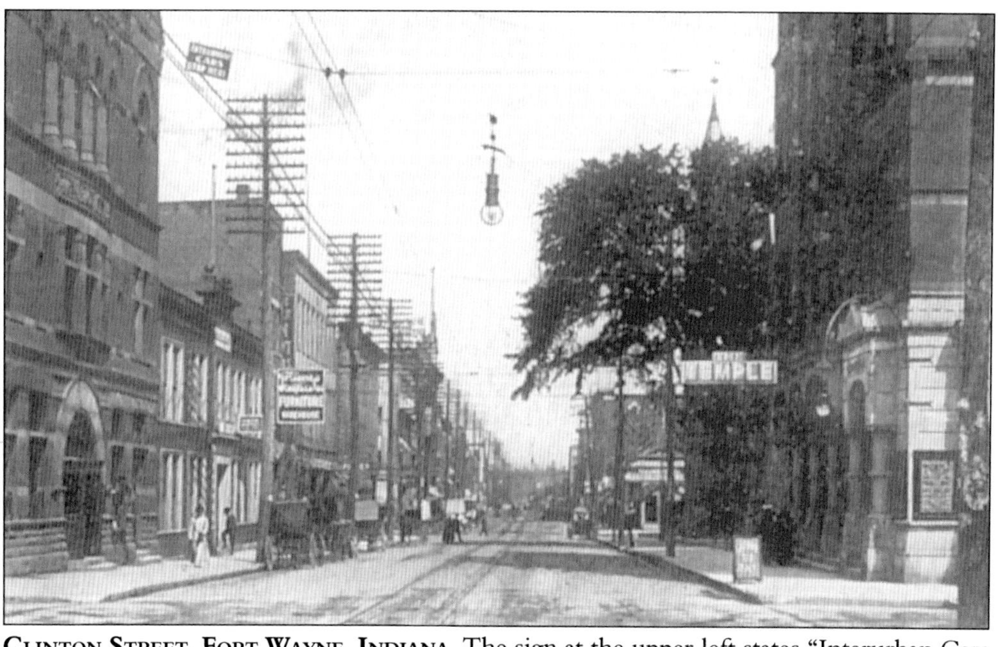

Clinton Street, Fort Wayne, Indiana. The sign at the upper left states "Interurban Cars Stop Here."

DOWNTOWN FORT WAYNE

MAJOR BUILDINGS

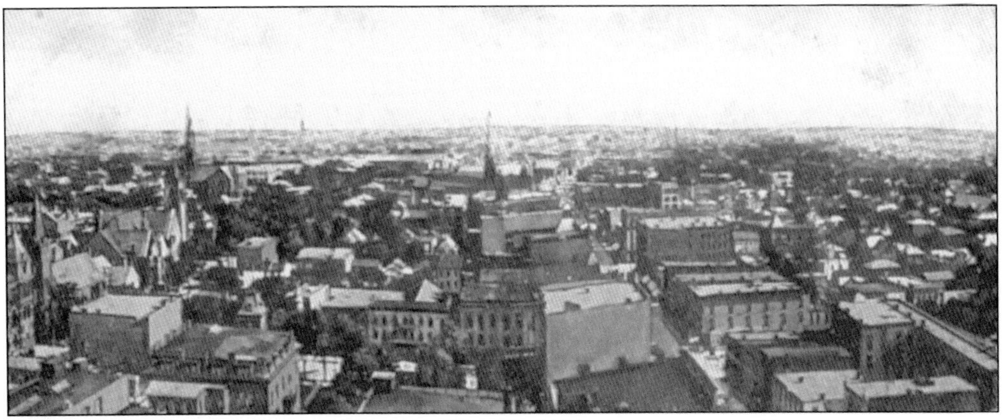

BIRD'S-EYE VIEW OF FORT WAYNE, INDIANA. This is a very early aerial view of the downtown area.

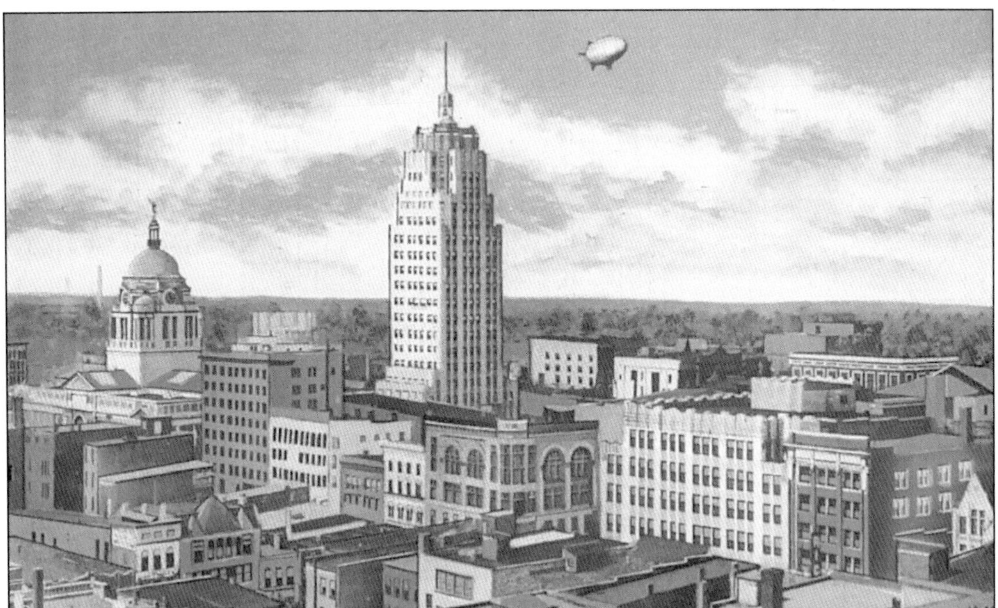

AERIAL VIEW OF BUSINESS SECTION, FORT WAYNE, INDIANA, C. 1944. A later aerial view is shown here, with the courthouse and Lincoln Tower being the prominent buildings.

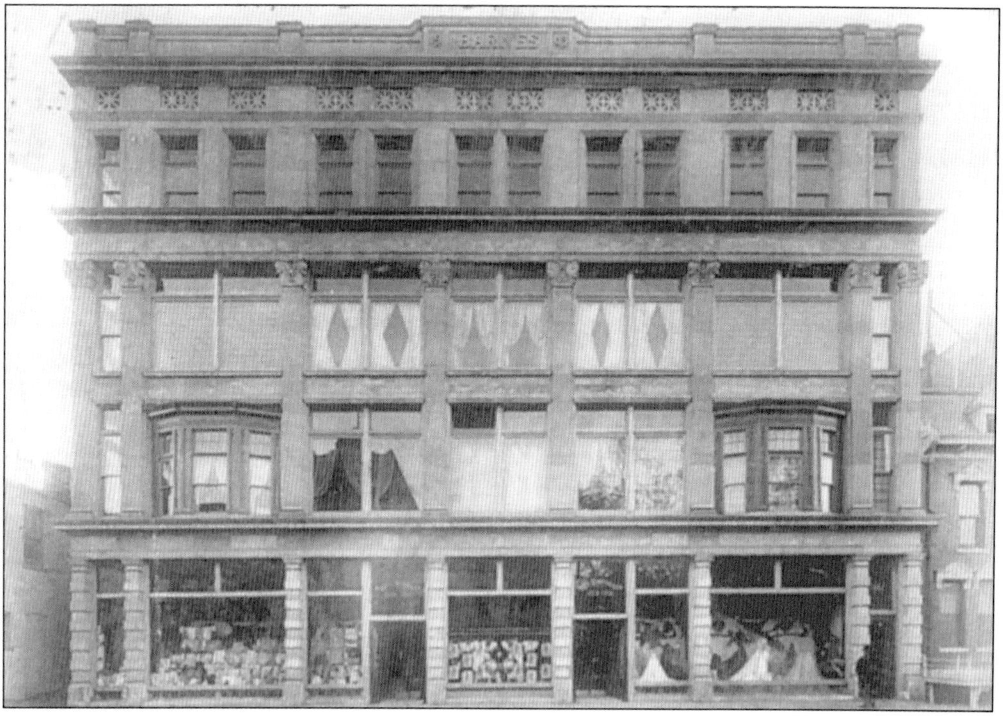

Wolf and Dessauer's Department Store, Fort Wayne, Indiana, *c.* 1907. The message on this card states: "Dear Grandma—This is the store where Wilbert works, the interior is very nice and up to date. Hoping you and Grandpa are well, I remain yours lovingly Wilbert." This was the first location of Fort Wayne's signature department store.

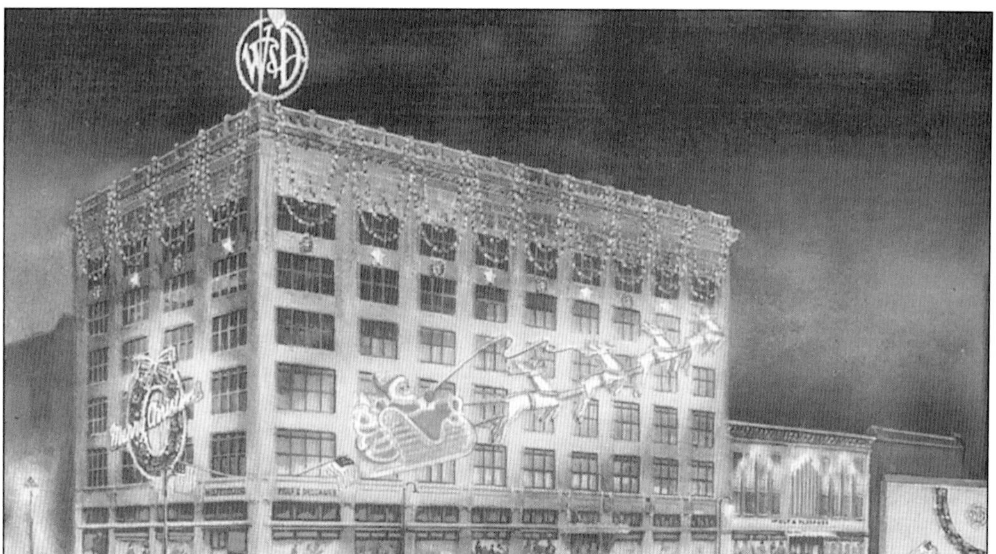

Christmas at Wolf & Dessauer, Fort Wayne, Indiana, *c.* 1946. This is reportedly one of the largest displays of lights in the U.S. The second location was famous for its Christmas displays. The street-level windows were decorated with animated Christmas scenes.

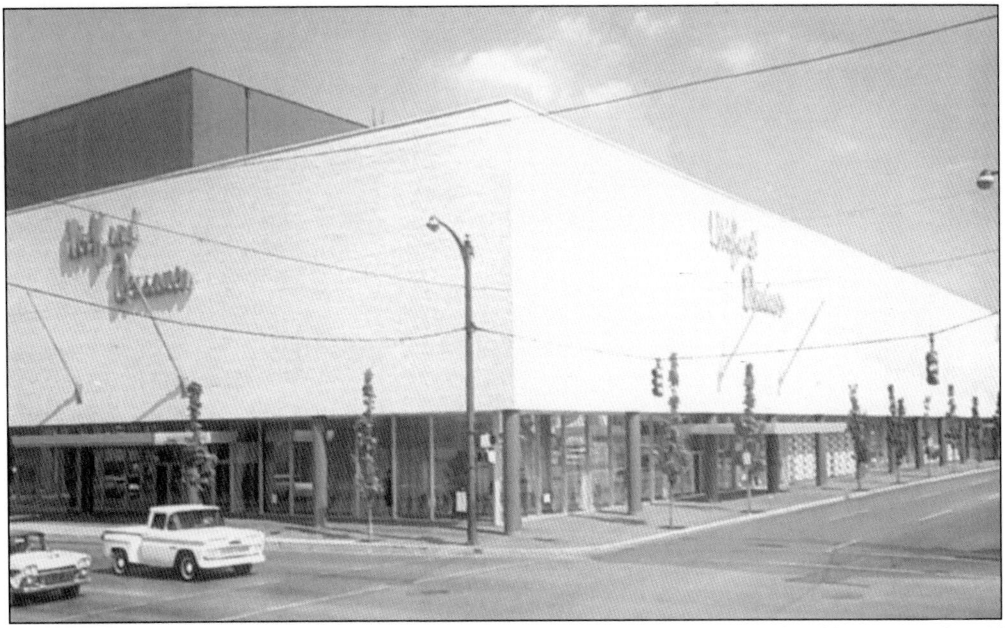

Wolf & Dessauer, Department Store, Fort Wayne, Indiana. The third location of Wolf & Dessauer was later acquired by L.S. Ayers Co.

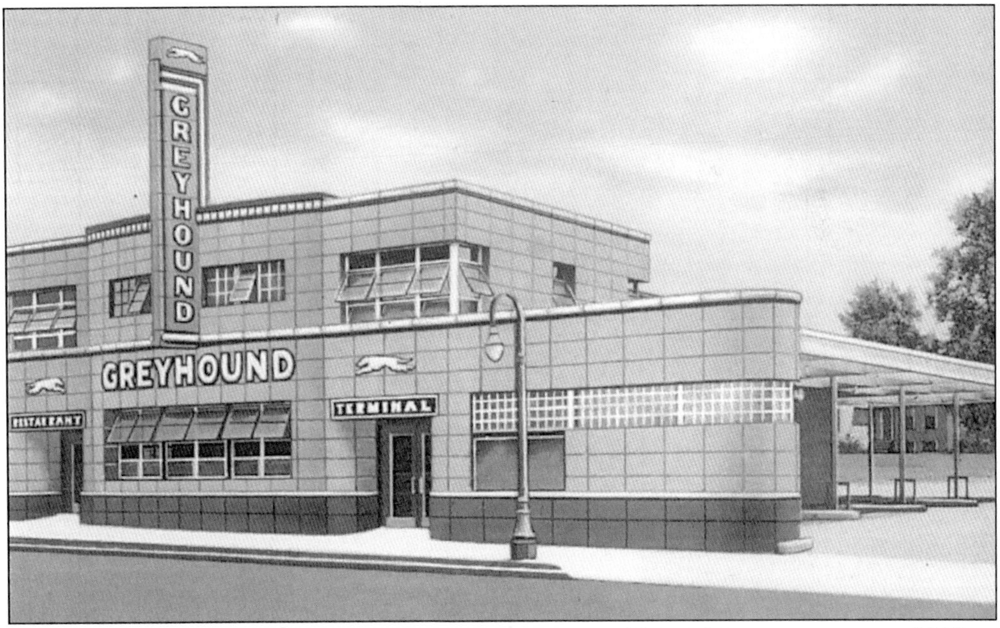

Greyhound Bus Terminal, Fort Wayne, Indiana, *c.* 1945. This message states: "Hi Pat. Yep I get way behind some-times. I work nights in a factory and take care of my child during the day. I'm divorced and live with my folks, they both work too. Am sorry. Deb Rackeweg." A handsome Art Deco building served bus passengers for many years.

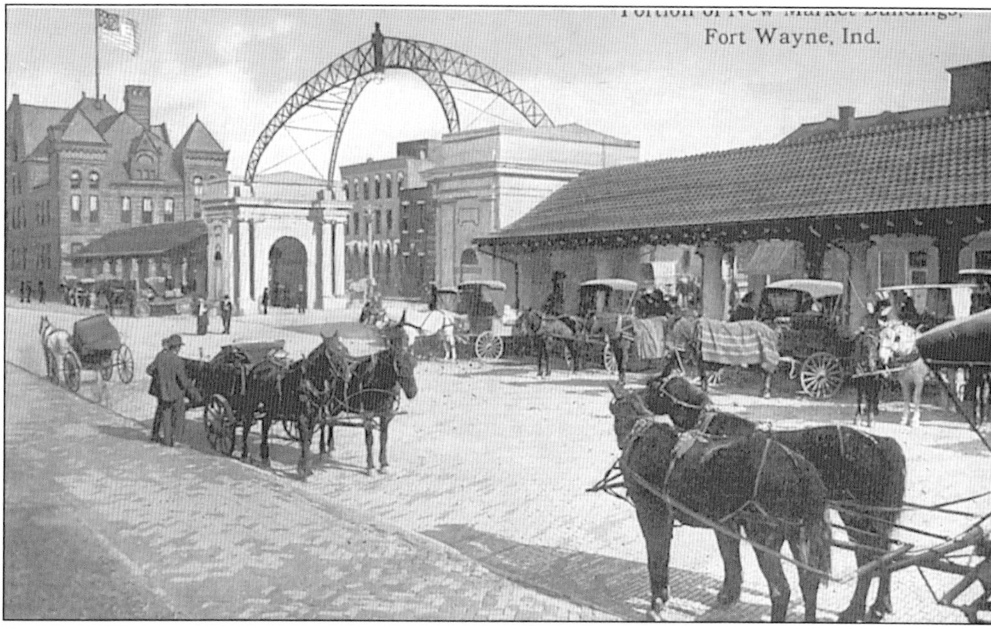

Portion of New Market Buildings, Fort Wayne, Indiana. Also known as "Barr Street Market," this pavilion provided a place for farmers to bring produce, eggs, meats, etc. for sale directly to consumers.

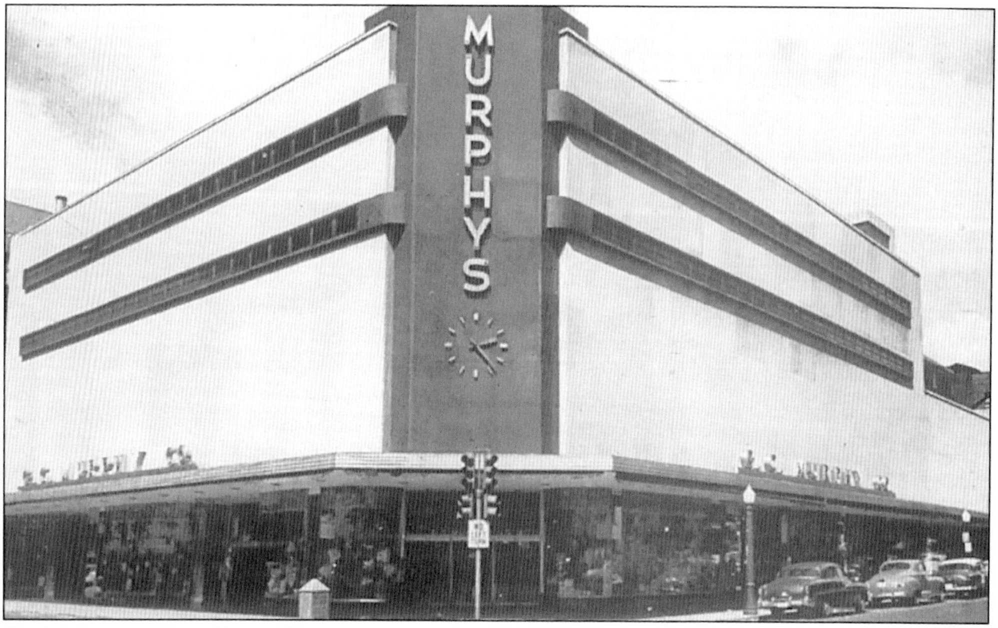

G.C. Murphy Co., Fort Wayne, Indiana. The cornerstone of downtown Fort Wayne, G.C. Murphy Co. was a variety store with a large toy department, a lunch counter, and a donut-making machine, which the author enjoyed watching in operation in the 1950s. It closed in 1992.

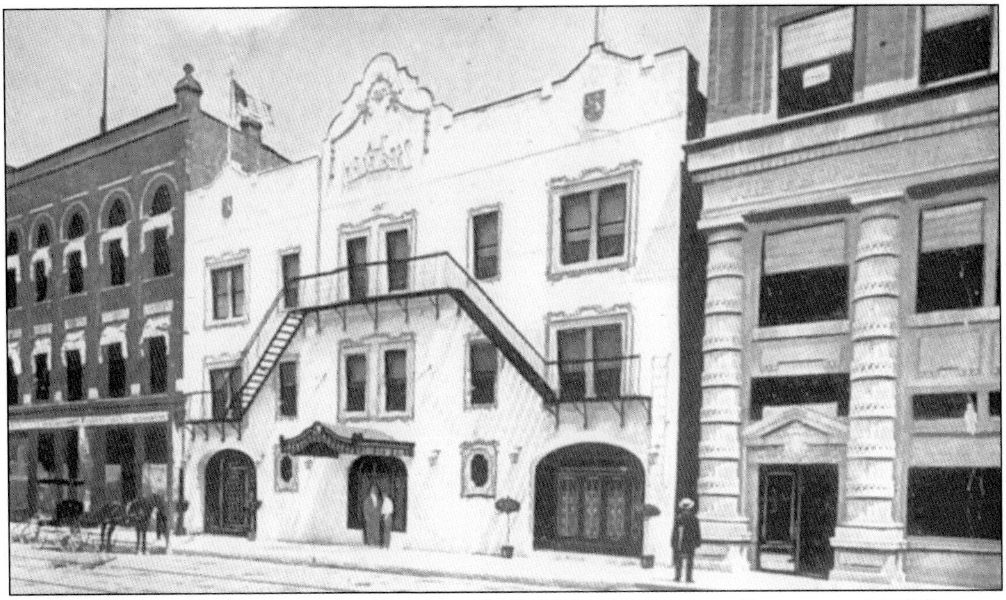

ALT HEILBERG, FORT WAYNE, INDIANA, *c.* 1910. Alt Heilberg was a German social club.

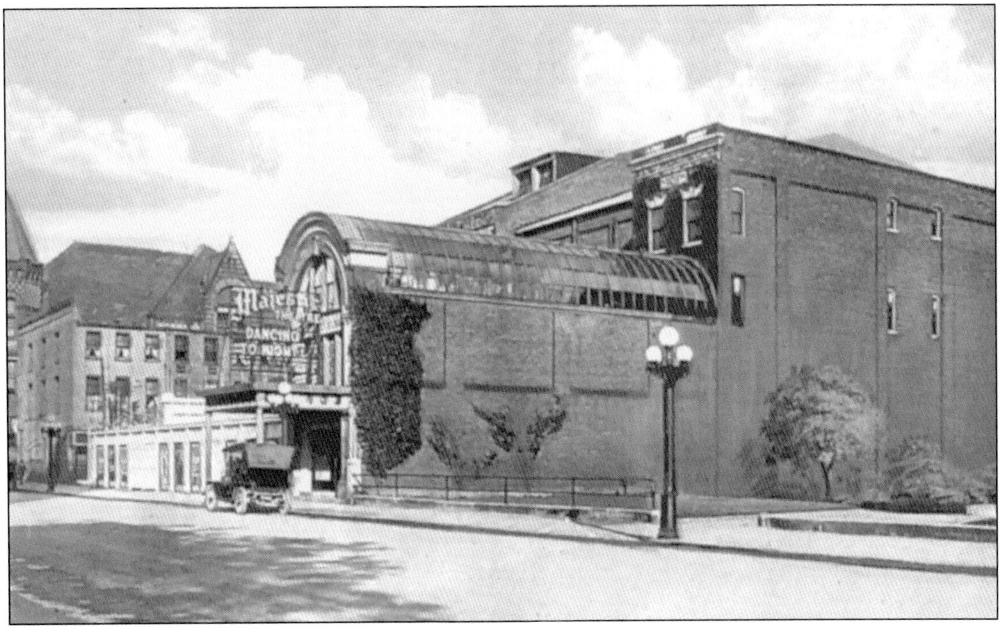

MAJESTIC THEATRE AND GARDEN, FORT WAYNE, INDIANA. The sign states: "Dancing Tonight."

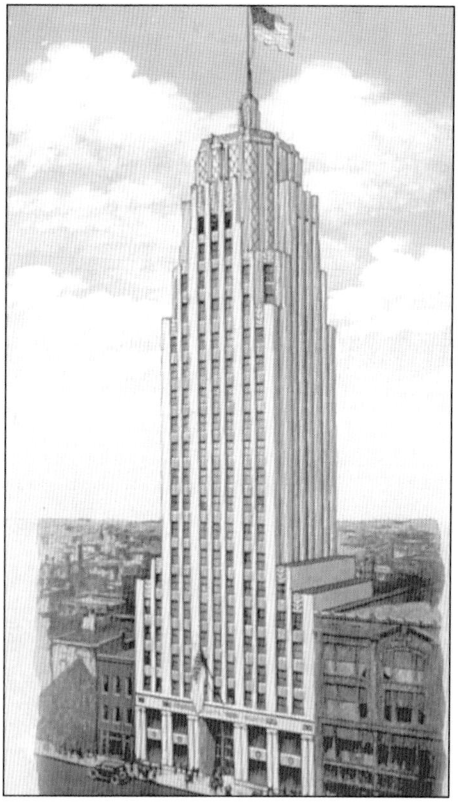

LINCOLN TOWER, FORT WAYNE, INDIANA. The 22-story Lincoln Tower was completed in 1930, and was the tallest building in Indiana for many years.

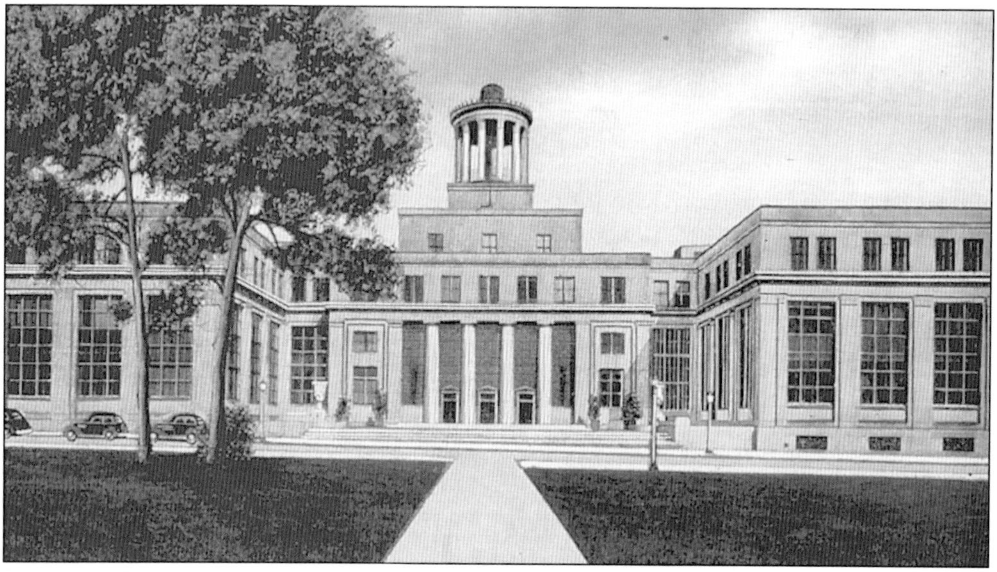

LINCOLN NATIONAL LIFE INSURANCE BUILDING, FORT WAYNE, INDIANA. Lincoln National Life Insurance Co. was founded in 1905. This building was built in 1923.

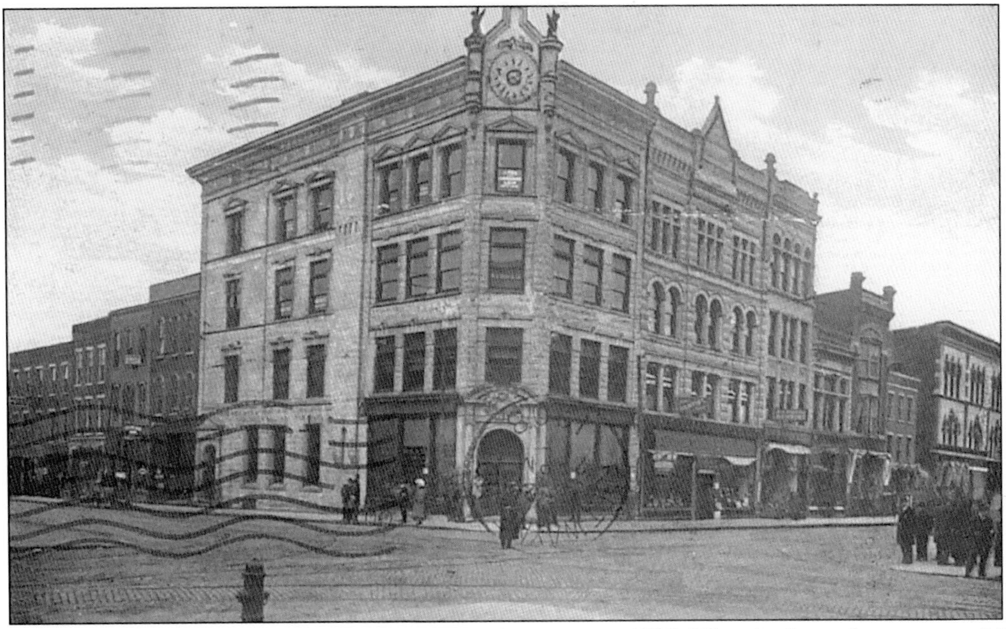

HAMILTON NATIONAL BANK, FORT WAYNE, INDIANA, *c.* 1908. The clock on the corner told the time at a glance.

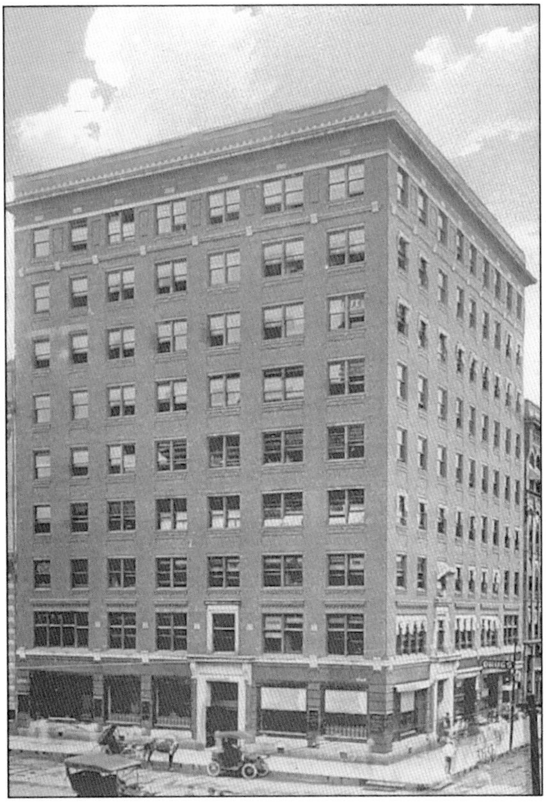

SCHOAFF BUILDING, FORT WAYNE, INDIANA. Storefronts were at street level, and offices were located in the upper stories.

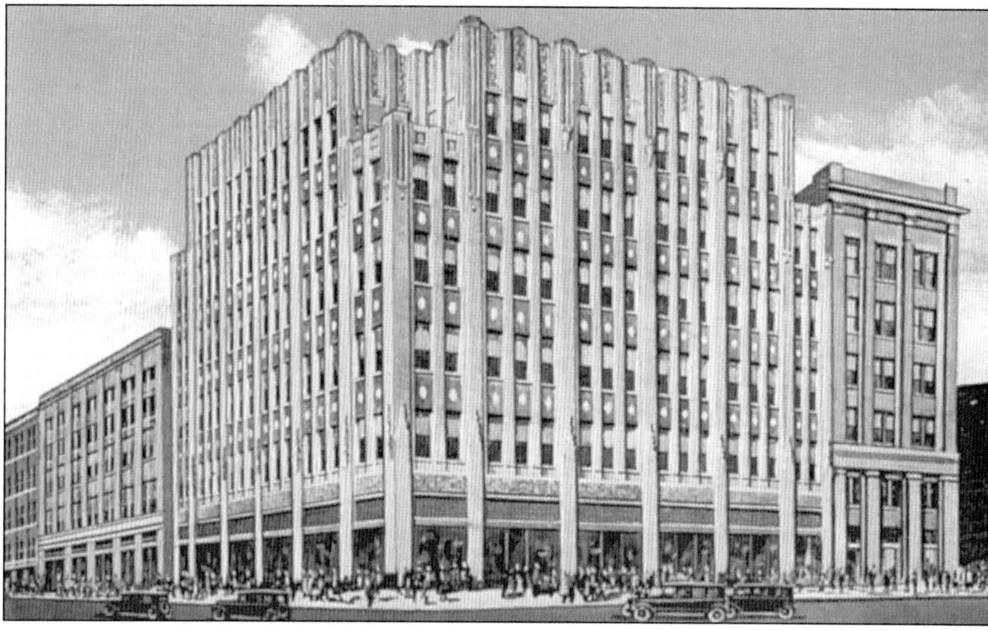

New Grand Leader Building, Fort Wayne, Indiana. Grand Leader was a prominent department store.

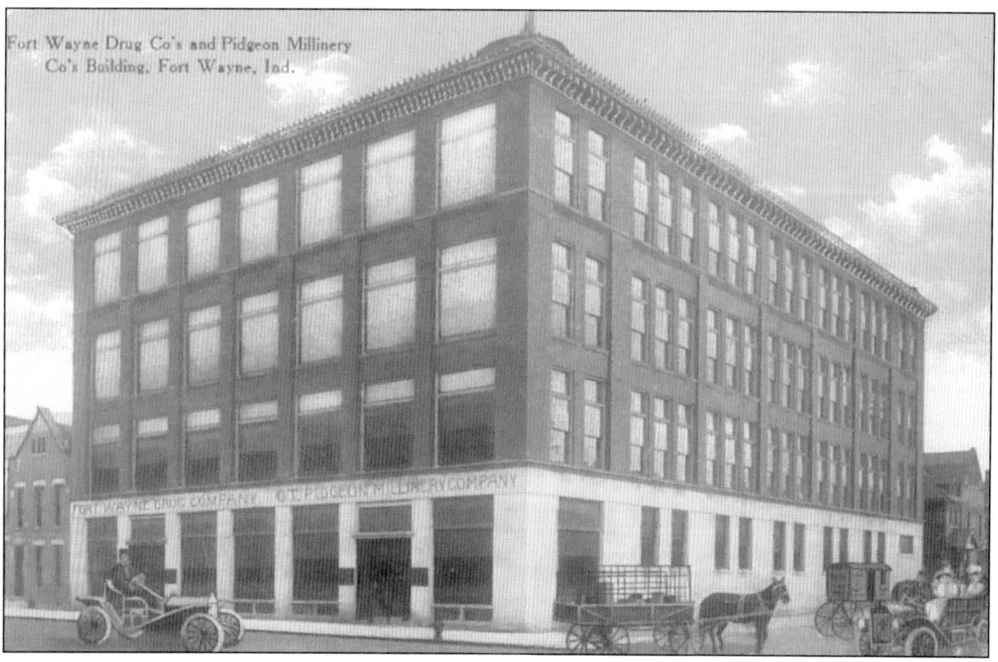

Fort Wayne Drug Co.'s and Pidgeon Millinery Co.'s Building, Fort Wayne, Indiana. Horse-drawn wagons and automobiles line the streets.

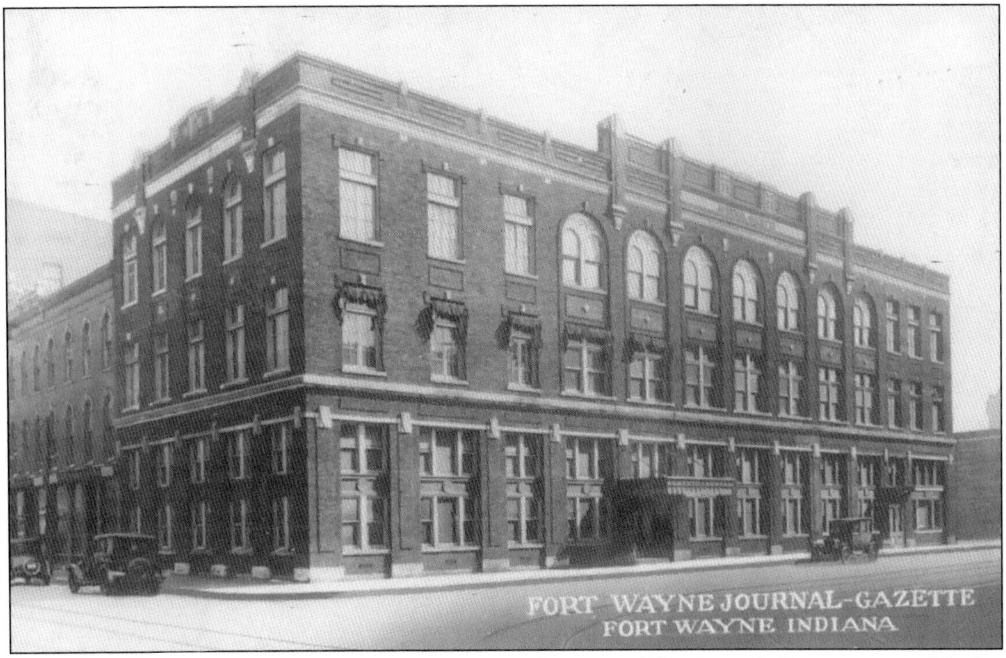

FORT WAYNE *JOURNAL-GAZETTE*, FORT WAYNE, INDIANA. The *Journal Gazette* was and is the morning newspaper.

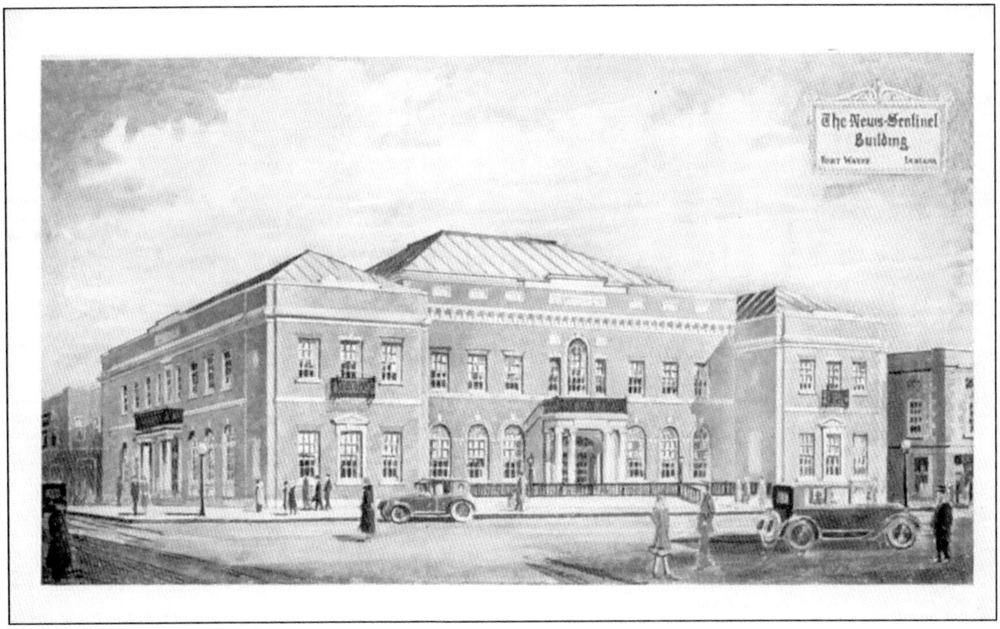

THE NEWS-SENTINEL BUILDING, FORT WAYNE, INDIANA. The artist's conception of the News-Sentinel Building was made to show the building before it was actually built to house the offices and printing plant of the evening newspaper.

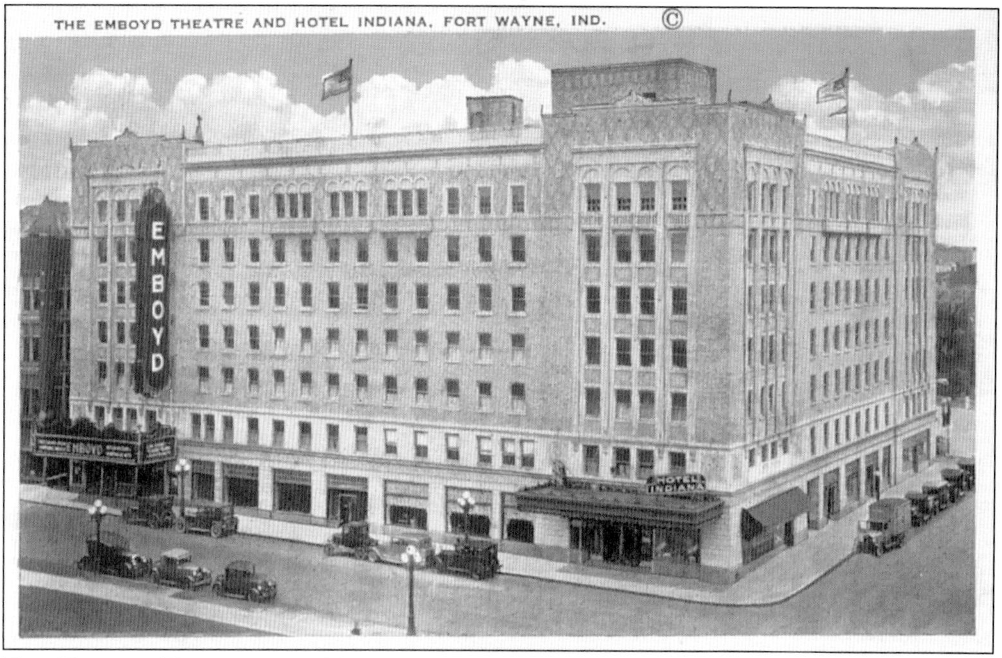

The Emboyd Theatre and Hotel Indiana, Fort Wayne, Indiana. The theater is now known as the Embassy and is one of the best restored theaters in the Midwest.

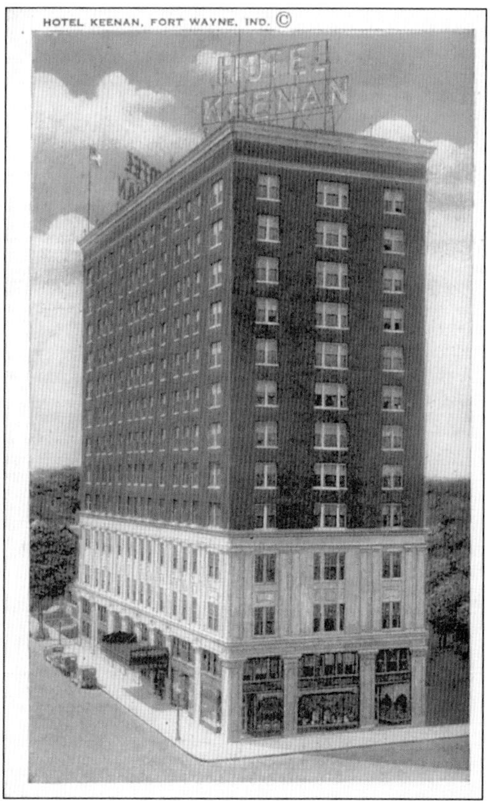

Hotel Keenan, Fort Wayne, Indiana. This was a popular place for business travelers.

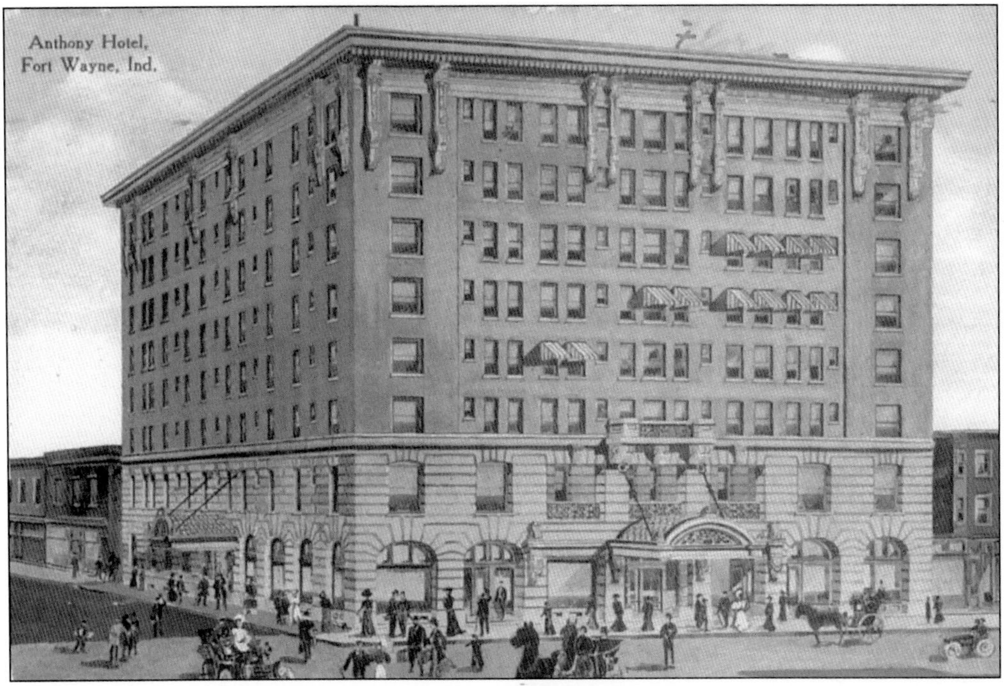

ANTHONY HOTEL, FORT WAYNE, INDIANA, *c.* 1910.

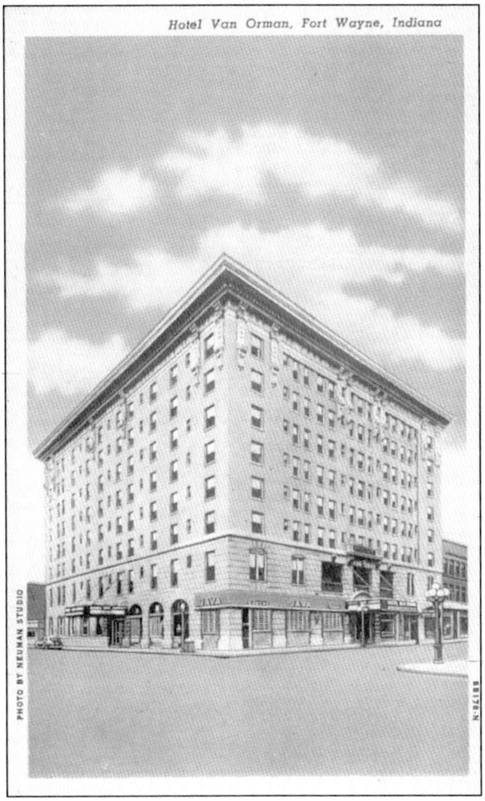

HOTEL VAN ORMAN, FORT WAYNE, INDIANA.

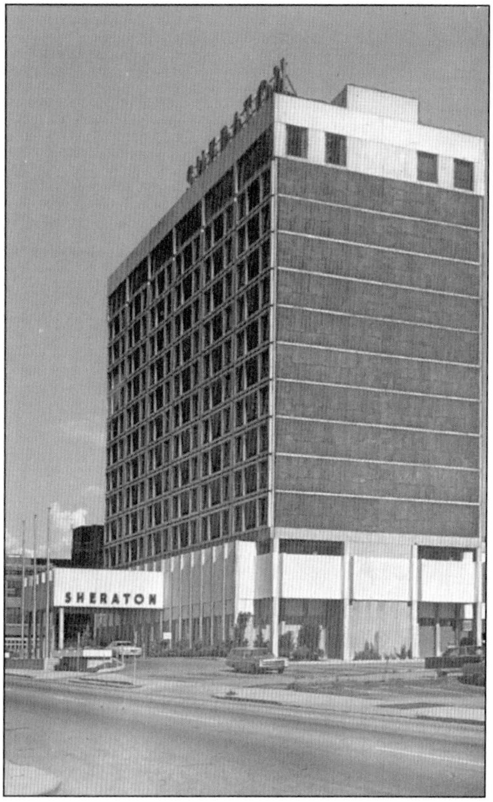

SHERATON MOTOR HOTEL, FORT WAYNE, INDIANA. The "Motor Hotel" and motels in the outlying areas resulted in the demise of Fort Wayne's fine downtown hotels.

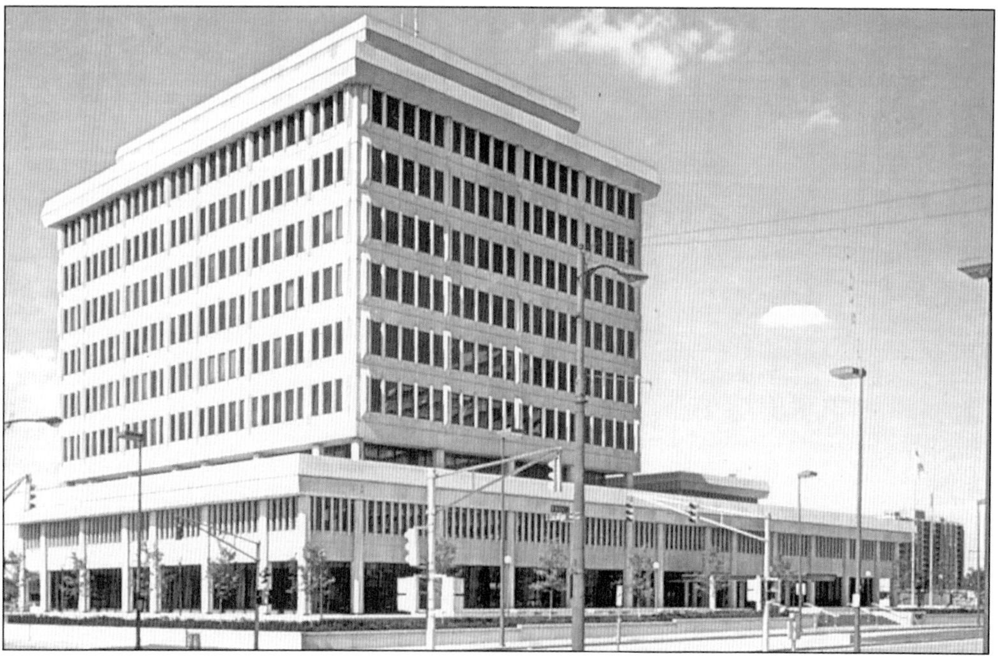

CITY-COUNTY BUILDING, FORT WAYNE, INDIANA. With groundbreaking ceremonies October 10, 1968, the new building was dedicated September 17, 1971.

Three

GRABILL

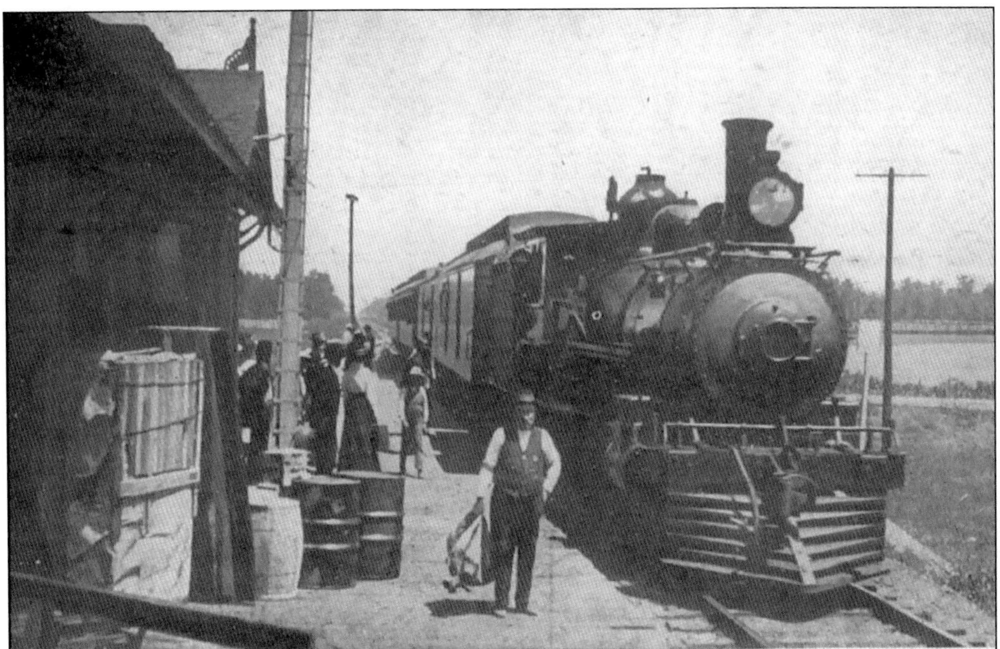

WABASH DEPOT, GRABILL, INDIANA. The Wabash Railroad was the principle means of transporting freight and passengers in and out of Grabill. The man in the foreground is holding a mail sack.

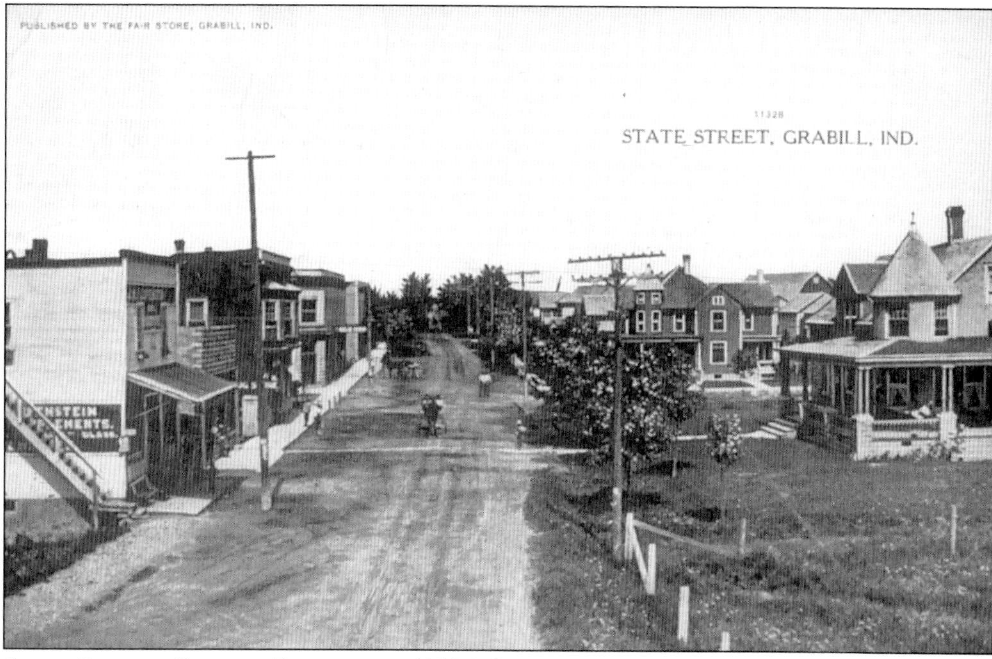

State Street, Grabill, Indiana, *c.* 1909. This message states: "Dear Friend: Called at the Hospital yesterday to see you, but the nurse said she allowed no one in. Gave her a bunch of flowers to give to you. Did you get them? Hope you are getting along alright. From one of your friends, Miss Emma Klopfenstein."

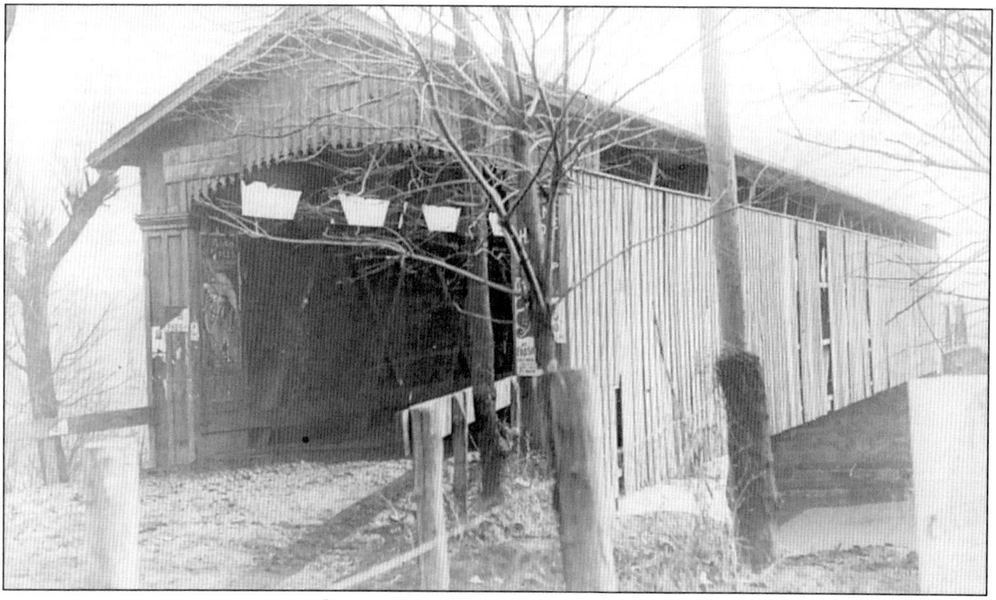

Covered Bridge, Grabill, Indiana. While the card is not labeled, this covered bridge is believed to have been located near Grabill.

Four

HUNTERTOWN

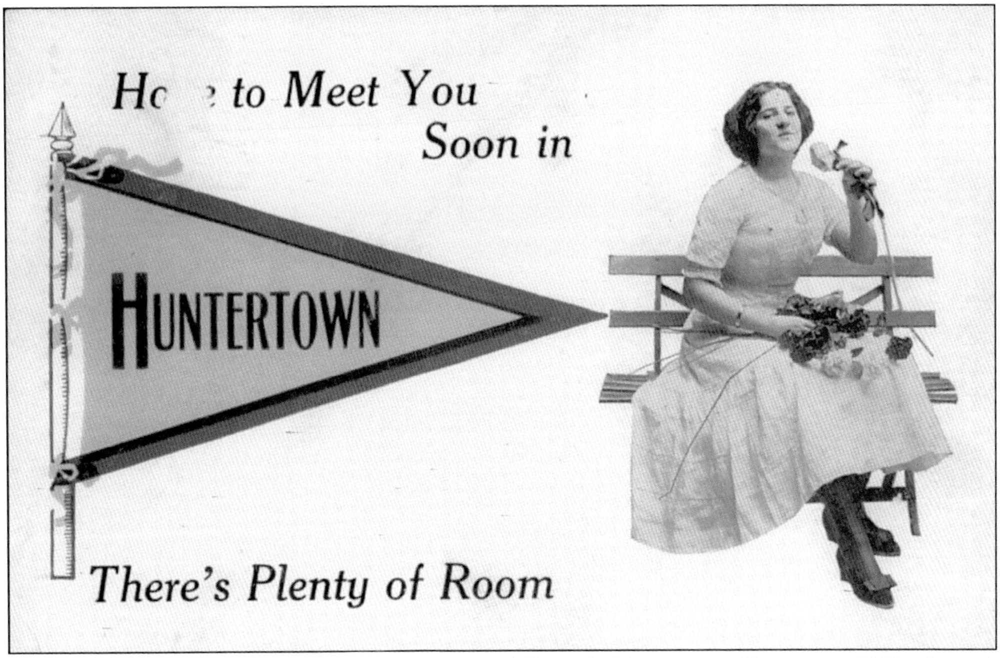

HOPE TO MEET YOU SOON IN HUNTERTOWN, THERE'S PLENTY OF ROOM, C. 1913. A stock card was overprinted with "Huntertown."

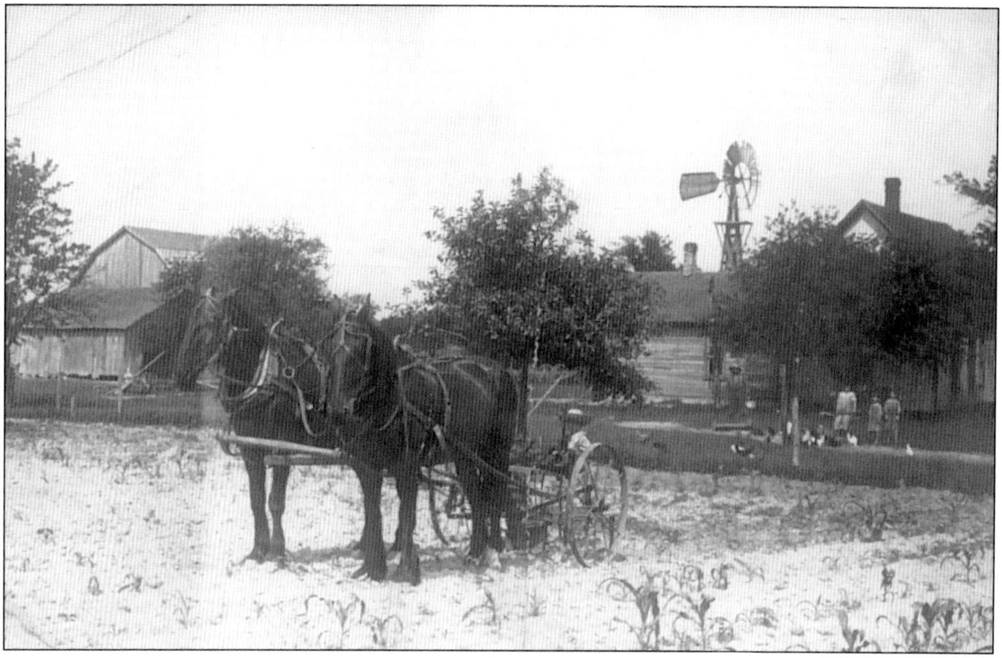

An Allen County Rural Scene. The location is "Seth Bonar Farm, Churubusco, Indiana."

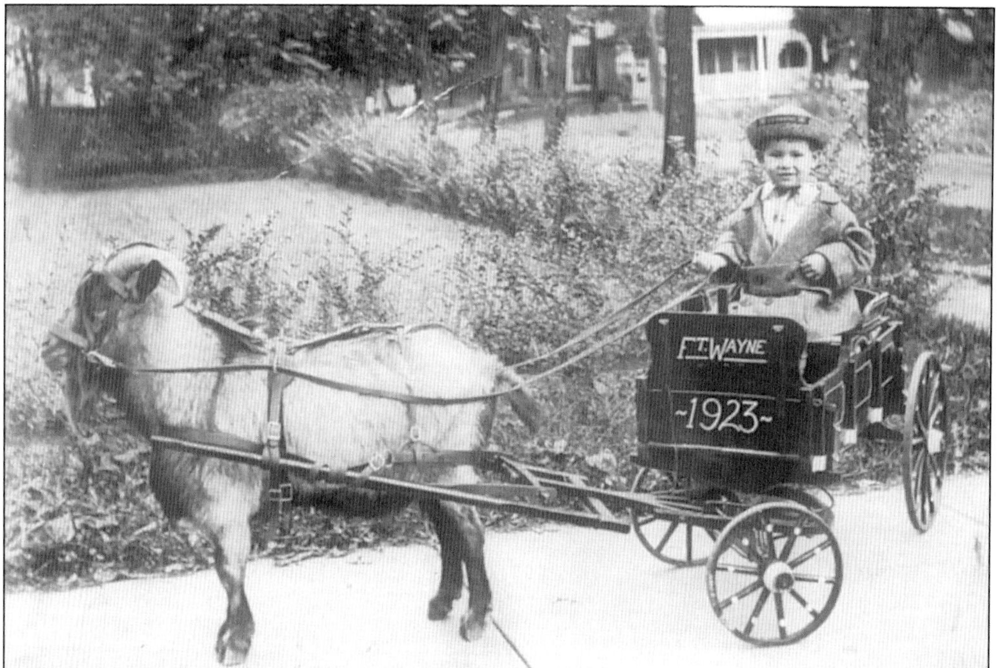

Fort Wayne, 1923. A young boy poses proudly in his toy wagon hitched to a sheep.

Five

NEW HAVEN

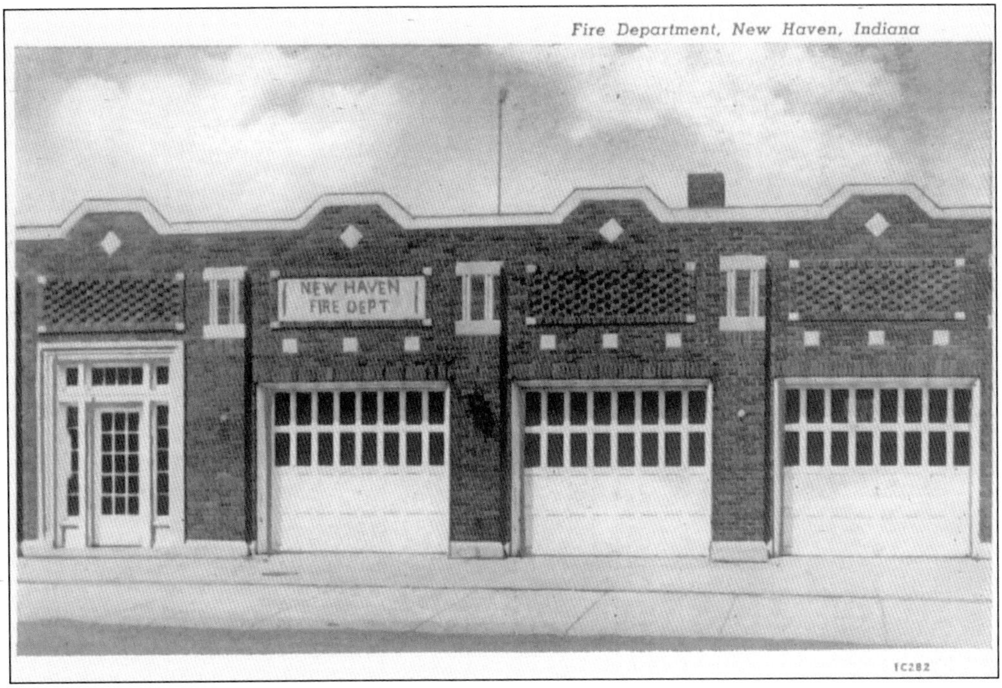

FIRE DEPARTMENT, NEW HAVEN, INDIANA.

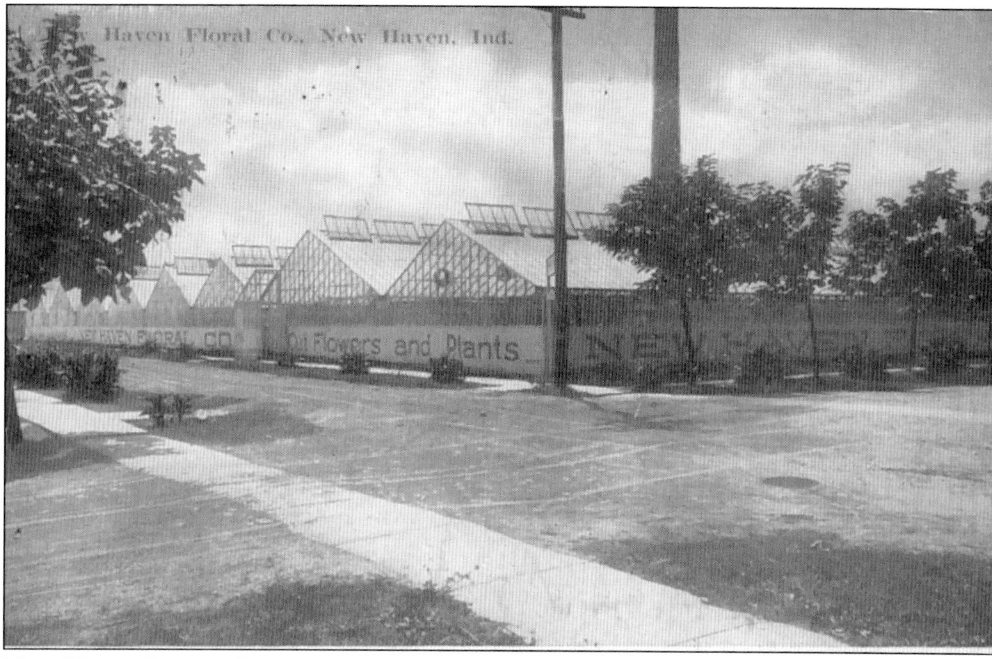

New Haven Floral Co., New Haven, Indiana. The sign states "New Haven Floral Co.—Cut Flowers and Plants."

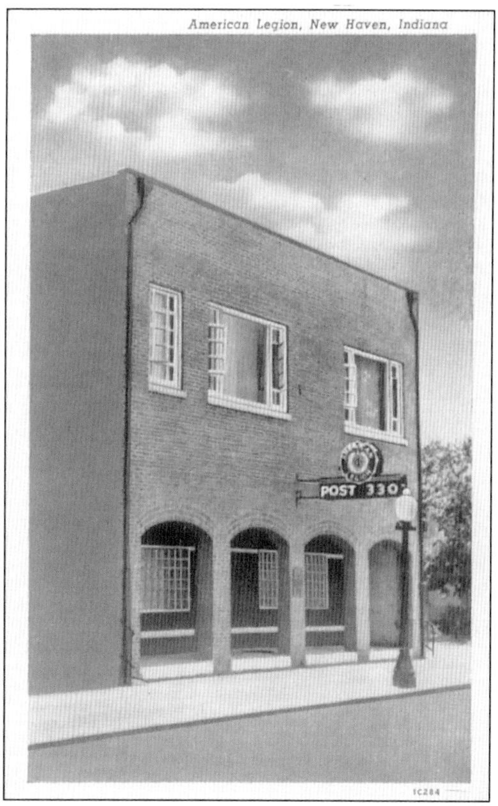

American Legion, New Haven, Indiana. Post 330 is located at New Haven, Indiana.

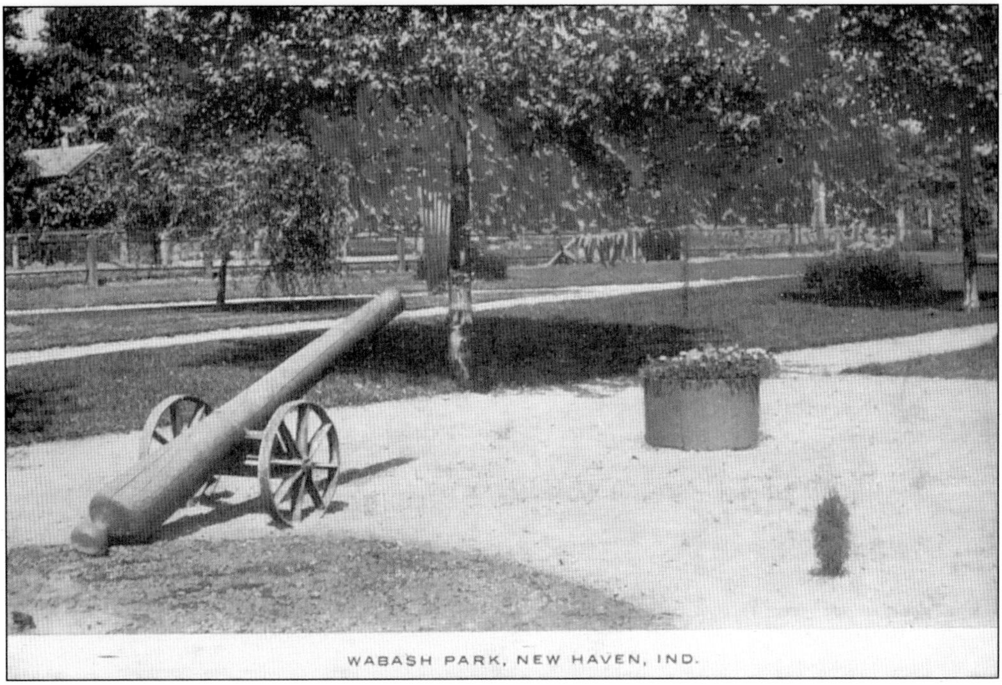

WABASH PARK, NEW HAVEN, INDIANA. Kids liked to climb on the cast iron cannon.

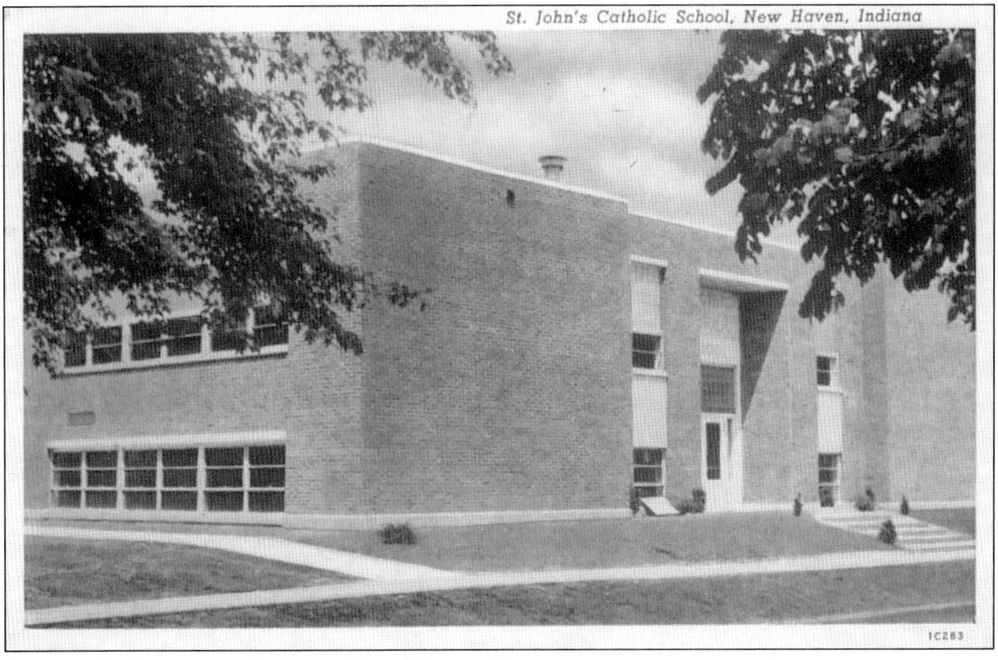

ST. JOHN'S CATHOLIC SCHOOL, NEW HAVEN, INDIANA.

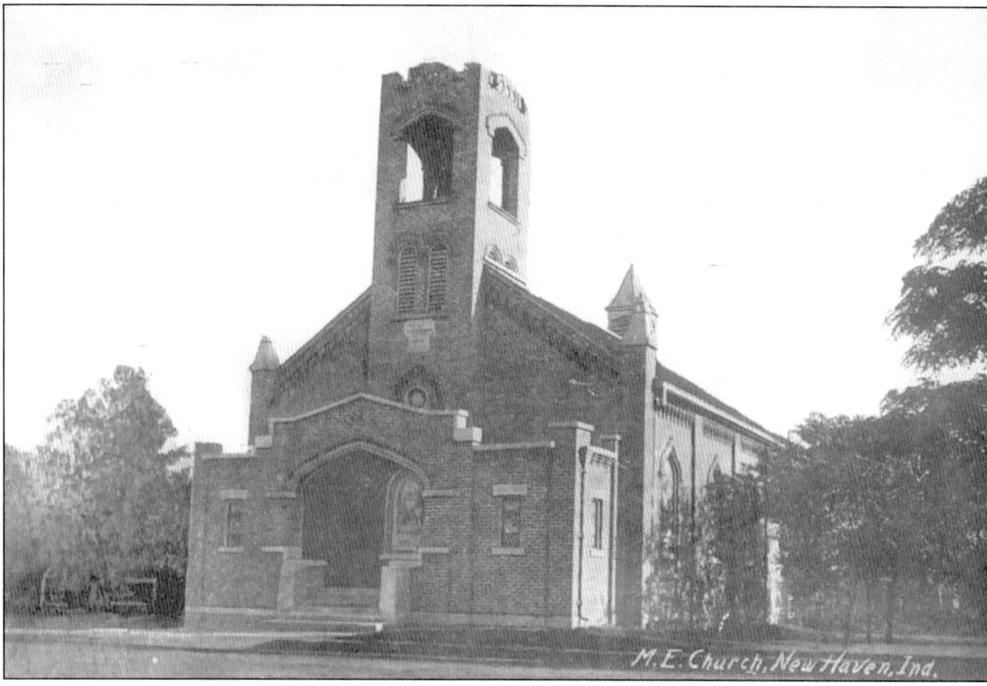

M.E. Church, New Haven, Indiana.

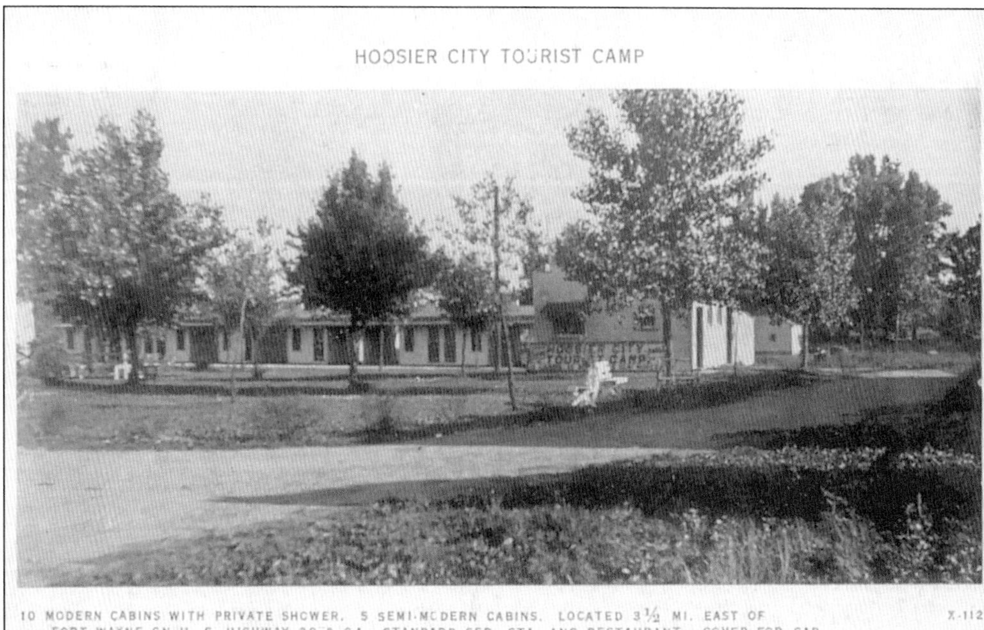

Hoosier City Tourist Camp. Ten Modern Cabins with Private Shower. Semi-Modern Cabins. Located 3 1/2 Mi. East of Fort Wayne CN U.S. Highway 30 & 24. Standard Ser. Sta. And Restaurant. Cover for Car, *c.* 1937.

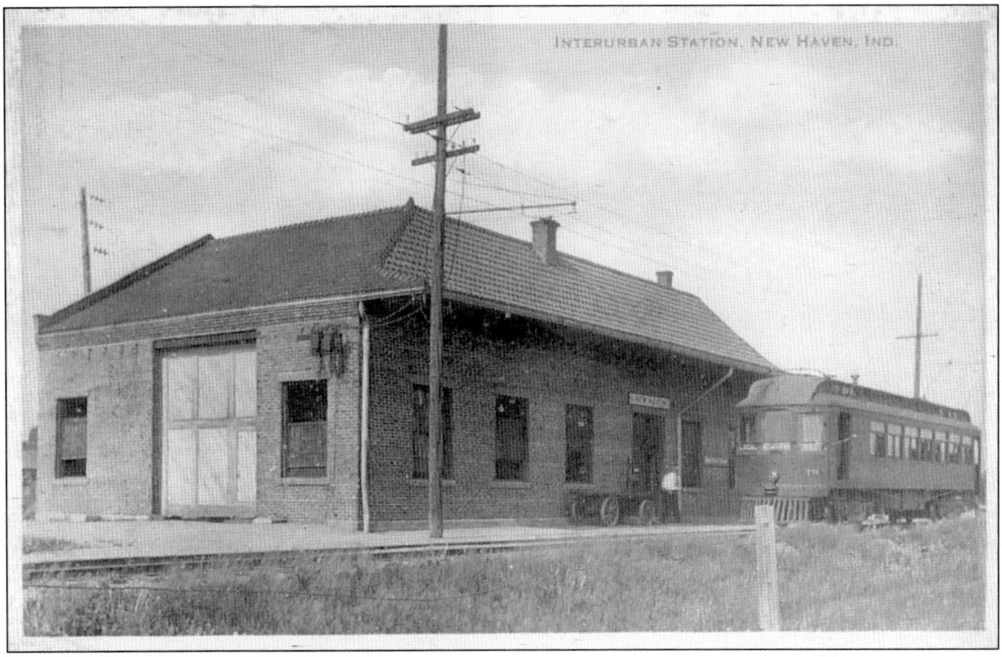

INTERURBAN STATION, NEW HAVEN, INDIANA. This line provided service to Fort Wayne and then connecting lines to the north and south.

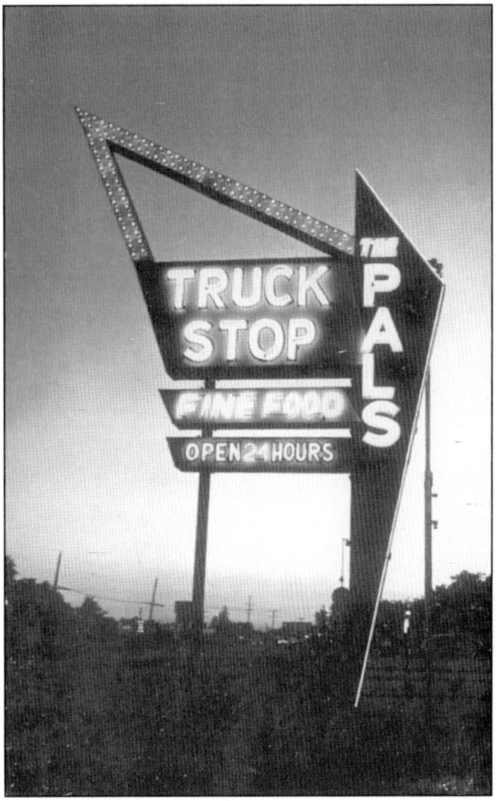

THE PAL'S TRUCK STOP. "YOUR HOME AWAY FROM HOME." This was located 3 miles east of Fort Wayne at the junction of Highways 30–24–14, New Haven, Indiana. The message states: "Hi Terry, This is a truck stop that I stop at—I am in Chicago Ill now. It's cold here. Wild Bill, King of the Road."

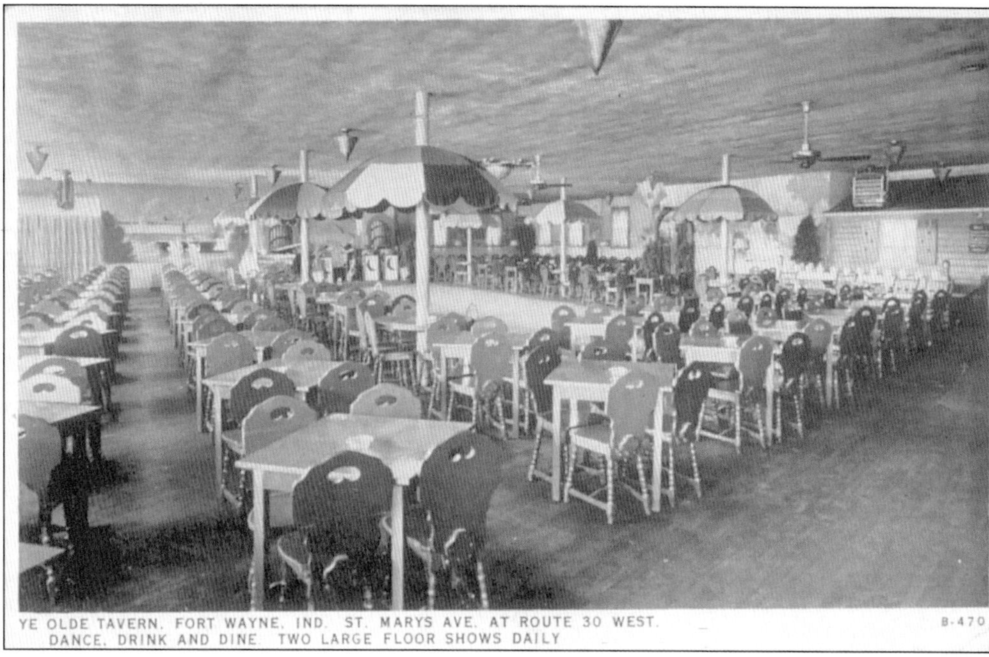

YE OLDE TAVERN, FORT WAYNE, INDIANA, ST. MARYS AVENUE AT ROUTE 30 WEST. DANCE, DRINK, AND DINE. TWO LARGE FLOOR SHOWS DAILY.

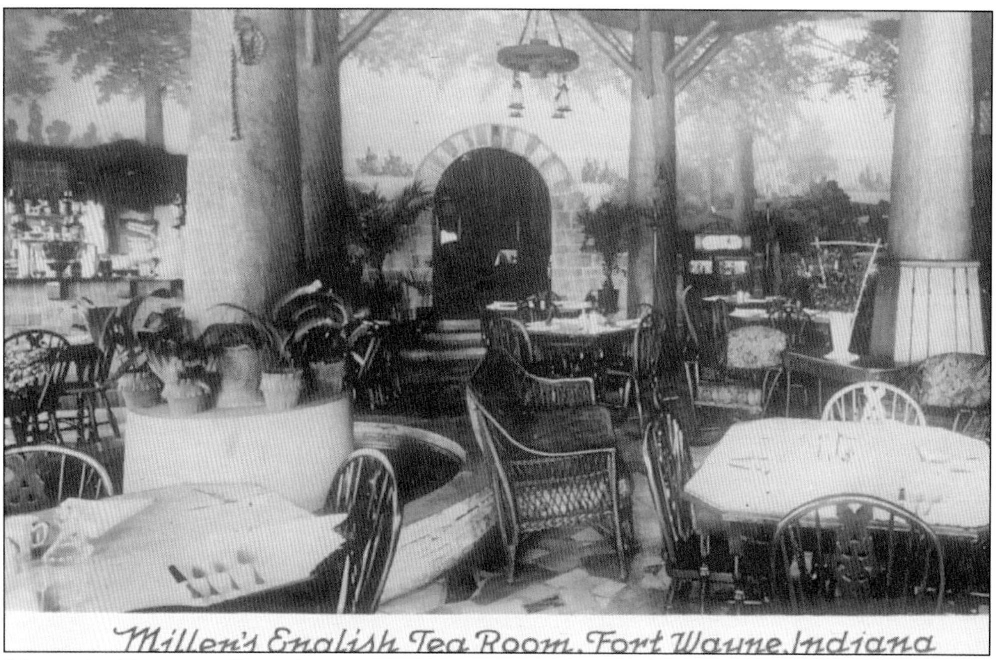

MILLER'S ENGLISH TEA ROOM, FORT WAYNE, INDIANA. This was a popular place for shoppers.

Six

Monroeville

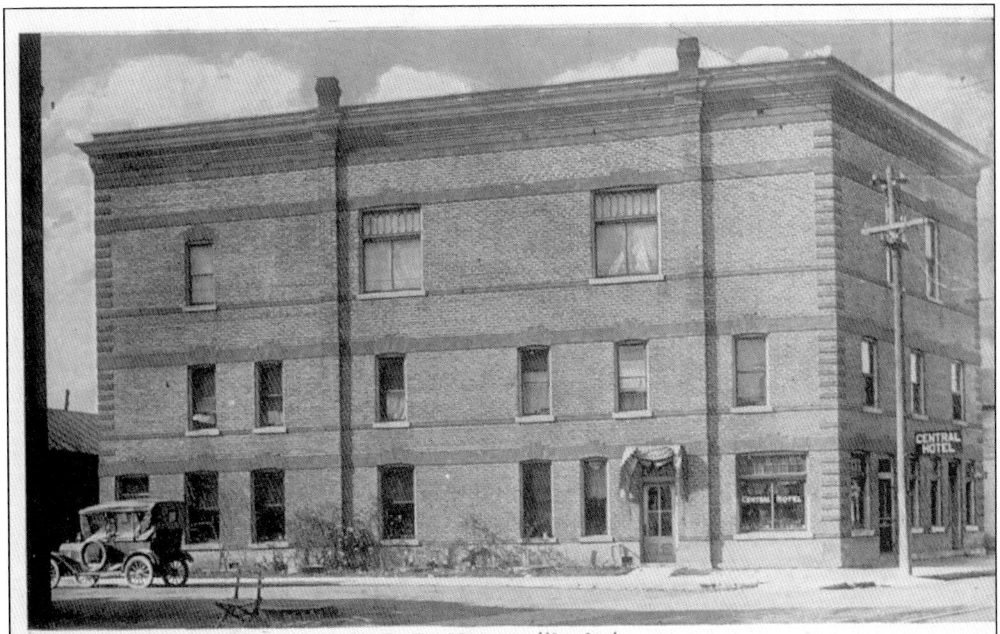

I.O.O.F., Monroeville, Indiana. Pictured here is the Independent Order of Odd Fellows Lodge Building. The Central Hotel occupied the first and second floors, and the lodge rooms were on the third floor.

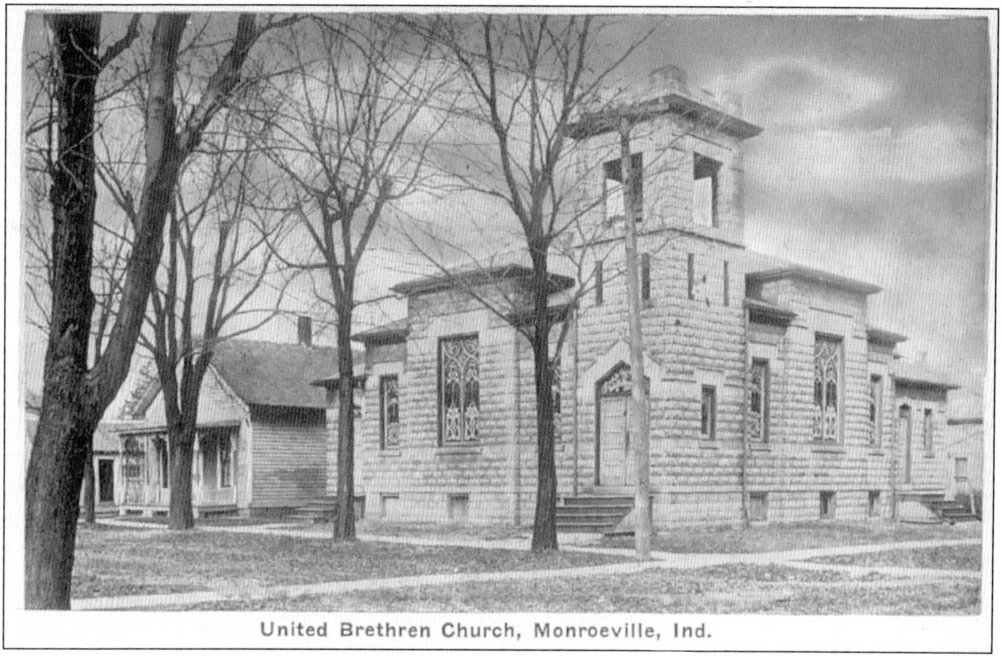

UNITED BRETHREN CHURCH, MONROEVILLE, INDIANA.

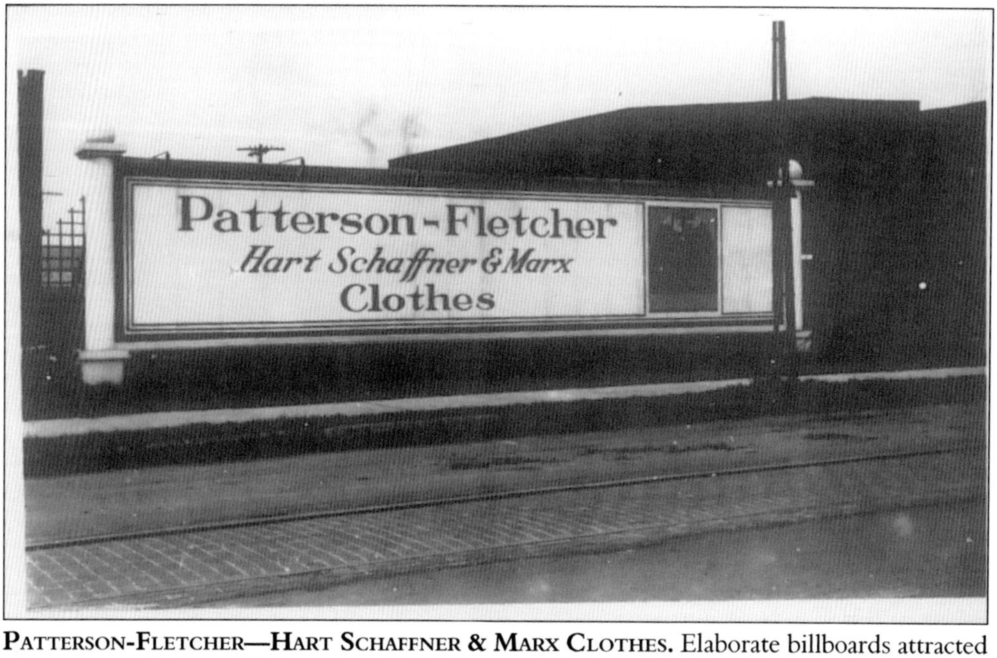

PATTERSON-FLETCHER—HART SCHAFFNER & MARX CLOTHES. Elaborate billboards attracted customers to the E.F Brinkman Co. Fort Wayne stores.

Seven

ZANESVILLE

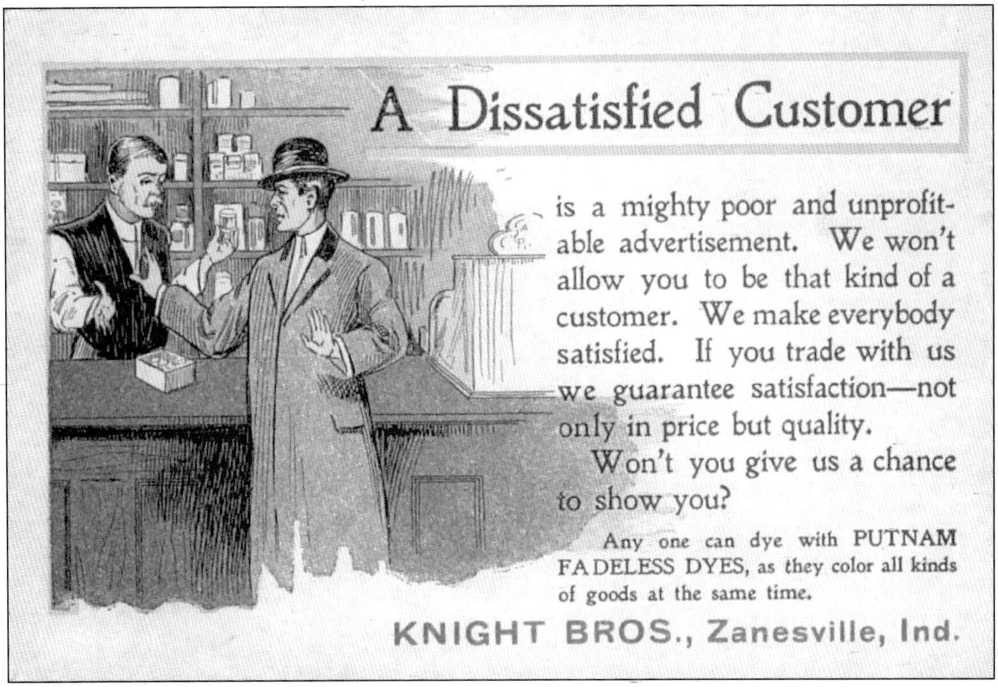

KNIGHT BROS., ZANESVILLE, INDIANA. This is an advertising card for Knight Bros., located at Zanesville.

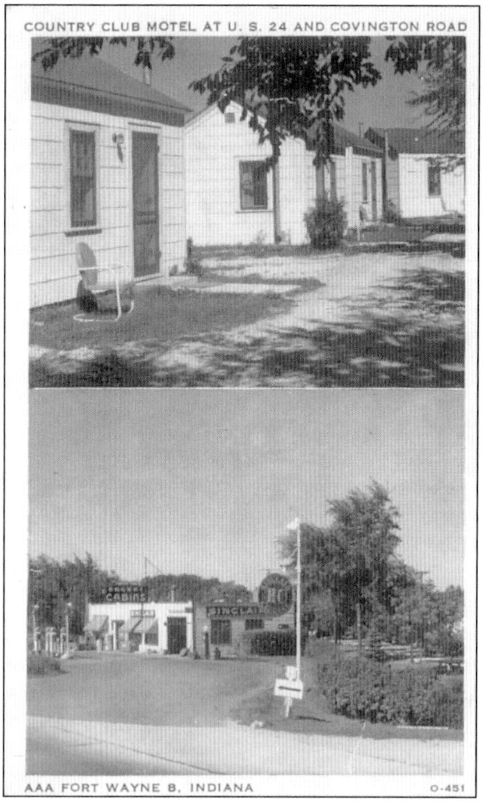

COUNTRY CLUB MOTEL AT U.S. 24 AND COVINGTON ROAD—AAA FORT WAYNE 8 INDIANA. The printed caption on the back states: "This camp is located at the division point of the water shed between the Mississippi and the St. Lawrence Rivers."

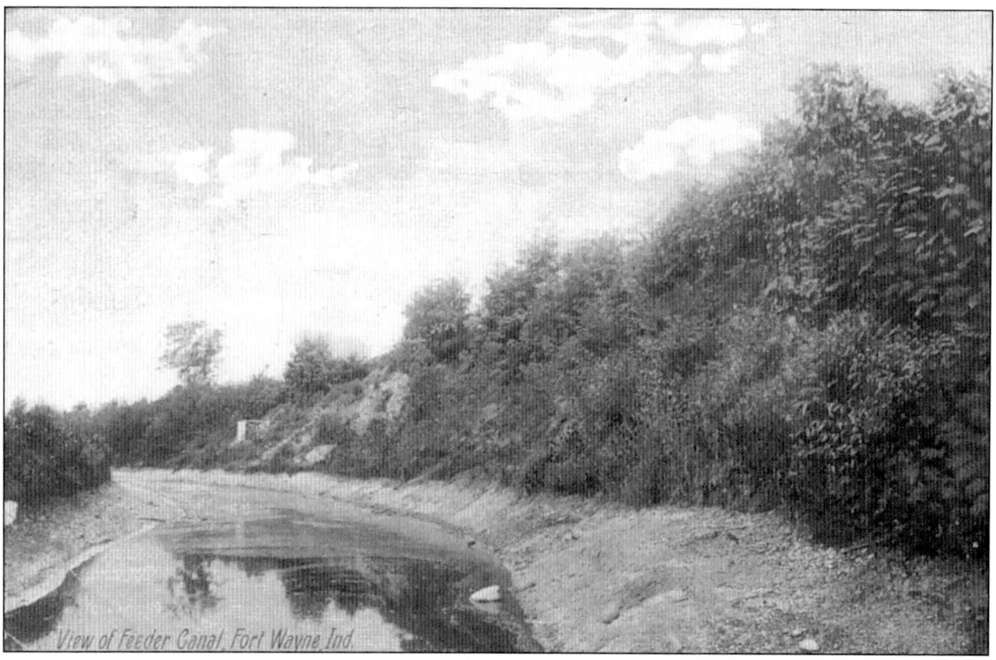

VIEW OF FEEDER CANAL, FORT WAYNE, INDIANA. The feeder canal supplied additional water to the canal system in periods of low water level.